Women's Bodies as Battlefield

Other Works by
Susan Brooks Thistlethwaite

#OccupytheBible: What Jesus Really Said (and Did) about Money and Power. Eugene, OR: Wipf and Stock, 2013.

Interfaith Just Peacemaking: Jewish, Christian, and Muslim Perspectives on the New Paradigm of Peace and War. New York: Palgrave Macmillan, 2012.

Dreaming of Eden: American Religion and Politics in a Wired World. New York: Palgrave Macmillan, 2010.

Adam, Eve, and the Genome: The Human Genome Project and Theology. Minneapolis: Fortress, 2003.

With Brock, Rita Nakashima, *Casting Stones: Prostitution and Liberation in Asia and the United States.* Minneapolis: Fortress, 1996.

With Mary Potter. Engel, eds. *Lift Every Voice: Constructing Christian Theologies from the Underside.* Maryknoll, NY: Orbis, 1998.

Sex, Race, and God: Christian Feminism in Black and White. New York: Crossroad, 1989.

Women's Bodies as Battlefield

Christian Theology and the Global War on Women

Susan Brooks Thistlethwaite

palgrave
macmillan

WOMEN'S BODIES AS BATTLEFIELD
Copyright © Susan Brooks Thistlethwaite, 2015.

First published in 2015 by PALGRAVE MACMILLAN® in the United States—a division of St. Martin's Press LLC, 175 Fifth Avenue, New York, NY 10010.

Where this book is distributed in the UK, Europe and the rest of the world, this is by Palgrave Macmillan, a division of Macmillan Publishers Limited, registered in England, company number 785998, of Houndmills, Basingstoke, Hampshire RG21 6XS.

Palgrave Macmillan is the global academic imprint of the above companies and has companies and representatives throughout the world.

Palgrave® and Macmillan® are registered trademarks in the United States, the United Kingdom, Europe and other countries.

ISBN: 978-1-137-46814-7

Library of Congress Cataloging-in-Publication Data

Thistlethwaite, Susan Brooks, 1948–
    Women's bodies as battlefield : Christian theology and the global war on women / Susan Brooks Thistlethwaite.
        pages cm
    Includes bibliographical references and index.
    ISBN 978-1-137-46814-7 — ISBN 978-1-137-46814-7
    1. Women in Christianity. 2. Women—Religious aspects—Christianity. I. Title.

    BV639.W7T47 2015
    261.8′73082—dc23   2015003957

A catalogue record of the book is available from the British Library.

Design by Scribe Inc.

First edition: July 2015

10 9 8 7 6 5 4 3 2 1

Printed in the United States of America.

Contents

Acknowledgments

It is very tempting to turn away from all the violence in the world, both the violence of the War on Women and of war itself. Being a witness, refusing to look the other way, is so very hard and can be nearly impossible without loving support and care.

I must acknowledge the love of my family as a constant source of the love that allows me to dare to witness. My husband, Dr. Dick Thistlethwaite, has always been that source for me, and his love and faith in me has enabled me to be a more courageous person. Our children, their spouses, and our grandchildren are a constant source of joy and a reminder that the pain of the world is not all there is. And I must acknowledge my friends and colleagues around the world, many of whom work on these same issues, who are a constant source of inspiration to me as we try over and over to bring peace where there is no peace and to bring justice where there is no justice.

In particular, I want to thank President Jimmy Carter for his decades-long, principled leadership to end violence and suffering and bring about lasting peace. My volunteer work with the Carter Center has been a source of tremendous hope to me. President Carter and the Carter Center staff, and especially Karin Ryan, work tirelessly not just to identify problems but to work collaboratively with people around the world in bringing about more peace and greater justice.

I must thank Burke Gerstenschlager, former editor at Palgrave Macmillan and now history and classics editor at Oxford University Press, for his tremendous interest and encouragement in this project and for his many astute critiques of the fundamental premise of the book.

I would also like to thank the editorial staff at Palgrave Macmillan for their work with me on completing the manuscript.

I want to thank the administration, faculty colleagues, and students at Chicago Theological Seminary (CTS) for being a community which values and supports witnessing to the myriad ways people are violated around the world and for their collective commitment to witness to such violations and to end them.

In particular, I would like to thank Dean Ken Stone for conversation and for lending me books to examine issues in the Hebrew Bible. I would like to thank Melanie Jones, CTS PhD student, and other womanist scholars at CTS for invaluable discussions around method. I would also like to thank Jason Frey, CTS PhD student and my excellent editorial assistant.

I would also like to acknowledge you, the reader, for refusing to turn away from the complex and painful realities of the War on Women and war itself. Be sure to reach out for support as you engage this book, especially if the issues connect to painful experiences in your own life. As we acknowledge each other in the struggle, we realize we are not alone.

Introduction

Rapists are the "shock troops of patriarchy" and batterers are the army of occupation.

Susan Brooks Thistlethwaite

All day long, all night long, every day and every night, the bodies of women and girls are turned into battlefields. Their bodies are penetrated against their will; they are burned, maimed, bruised, slapped, kicked, threatened with weapons, confined, beaten with fists or objects, shot, and knifed; their bones are broken; and they lose limbs, sight, hearing, pregnancies, and their sense of personal and physical integrity. They are terrorized and they are killed.

This is what battlefields in war are like. Bodies are damaged, flesh is ripped apart, and minds and lives destroyed. In *All Quiet on the Western Front*, Erich Maria Remarque shocked Europe out of its heroic delusions about war with an unrelenting portrait of men locked in trench warfare over a destroyed landscape. The battlefield in this novel is central—a gore-filled, body-destroying wasteland: "Haie strikes his spade into the neck of a gigantic Frenchman and throws the first hand-grenade; we duck behind a breastwork for a few seconds, then the straight bit of trench ahead of us is empty. The next throw wizzes obliquely over the cover and clears a passage; as we run past we toss handfuls down into the dug-outs, the earth shudders, it crashes, smokes and groans, we stumble over slippery lumps of flesh, over yielding bodies; I fall into an open belly on which lies a clear, new officer's cap."[1]

"Slippery lumps of flesh" and "yielding bodies" that are torn open are what battlefields make of bodies.

Torn flesh and yielding bodies also can describe the experience of rape for women. In 1984, Sherry Kurtz was a brand-new recruit sent to Germany by the US military. She was gang raped by her "brothers in arms":

"Do you want a beer?" he asked. "Sure" I replied. The next thing I knew is I was waking up. (I know now something had to be in that beer.) I felt like I was dreaming, only I felt hands on me. I felt touching, and I felt a guy on my back. I knew from the pain that I felt what he was doing to me. He was sodomizing me, and he wasn't the only one to do that. I remember he used one arm to just flip me over; I kept my eyes closed trying to figure out why this was happening. I was in a fog, I knew and felt what was going on, but I had no strength to stop it . . .

Finally, I opened my eyes because I had to see. I was trying to get my arms free, I couldn't free them. I felt like [there] were bugs crawling on me and something was sitting

on my body. I felt like I could get no air. I remember thinking "I have a headache and feel
very fragile at this time. I see one on each arm, and leg, I feel as though I might throw
up. I can feel this one inside me and I see faces like in a fog. I don't know all of them, but
I have seen them."[2]

It is important to understand the War on Women from the perspective of the body as battlefield because that is where we can actually see the carnage and acknowledge the pain. The damage to the body is an undeniable fact of violence; so too are the threats of violence that are carried not only in the mind but also in physical changes due to stress. The fact of the physical effects of violence on women's bodies, however, is aggressively hidden, qualified, reframed, reorganized, catalogued, excused, and ultimately authorized. This is how such a monumental amount of carnage continues almost unabated with very little public outcry or sustained efforts to stop it. To prevent and reduce violence in the War on Women, and indeed to prevent and reduce the violence of war, the facts of physical injury and death on these related battlefields must be exposed and seen in all their reality. This is a crucial starting place.

Seeing Violence against Women

One way to actually begin to see the violence perpetrated against women's bodies is through a health-crisis model.

The advantage of the "health-crisis" model is that it is backed up by statistical analysis. The World Health Organization (WHO), for example, has issued a comprehensive, multicountry report on the incidence of violence against women worldwide.[3] WHO has concluded that 35 percent of women around the world, or more than one in three women and girls aged 15 and above, experience sexual or physical violence at least once in their lives. WHO found that such violence is most commonly at the hands of an intimate partner; in fact, 30 percent of women globally are shown to be victims of domestic violence.

Given their mandate on health, it is unsurprising that WHO researchers call these horrifying statistics a "global public health problem that affects approximately one-third of women globally."[4] The negative health effects are well documented, and there are recommendations for health-system changes as part of an overall strategy to combat violence against women. These are practical and provide a crucial way that societies can confront this alarming rate of violence against women.

The WHO report gives a baseline calculus of the enormity of the incidence of violence against women and shows that this is a world crisis, and indeed a world health crisis. But statistical analysis and the health-crisis framework are not enough. They do not get at what drives this massive problem, nor is the "health-crisis" model compelling enough to break through to public consciousness.

Personal stories are more compelling than public-health statistics, though actual data are important to ultimately crafting a comprehensive response to the extent of violence against women.

Stories—especially in the age of new media where they can be replicated with remarkable speed and visual impact—are crucial. Personal testimony to what actually happens to women's bodies can move people to awareness and break through the silencing. This happened following a shooting spree in Isla Vista, California, where the male shooter was discovered to have posted and filmed women-hating, racist messages, which produced a viral Twitter hashtag, #YesAllWomen. The thousands and thousands of messages posted in just a few hours after the hashtag's creation started to give testimony to the widespread culture of violence against women and how it is so common and so accepted. The #YesAllWomen Twitter tag was framed as a furious rebuttal to the familiar "not all men" argument that deflects analysis of rape culture and redirects it to individual male behaviors.[5] Reading the tweets provides a virtual tour of the battlefield of women's bodies in the War on Women.

Data, like that contained in the WHO study, are important, of course, but it is crucial to confront the massive amount of violence against women at ground zero. *Ground zero* is defined here as the painful injuries to women's bodies and the threat of this pain, even to death, that causes widespread fear. Stories begin to address this physical level. Staying with the body and what happens to the body begins to expose the gaping wounds caused by violence. The wounding of bodies, sometimes even unto death, poses an existential claim that is less easily dismissed than statistics, though the drive to dismiss, deny, minimize, or even authorize these wounds is strong.[6]

This Is My Body

The wounded, bleeding, maimed, and destroyed bodies of women are nonnegotiable; they are what they are. They are not "the body" in general but individual women's bodies that are violated and wounded and sometimes destroyed. These are bodies that can carry the scars and memory of painful mistreatment as long as they exist. These are bodies that have been forced to endure painful injury, as Susan Brownmiller wrote, "Against Our Will."[7]

The body is the way we exist in the world, and despite millennia of trying, Western philosophy and religion have been unable to get around that inescapable fact. Women have, for far too long, been denigrated as "the body," identified with the problem of embodiment, and embodiment itself has been denigrated as a prison of the soul. Embodiment is not a problem; violence is the problem.

When we make the body our touchstone of what it means to be human, the body/soul dualism that has so plagued philosophy and religion, particularly in the Christian-dominated West, is profoundly challenged. The real separation is not body and soul but body and will. Force or the threat of force used on bodies is an attack on the integrity of the human person, body and soul together.

Violence thus enters into the analysis offered in this book in a primary way. Western Christian theology and the biblical and philosophical sources that have been so influential in its formation have misunderstood, misnamed, and misdirected the primary existential issue of the human condition. The primary existential crisis of the human condition is violence, not a body/soul dualism and its attendant dualism of sin/grace. This misnaming and misdirection has led Christian theology into a profound complicity with both intimate and societal violence, where violence itself is lauded as a divinely authorized rule instead of being seen as the ultimate insult to God's work in creating human beings and the world.

The reality of women's bodies as battlefields reveals the legacies from Western philosophy and theology that support not only the War on Women but also war in general.

There are social, cultural, and religious supports that a society needs to employ in order to ensure that more than a third of women in that society can be treated violently, or threatened with violence, without mass outcry and rebellion. These social, cultural, and religious supports overlap with many of those that are necessary for societies to be willing to send the young, healthy bodies of its citizens into war, where many of them will be maimed or killed, also without mass outcry or rebellion.

The Western biblical, philosophical, and theological legacies that provide these supports for both the War on Women and war in general are the desire for power, hierarchical authority structures, and contempt for the body. Moreover, it will be shown in this argument that war and violence against women not only have some of the same social, cultural, and religious roots, but these roots are also mutually reinforcing. War is a model for violence against women; the widespread acceptance of violence against women is a template for war.

The body as injured, in pain, and killed is the starting place. This volume, therefore, attempts to focus the gaze on what happens to the bodies of women in the War on Women, and to bodies in war, and to show how these are related and also how they are different. Really seeing the injury to bodies is an attempt to expose, by comparison, all the ways that the injuring of women's bodies in the War on Women, and the injuring of bodies, civilian and combatant, that happen in war, are ignored, sidelined, justified, and even celebrated. It is also specifically a way to keep focusing on the injuries to bodies to empower a movement to resist this in all its forms.

It is crucial to actually work to witness to this injuring in the War on Women and in war because, while these forms of violence are everywhere, strong social, cultural, religious, and economic forces conspire to hide them.

But physicality cannot be the only starting point. There is a real risk that if we witness to all these forms of violence equally, we will not actually see the very different forces that act so that certain bodies are made available to certain forms of violence in certain ways and at certain times. The book is an attempt to stay with the injuring of bodies but not collapse "the body" or "women's bodies" into one abstraction.

"Critical physicality" is a term of my own invention, and I use it to describe the method I am attempting to employ in this book. The term "critical physicality" is partly related to the work of Elaine Scarry in *The Body in Pain: The Making and Unmaking of the World* and especially to Scarry's unrelenting focus on the irreducibility of bodily pain.[8] Whatever else we may say about the War on Women, and about war, it is undeniable that pain is caused to the living body. That is a profound existential starting point, as bodies that are not alive cannot feel pain. Life itself is at stake when violence is done to the physical body.

It is important, however, to employ critical theory at every step of this analysis; hence the modifier "critical" is used along with physicality. All bodies are not equally accessible for injury, and the method used in this book employs critical theory to keep that fact in view. Different women's contexts matter immensely when we try to join together to create a movement to stop violence against women. Thus, while it is important to say #YesAllWomen by virtue of being female, at risk in the War on Women, we must also say "#YesAllWomenDifferently."[9] If we do not think and act on the premise of #YesAllWomenDifferently, the solidarity so needed for movement building to prevent and reduce violence is not created; it is destroyed.

Bodies have races, sexual orientations, sizes, reproductive organs, religious and cultural meanings, and social locations within states and economies. These must not be ignored even as physicality itself is the focus. Critical physicality must adopt a position outside the regular mechanisms that essentialize the body in order to actually witness to the multiple violations of bodies.[10] Liberation feminism, Womanism, queer theory, and postcolonialism in particular are crucial to displacing the vast amount of injury and death of women from within the power structure of dominance and submission where it has been normalized and to place it outside.[11] Then, injuring women's bodies and injuring bodies in war, even to death, can be seen as beyond the confines of "normal." Even further, how the normal is constructed from the various mechanisms of domination can perhaps be seen.

Gender and sexual orientation, as they function in Western culture, are constructed as relationships of power in dominance and subordination. The unequal social relations that are produced, maintained, policed, and punished if transgressed must be the focus of critical theory. Theory reveals that heterosexuality is compulsory and thus must be a crucial framing device for examining violence against women, even as the very category of "women" as defined by heteronormative patriarchy must be constantly highlighted and challenged as an oppressive construct.

Race and racism must not be reduced to individual "prejudices" best addressed through "dialogue" and "inclusion," but as a major part of the way Western societies have developed law, economics, politics, and religion and anchored them in racism. Critical race theory provides a way into the critical consciousness needed to expose this at the foundations.

Critical scholarship also demands an acknowledgment of the scholar's own context. I am a white, middle-class, female academic. I have been a domestic violence counselor, and I continue to be a volunteer advocate to end violence against women. When I was a sophomore in my high school, many friends who had already graduated began to come back in body bags from Vietnam. I became a peace activist. Peace activism led me to the Civil Rights movement and the recognition that racism fueled both the war in Vietnam and the violence against African Americans at home.

Yet none of these commitments or social locations provides me an "innocence" from which I can take a stand without constant work, with the aid of critical theory, to expose my own immersion in the multiple sources of power, authority, and contempt for the body that are built into the very fabric of the society in which I have lived all my life. This is a given. There is no escape from our social locations, only constant effort to achieve critical consciousness and to build solidarity through complex movement building.

I work, therefore, within Euro-Atlantic culture and examine it in regard to its role in the War on Women and in war. This stance can reveal how these wars set the parameters of not only how bodies become battlefields within Western culture but also how they exercise power globally. Increasingly, the model of women's bodies as battlefields, in particular, is coming to be the model for globalization, and the role of war and the War on Women is seen as advancing the interests of global economics.

There must always be a dynamic tension between the particulars of the social construction of bodies in Western culture and the sustained analysis of what this construction means in terms of the widespread acceptance, even valorization, of many forms of violence.

There is a further challenge and the particularities of all bodies matter immensely in meeting this challenge. All this analysis, no matter how detailed and intricate, will mean little without the movement building that is required to actually prevent and reduce both violence against women and the violence of war.

Unless we can find a way to witness to the injuring of the bodies of all women (and all women differently in a complex solidarity), and unless we can find a way to witness to the injuring of the bodies of all those in war and to probe at why war actually continues unabated, we will make no real impact.

That is in part why theories of war and peace, for example, have almost completely failed to either prevent or control war. These theories have not even been applied as an attempt to end the War on Women.

Theories of War and Peace

The goal of this volume is to examine violence against women in relationship to the models of war and peace that exist in Western thought. These models are primarily Pacifism, Just War, and Just Peace. These paradigms are potential resources in the struggle to curtail and end violence against women. Tragically, however, the analyses in this book also expose flaws within all of them when it comes to understanding the body as the primary object of war making and the body as the primary object of peacemaking. All three of these theories need to be rethought from the perspective of critical physicality, with reconstructing Just Peace a primary goal of this work.

The War on Women and war have common supports, and theories of peace and war should account for these. But the War on Women and wars between nations also have crucial differences. According to Scarry, two facts are essential to comprehending the activity that is war, "first, that the immediate activity is injuring;

second, that the immediate activity of war is a contest." War is "reciprocal injuring where the goal is to out-injure the opponent."[12]

When we consider women's bodies as battlefields, the injuring of women's bodies comes into clearer view and does pose an existential claim as noted earlier. The War on Women is a war primarily because of this embodied link: war and the War on Women are about injuring the body.

But when it comes to the second part of Scarry's definition of war, that of contest, there is a difference. The "War on Women" is not a war between combatants engaged in mutual injuring, each side struggling to out-injure the other. It is not, then, a war between men and women, where men and women are both duly authorized combatants, it is a war *on women*, where women are categorically more like noncombatants or civilians who are being attacked. Women are not equally authorized by their societies to use violence; even when women use defensive violence in the case of attack, women are often more harshly punished than the men who beat them. "The average prison sentence for men who kill their intimate partners is 2 to 6 years. Women who kill their partners are sentenced, on average, to 15 years."[13] In 2012, Marissa Alexander of Jacksonville, Florida, received a 20-year prison sentence for firing warning shots against her allegedly abusive husband. The judge rejected a defense under Florida's "Stand Your Ground" law. She told police it was to escape a brutal beating by her husband, against whom she had already taken out a protective order. Alexander had never been in trouble with the law before.[14]

Women's bodies are the battlefields where violence takes place, but often the contest is not with them but rather about them. The goal of establishing control over women through violence or the threat of violence is only apparently about women; it is frequently, instead, about using the control of women in a contest with other men. Gang rape exhibits this characteristic to a great degree, where men use violence on a woman's body to gain power and status with and over other men. There are also aspects of domestic violence and ideologies of the "head of the household" where masculinity is defined as control of women backed up by force and is thus a way to establish "maleness" vis-à-vis other men, not merely contesting with women.

While the War on Women and war will be treated in tandem and subject to the multiple analyses provided by critical physicality, they will not be conflated. Generalities do not help prevent or reduce violence that is so vast and so well-established in law, custom, politics, economics, and religion. When power is so diffuse, as Michel Foucault has pointed out, there must be multiple forms of resistance to address it.[15]

The diffusions of power and the multiple paths of resistance to them is actually the good news. While there are no easy answers or fixes for the ubiquitous role violence plays in Western society, there are multiple ways to identify and subvert it.

But in order to subvert violence, you have to actually begin to see it for what it is.

Injuries and Bodies

Chapters 1 and 2 describe what happens to bodies in war and in the War on Women. Battlefields in war are the sites of horrific injuries to those engaged in combat and to noncombatants. Twenty-first-century wars are now conducted on the bodies of more noncombatants than combatants, and as Jeremy Scahill documents in *Dirty Wars*, the whole world became a battlefield for the Bush administration, and this is now the new pattern for global conflict. The world is a battlefield, according to Scahill.[16]

There is a War on Women in war that is part of the chapter on war, including the extent of sexual assault in the military as well as rape in war. War, as it is conducted in many times and places, includes systemic sexual abuse. Violence against women and girls has been called *War's Dirty Secret*.[17] Dirty Wars, in other words, have dirty secrets.

The War on Women is a war, and we know this because of the amount of injury and death suffered by women's bodies at the hands of others, primarily men whom they know or who are their intimate partners. This war is global and there are signs it is accelerating as women's bodies pay the price for anxieties and dislocations created by globalization. Failed or failing nation-states cannot enforce the meager laws that are designed to protect women from the War on Women, and too few states have such laws or are willing to enforce them.

Philosophy and Theology

The foundations of Western thought on the body, women's bodies, and war are taken from Greek philosophy (Plato and Aristotle) and from Christian theology (Augustine and Aquinas). Chapters 3 and 4 examine in greater depth the common roots of war and the War on Women in these crucial thinkers and examine the development of militarism and a denigration of the body and sexuality.

The Heroic and the Erotic

The massive amount of injury that both the War on Women and war entails, numbering in the millions every year, must be hidden from view to be tolerated by societies. Both the War on Women and war are hidden by being fictionalized, but in different ways. These fictionalizations are aided and abetted by aspects of Christian theological development in regard to the body, sexuality, and the use of force, but they have enormous social and cultural sources as well.

Chapter 5 examines the way war is fictionalized as heroic, and especially the conquest of the female, while Chapter 6 explores how the War on Women and war are fictionalized as erotic.

Pacifism, Just War, and Just Peace

Chapter 7 goes into more detail on the way in which Just War—a theory of war that draws on both Western philosophical and theological sources—authorizes militarism and is also a normative frame for authorizing and conducting violence against women. Major flaws in Just War theory are revealed by the way in which violence against women has so often been considered "just" in Western culture.

Pacifism and Just Peace are examined in Chapter 8. Pacifism in a historical context arises from eschatological and sectarian impulses rather than a repudiation of violence per se, though there are voices in Western philosophy and theology that do contend just that. But Pacifism has never included opposition to violence against women in a central way. A weakness of Pacifism, in a contemporary context, is the conviction by its adherents of their own "innocence" in regard to violence, and this hides actual violence against women in pacifist communities.

Just Peace was developed as a concrete set of practices that prevent or reduce violence in war and that are designed to create a sustainable peace. Just Peace was influenced, in its development, by Christian sectarian Pacifism, liberal Christian theologies, Catholic moral reasoning, and by Western understandings of human rights and international law. Yet it will be argued that so far in its development, Just Peace lacks sufficient attention to the way in which the War on Women, and the denigration of the body itself, can continue even through many of the practices of Just Peace. Just Peace also lacks a sustained analysis of power and hierarchy.

A Just Peace theology of critical physicality is proposed in Chapter 9. This is not set out as a solution, but more of an invitation to a path forward, one that does not flinch from going through the horrors of what happens to bodies on the battlefields of the War on Women and in war, one that forthrightly rejects aspects of Western philosophy and Christian theology that have so far enabled—even demanded—war and the War on Women and one that leads to deepened and expanded practices that put ending the War on Women, and war itself, at the center of the Christian theological and ethical task.

The conclusion is called "Can I Get a Witness?" and sketches out what happens in Just Peacemaking when a critical focus on the body encounters what are called the "practice norms"—that is, the specific tenets of the theory.

The Honored Dead and Living

After the battle of Gettysburg, a defining battle of the American Civil War, the dead (especially the Confederate dead) lay for days in the sun and rain, and many were hastily shoved into mass graves. For years afterwards, dead bodies or parts of bodies would heave up in the spring from the thawing ground.

On November 19, 1863, President Abraham Lincoln gave what is arguably his most famous speech over the freshly dug graves at Gettysburg. Lincoln said that those in attendance on that day were met on a "great battlefield," a battlefield not only of a single engagement at Gettysburg but a struggle over the very definition of the nation. This was the consecration of this battlefield, Lincoln contended, not any words said on that day. It was "[t]he brave men, living and dead, who struggled here, [who] have consecrated it, far above our poor power to add or detract." The cause for which they fought and died, Lincoln concluded, was to ensure that a "government of the people, by the people, for the people, shall not perish from the earth."[18]

Lincoln believed the mass death at Gettysburg "hallowed" the ground as no dedication could do, for it was their deaths that provided the consecration. So much is true.

Yet, even in this remarkable speech, there is a flaw, a flaw we inherit as a nation. This flaw is the idea that the obscenity that is the suffering and death from violence inflicted by one human being on another can become "sacred" when cast as a "sacrifice." The "honored dead" deserve respect, of course, but let us not delude ourselves that these deaths are sacrifices that make something as unholy as war sacred. "Government of the people, by the people and for the people" has not yet been achieved, and much of the blood spilt on the battlefield at Gettysburg has seeded continued national division, especially in regard to race. No, Gettysburg was not "hallowed" but, in following what happens to the body on battlefields, it was a mass grave resulting from mass injury and death.

The War on Women has its own battlefields—that is, the bodies of those who are killed in what is now called "femicide," the "killing of a woman because she is a woman, the killing of a girl because she is a girl."[19] Those killed by femicide do not even get the recognition of big public speeches, and the places they are injured and buried are not made into national monuments consecrated by their deaths. Their fatal injuries are not regarded as marks of honor.

Women activists, however, have made their own memorials, as represented on the cover of this book. Crosses with the names of women who had been victims of femicide and domestic violence in Bolivia were attached to a fence as a memorial and a protest. Bolivia is considered to have the highest rate of domestic violence and femicide in Latin America.[20]

Women's bodies can no longer be hidden, but like the thawing bodies at Gettysburg, they are heaving up and demanding their lives be valued and their loss mourned as a vast human atrocity. They shall not indeed have died in vain if we commit ourselves to end the scourge of the War on Women. Their suffering and woundedness shall no longer be hidden, excused, or even deemed their own fault. And women around the world who live in thrall to fear and suffering inflicted on them shall too be valued, and their value made plain so that women's bodies can no longer be a place where violence can be enacted as justified or even sacred.

And from this we will learn to study the War on Women, and war itself, no more.

1

Injuring in War

They were going to look at war, the red animal—war, the blood-swollen god.

Stephen Crane, *The Red Badge of Courage: An Episode of the American Civil War*

War fascinates because it is such a spectacle of power. War poses an existential threat to life and thus is also often equated with the power of life and death of a god, whether for good or for ill. No other human activity can loom so large in consciousness as war and yet, at the same time, be so hidden and so poorly understood.

This is by design. If war were known in full, it would be far and away more difficult for nations to wage it.

But how to know war? One way is to know the injuries to bodies that are the true goal of war. Injuries to bodies in war are war's reality.

The names given to wars, by contrast, are not real. Indeed, the unreality of the reason(s) for a war, as often represented in the name of a war, is on display in the naming. Names given to war reveal such a studied unreality that it is difficult to believe it is not deliberate. By contrast, the dead and injured bodies simply are the reality of war. They exist. While often covered up and hidden, the body count of dead and injured is real. The dead and the injured can be counted. They can be named. The name of a war, on the other hand, is about the unreality of war.

Consider the names given to America's longest war, the war in Afghanistan.[1] When the United States was preparing military action against Afghanistan following the attacks on 9/11, it was originally called "Operation Infinite Justice." Then the official name was changed to "Operation Enduring Freedom." In announcing the name change, Defense Secretary Donald Rumsfeld "said the administration had quickly reconsidered the original name because, in the Islamic faith, such finality is considered something provided only by God." Following on President Bush's dubbing the "war on terror" a "crusade," this was apparently an attempt by the administration to avoid more Islamic backlash.[2] It was wholly and completely not an attempt to more realistically name the war.

Neither "Infinite Justice" nor "Enduring Freedom" means anything real. Infinite justice must be attributed to divinity, as it cannot be attributed to the activities of finite human beings. So a war named "Infinite Justice" cannot, by definition, even exist in human history. "Enduring Freedom" is also unreal. If taken to refer to freedom for Americans, this has never completely existed for the American democratic experiment. From the genocide of Native Americans, to slavery, to Jim and Jane Crow, to the school-to-prison pipeline, and to inequality of rights for women and LGBT citizens, freedom has been partial and so cannot actually "endure" as it has not ever fully existed. If "Operation Enduring Freedom" was meant to refer to Afghanistan, however, it is even less real. As the war went on, "Enduring Freedom" retreated further and further from reality as "freedom" for the vast majority of Afghans was not attained nor did whatever actually was attained endure.

This does not matter in the naming of wars. Naming wars is an exercise in unreality for the purposes of obscuring the real goal: out-injuring the enemy in a contest for domination of territory and ideology.

All you can really know about war from the names given to war is what war is not. Probably the best example of this is the popular name given to World War I, the "War to End All Wars." It is now a term used in derision about that war, as it was in reality the war that ended peace in Europe, and indeed in the world, for two generations. It is a war best known for the staggering death (16 million) and injury (20 million) totals. It is, in some ways, still the epitome of war as injuring.

Mapping the injuries to bodies, the death, disfigurement, and dismemberment, is a way to know war. Beyond counting, knowing the specific forms of injuring and death in war is a way to know war more deeply. It is not a way without difficulties, however, since, unless the injuries are your own, you are an observer, a witness to injury and death.

There is a profound difference between being a witness and being an observer, or even worse, a voyeur. An observer merely looks and perhaps records. It is understood to be the neutral gaze. A voyeur is an obsessive who likes to look at a sexual or violent act being performed. Voyeurism is about personal gratification; it is a profoundly selfish gaze.

Being a witness is something else. It is active. Witnessing can involve community participation. In some Christian churches, someone may cry out, "Can I get a witness?" What she or he means is, "can anybody else can give testimony to the movement of God in my life that I am sharing?" This is communion as spiritual participation.

If we wish to be witnesses to war, we must struggle for some of this communal grasping of a profound reality; in the case of church, it is grasping a spiritual reality. In the case of injury in war or the War on Women, it is grasping the physical reality, but not without critical reflection on the multiple contexts and meanings of bodies. This kind of critical reflection then can help build more complex movements to prevent and reduce violence.

Communal witnessing is not enough when it comes to the injuries to bodies. "Witness for Peace" has it right. In the 1980s, Witness for Peace (WFP) was founded by people of faith concerned about the US support of the "Contras" in Nicaragua. WFP sent thousands of Americans to that country to witness the devastating effects of US-sponsored "low-intensity warfare." They have turned that witnessing into "changing U.S. policies and corporate practices that contribute to poverty and oppression in Latin America and the Caribbean."[3]

Witnessing in this way is part of a "praxis" to end violence. By praxis, I mean an engaged process of really seeing the complexities of injuring and death and working to change the policies and/or societal norms that give rise to the injuries and death in both the violence of war and the violence of the War on Women.[4]

In the work of movement building to end the War on Women and war itself, actually seeing injuries and death is the indispensable starting place.

"Ashes to ashes, dust to dust"

Prior to the nineteenth century, it was relatively rare that injuring in war could be "seen" by noncombatants unless one was an unfortunate civilian thrust into conflict or went deliberately to observe war as did the foolish citizens of Washington, DC, who decided to do some picnicking and watch the Battle of Bull Run. When the Union Army was overrun, spectators, including some Congressmen, were injured, killed, or even captured, and they ceased being spectators.[5]

Injuring in war has been depicted in narrative and art throughout human history. Vast scenes of battles cover huge swaths of walls in museums like the Louvre. These are commemorative and are closer to the "naming" of war than they are a way to observe war, and certainly they are not a way to witness to the injuring in war. Rarely, until recently, has art striven to present injury in war as it really is.

There are classical exceptions. Leonardo da Vinci, the artist and weapons maker, gave instructions for painting a battle, and in these instructions, he insists that artists have the courage and the imagination to show war in all its ghastliness, as da Vinci instructs, "Make the conquered and beaten pale, with brows raised and knit and the skin above their brows furrowed with pain . . . and the teeth apart as with crying out in lamentation . . . Make the dead partly or entirely covered with dust . . . and let the blood be seen by its color flowing in a sinuous stream from the corpse to the dust. Others in the death agony grinding their teeth, rolling their eyes, with their fists clenched against their bodies, and the legs distorted."[6]

The "dead partly or entirely covered with dust" represents the physical location of the battlefield and is also highly evocative of the return of dead bodies on a battlefield to the dust from which they came. The bodies of human beings are mortal, and as such, they are earthly and return to the earth. "For you are dust, And to dust you shall return" as in the book of Genesis (2:19). But the book of Job (30:19) goes much further. Far from simply attributing the suffering induced by injuries to the body to the trials of finitude, or even to deserved punishment for sin, Job protests the conditions of suffering and death for human bodies. Even more, Job attributes his plight to God: "He [God] has cast me into the mire, And I have become like dust and ashes." It is a challenging question: whether it is ultimately God who is the author of bodies being cast into the muddy ground of mortality or whether the injury and death of bodies is, instead, an offense to God, and whether this is caused by human sin. Christian theology has argued this many ways, as we shall see in Chapter 4.

But whatever the theological view, staying with injuring bodies in war reveals that war is, at bottom, about injury and death, the damage to, and sometimes the end of, the vitality of living human tissue. When this comes into view, war is seen and thus can actually be known for what it is.

Seeing War

The first war where injury and death was really "seen" because it was documented with the new medium of photography was the US Civil War. President Abraham Lincoln gave Matthew Brady (and his assistants who took many of the photos) unprecedented access to the battlefields and camps.[7]

A *New York Times* review of some of photographs of the war exhibited at Brady's Manhattan Gallery a month after the Battle of Antietam testifies to the power of the images of injury and death displayed and how rare it was for people to see war this way.

> [T]he dead of the battle field come to us very rarely even in dreams. We see the list in the morning paper at breakfast but dismiss its recollection with the coffee. But Mr. Brady has done something to bring home to us the terrible reality and earnest-ness of war. If he has not brought bodies and laid them in our dooryards and along the streets, he has done something very like it . . . These pictures have a terrible distinctness. By the aid of the magnifying-glass, the very features of the slain may be distinguished. We would scarce choose to be in the gallery, when one of the women bending over them should recognize a husband, a son, or a brother in the still, lifeless lines of bodies, that lie ready for the gaping trenches.[8]

The photographs do what the lists of the dead cannot; they enable people to "see" the injury and death. Susan Sontag comments on Virginia Woolf's powerful essay, "Why War," a reflection on a series of photographs of war, "Look, the photo-graphs say, *this* is what it's like. This is what war *does*. And *that*, that is what it does too. War tears, rends, War rips open, eviscerates. War scorches. War dismembers. War *ruins*."[9,10]

Photographs compel us to see war because they are records of "what hap-pened." Even though it is now known that photographs in war have been staged and, due to the technological difficulties of the time, many in the Civil War were "stage set," yet photos retain that sense of authenticity because they are made by shards of light from the event itself and impressed on film; in a sense, they *are* a little of the ghost of what happened. At least that physical connection was true until the digital age.

But that is not to say that artistic representation is powerless to convey injur-ing and death in war. Perhaps the most famous artistic interpretation of war as injury and death is Pablo Picasso's *Guernica*. Three-quarters of a century have passed since Picasso painted this nightmare come to life of the bombing of the Basque village of Guernica in northern Spain by German and Italian warplanes at the request of the Spanish Nationalist forces in the Spanish Civil War. The black, white, and grey of the artist's pallet has a timeless photographic quality. The move-ment of the painting is toward the center as a woman's arm holds a lamp to illu-minate the death and injury. This is what you need to see. All is compressed into a room that contains the carnage. A woman weeps over a dead child, a dead soldier lies below with a severed arm and a broken sword, an injured horse cries out in pain under an evil eye with a light bulb, the Spanish word for light bulb and bomb being the same. A bull menaces from beside the evil eye. It is impossibly intense.

That is why, conceivably, a tapestry reproduction of *Guernica* at the United Nations was covered up with a blue cloth during a press conference in February 2003 when Colin Powell gave his error-filled speech on going to war in Iraq. *Guernica* became "An Inconvenient Masterpiece" for its evocation of the reality of what war is really like.[11] The reality convened by *Guernica* was "inconvenient" when placed next to the completely unreal explanation by Colin Powell to the Security Council of why the United States wanted to attack Iraq. Seeing war as injury and death had to be covered up so that the unreality of "reasons" for the Iraq war could progress unimpeded.

Thus "seeing" can occur through art and, as with texts like *All Quiet on the Western Front, Red Badge of Courage*, and many other compelling narratives about war, "seeing" can occur through reading profound writing.

We cannot deny, however, that "ghosts" of the real attach themselves to film in such a powerful way that photographs of war pose a particular claim on the viewer. But while photographs of war do have this kind of power, so too do the moving photographs: the televised pictures and films.

The Vietnam War was the first televised war. The war was brought into American living rooms every evening. The images of "body bags" being unloaded from planes were powerful witnesses to the mass death that was Vietnam.

President Lyndon Johnson came to believe this is why he lost support for his policy in Vietnam. The day after Johnson announced he would not seek reelection, April 1, 1968, he told a meeting of the National Association of Broadcasters how he felt that television coming into American living rooms doomed his policy in Vietnam.[12]

Yes, the intimate witness to injuring in war that television provided for American living rooms was a huge factor in declining public support, but what Johnson failed to understand was that this witnessing became profoundly connected to a praxis of resistance to the war that was widespread. It erupted into full visibility when President Nixon tried to name the Vietnam conflict "Peace with Honor" and couple that to widening the war into Cambodia in the spring of 1970. An already active antiwar movement accelerated. A "tidal wave" of protest by politicians, the press, students, professors, clergy members, business leaders, and many average Americans ensued. On May 4, 1970, at Kent State University in Ohio, National Guardsmen shot and killed four student protesters and wounded nine. In response, more than 400 colleges and universities were shut down, and 100,000 protesters surrounded the White House and various government buildings and memorials in Washington, DC.[13,14]

The Vietnam War continued, however, until March 29, 1973. During 15 years of military involvement, more than 2 million Americans served in Vietnam with 500,000 seeing actual combat. A total of 47,244 were killed in action, including 8,000 airmen. There were 10,446 noncombat deaths. There were 153,329 seriously wounded, including 10,000 amputees. More than 2,400 American POWs/MIAs were unaccounted for as of 1973.[15]

The televised body bags, and the photos and films of injuries and death, did not end the Vietnam War alone. It was the witness and the praxis as well.

This connection can be noted not only when it is present but also when it is absent. Photographs of returning American war dead were banned by President George W. Bush. Eighteen years later, the ban was lifted by President Barack Obama but only when the family gave consent.[16] President Obama went to Dover Air Force Base in 2009 and saluted the returning war dead as the coffins were brought off the plane. While this act did profoundly signal that the Obama administration regarded war not as some cosmic struggle between good and evil but as involving actual death, the photographs of the coffins, unconnected to a coherent American antiwar movement, have produced little in the way of protest against the staggering costs, in injury, lives, and money, of the wars in Afghanistan and Iraq.[17]

An exception may be the photographs of the torture at Abu Ghraib. In the fall of 2003, Iraqi detainees at the notorious Abu Ghraib prison in Iraq were brutalized and sexually humiliated by military and intelligence agents. Photos were taken and subsequently leaked to the press; an investigation followed and a report was issued.[18] Most people have seen some of these images, especially the hooded Iraqi standing on a box and linked to wires. Piles of naked bodies, simulated sex, intimidation with dogs, and even the hideous smiles and thumbs up over a dead body are more familiar. But subsequent images include bloodied prisoners and clear evidence of beating.[19]

These images spurred worldwide outrage; as I asked in May of 2004, when the photos were racing around the Internet and this evidence of American torture in Iraq became clear, "Can a Nation Lose its Soul?"[20] When a nation adopts torture as policy, the answer was and always will be, tragically, yes.

Torture did not end with the investigation at Abu Ghraib, and Guantanamo prison, for example, is not yet closed. The reaction to the prison hunger strike by the force-feeding of the hunger-striking prisoners is a form of continued abuse. A movement has formed to resist torture and is connected by a National Religious Campaign Against Torture (NRCAT) network that is very active in opposing the immoral wounding in war that is torture.[21]

Torture makes the body the sum total of the battlefield where injury and even death are inflicted in a wholly one-sided spectacle of power; torture is therefore strongly related to how women's bodies are battlefields. In addition, the modern trajectory of war is going this way. War is increasingly making the bodies of civilian noncombatants, as well as their means of life in animals, fields, and dwellings, the primary battlefields.

Battlefields

From Gettysburg, to the trenches of France, to the fields of Europe, to the rice paddies of Vietnam, the bodies of combatants have met on battlefields and injury and death have occurred. But over this period, the battlefields became harder and harder to discern. War is becoming more and more a total war, with no distinction between civilian and combatant, and the contest is literally waged in the injuring and death of whole populations. Africa as a continent has become a battlefield, from the Congo to Sierra Leone, Nigeria, Uganda, Chad, the Sudan, Somalia, the Central African Republic, and Ethiopia. But Africa is not alone in this. In the Middle East—from Yemen, to Gaza, Syria, Iraq, Afghanistan, and now Egypt—there are murderous conflicts where the primary battlefields are the bodies of civilians. Central and Latin America are not exempt from this description, nor are significant parts of Asia.

In 2010, *Foreign Policy* did a photo essay called "Planet War" on "the 33 conflicts" raging around the world in that year.[22] What is clear from these photos is that the world today is a battlefield, and a huge percentage of those injured and killed in war are noncombatants. Their bodies are the battlefields.

Hiding the death and injury, whatever the battlefield, has been crucial to continuing to prevent populations from becoming active, engaged "witnesses" to war and rebelling against the carnage—that is, why it is so critical to not look away from death and injury in war.

Mapping the Death and Injury

The Dead

LIFE magazine fought to get a picture by George Strock, another well-known photojournalist, past government censors. The photo showed three American servicemen sprawled on Buna Beach in New Guinea: two are face down, and one is on his back. One of the bodies is partially covered in sand, another partly in the water. The limbs are heavy, without life. It is a photo of death in war, without question. Printed on a full page, an editorial on the facing page explained the struggle to get the photo past government censors at the Office of War Information: "Well, this is the picture," they said. "And the reason we print it now is that, last week, President Roosevelt and Elmer Davis and the War Department decided that the American people ought to be able to see their own boys as they fall in battle; to come directly and without words into the presence of their own dead."[23]

The *Washington Post*, for one, celebrated the new policy. In an editorial on September 11, it said, "An overdose of such photographs would be unhealthy. But in proper proportion they can help us to understand something of what has been sacrificed for the victories we have won. Against a tough and resourceful enemy, every gain entails a cost. To gloss over this grim fact is to blur our vision. If we are to behave as adults in meeting our civilian responsibilities, we must be treated as adults. This means simply that we must be given the truth without regard to fears about how we may react to it."[24]

The irony of assuming there is any number of photographs of death in war that would be "healthy" is plain. "Proper proportion" in regard to "sacrifice" means that those who see these photos are being none too subtly reminded to be calm observers and not cross over into becoming witnesses to death in war and thus becoming activists raising questions about war's purpose.

When injury and death are seen, "sacrifice" is the category used to turn our gaze from what is actually occurring in the reality of war to an abstraction, that abstraction being something called "sacrifice." It is very close to the idea of something sacred, something holy. This serves to remove the injuring and death from their reality on the battlefield of blood, torn flesh, and disintegrating bodies to a level of unreality, the "sacrifice," and thus to justify it.

Injuring and death are war's reality. But injuring and death in war are used to project power when they are constructed as "sacrifice." Injuring and death in war are reconstructed, as in the *Washington Post* comment, as "gain." The one injured, the one killed, disappears and in his or her physical place is substituted the abstraction of the "cost" of victory turned to "gain." Even more remote, and unreal, the conversion of injury and death in war from "cost" to "sacrifice" drains the profanity out of injuring and death in war and replaces it with the sacred. But at the end of the day, the dead bodies of Gettysburg really did not "hallow" the ground. They just became dust and one with the earth.

The problem is that injury and death are war's purpose and really seeing, really stopping just to see and not drifting over into the abstractions of "cost" and "sacrifice" is clearly dangerous; too much seeing war for what it is triggers resistance. This happened in Vietnam, and thus censoring what is "seen" of war again became more the norm in America's wars following that conflict, though it had actually been the case before, in World War II.

There was, in this new century, a huge debate over a decision by the Associated Press (AP) to release a picture taken by photographer Julie Jacobson of a mortally wounded marine in Afghanistan. This debate was fueled in part by the fact that pictures of the extremes of wounding and death on the battlefields of Iraq and Afghanistan had hardly been shown at all to the American public to that point: "The photograph shows Lance Cpl. Joshua M. Bernard of New Portland, Maine, shortly after he was severely wounded by a rocket-propelled grenade during a Taliban ambush in southern Helmand province on Aug. 14. Two Marines are bending over Bernard, whose severed leg is bleeding profusely and whose face bears an expression of shock, with his mouth and eyes wide open. Bernard was evacuated to a hospital but died that day, according to the AP."[25]

Defense Secretary Robert M. Gates criticized the Associated Press for deciding to distribute a photograph of a mortally wounded Marine in Afghanistan over the objections of the Marine's father. The AP defended its decision, saying in an article that it released the photo to convey "the grimness of war and the sacrifice of young men and women fighting it."[26]

War is more than "grim" and it is obscured when it is shoved into the category of "sacrifice," even as AP did when it was defending its decision to show war's reality. War's reality is blood, severed limbs, and death. Photojournalists see that about war far better even than those who look at their photos, and some also see what seeing war can do to those in whose name war is waged.

John G. Morris wrote regarding the controversy over the AP publishing the photo of the dying Marine in Afghanistan,

As picture editor of The New York Times during the Vietnam War, I argued for prominent usage of the pictures by the A.P.'s Eddie Adams of the execution of a Vietcong suspect, for the publication of the photo by the A.P.'s Nick Ut of a naked Cambodian girl running from napalm, of the picture by John Filo of the shooting of a student at Kent State by National Guardsmen. If those pictures helped turned the world against continuation of the Vietnam war I am glad . . . If Julie Jacobson's picture awakens even a few more of our fellow citizens to the necessity of finding a non-military solution in Afghanistan, I shall be eternally grateful.[27]

Seeing war itself, seeing it as injury and death, is dangerous. Seeing their injuries and death does not pose a danger to those involved in the fighting, the dangers to them are far more concrete, the dangers of bodies placed in proximity to bombs and bullets. The real danger of seeing war as injury and death is to those who would persuade their nations that war should be waged and "sacrifices" made.

Death is ever present in war, and the reality of death is the reality of war whether on traditional battlefields or in the total wars of today's conflicts, where the bodies of those who live in a whole country or even region can be the battlefield.

But death in war itself may be changing as war changes. In the "Planet War" photo essay, the dead are civilians and combatants alike. In today's total wars, the bodies are so literally the battlefield, it is sometimes nearly impossible to count the dead.

This is the case for a giant conflict that has been raging for just short of 20 years in the Congo. Jason Stearns's book *Dancing in the Glory of Monsters: The Collapse of the Congo and the Great War of Africa* describes the extraordinary complexity of this war: how to even begin to describe a war that has involved "at least twenty different rebel groups and the armies of nine countries, yet does not seem to have a clear cause or objective?"[28] This is a "war" that "thus far cost the lives of over five million people. The Congolese war must be put among the other great human cataclysms of our time: the World Wars, the Great Leap Forward in China, the Rwandan and Cambodian genocides."[29] Yet this giant, lengthy war that has killed and injured so many is receiving little or no attention from the world.

What do we do with these kinds of wars around the globe today, when even the one thing that is supposed to be real about war, the dead bodies, can hardly be determined, let alone grasped? The "mortality figures are so immense that they become absurd, almost meaningless."[30] What do you do with war when death itself seems not only to be the reality of war but actually its objective? And what do you do with a war that is compared to World Wars I and II in the immensity of its lethality and yet is nearly invisible to the world?

In the summer of 2014, the war between Israel and Gaza resulted in more than 2,100 Palestinian casualties and 73 Israeli casualties.[31] There was extensive coverage in the world press. Now, death in war is always the reality we need to know, but it is significant that there is, by contrast, so much media coverage to the conflict between Israel and Gaza and so little media attention given to the massive war and the immense casualties in the Congo. The Congo, thus, has been called a "Stealth War."[32]

There are a multitude of reasons for the extensive coverage of the conflict between Israel and the Palestinians, like the apparent link to "terrorism" in Middle East conflicts that drives reporting. The conflict in the Congo is complex and multilayered, without the "good guys versus bad guys" frame that the media often follows in reporting on war. And there is, importantly, the racism and the willful blindness in white-dominated Western countries as to how their own colonial ambitions set up Africa for violence, and thus there is a need to turn away from the consequences.

But perhaps that is not even deep enough to account for the lack of attention to 5.4 million dead. When we apply critical analysis to physicality, it is crucial to realize the reason the war in the Congo is hidden is global capitalism. "The DRC [Democratic Republic of the Congo] is rich in natural resources linked to products sold in high-income countries, of particular importance 'conflict minerals' used in information technology."[33] Control of the "slave-based" mines is critical to this supply and "follows a system characterized by horrific physical and sexual violence."[34]

This is the new reality of war, where bodies are the battlefields and much of the conflict is complexly intertwined with global capitalism and its interests. It is a hidden war that feeds on history, culture, and religion, setting up the conditions for permanent war, war without end. The goal is not to dominate territory or enforce a rival ideology. It is about the supply chain of production of goods. This permanent form of war involves far more bodies of civilians than soldiers, and women are very often targets for injury and death. There are no "lines" or even "battlefields," only death and injury on an unimaginable scale. That is what "critical physicality," as a method to examine war and the War on Women, can reveal.

The resistance to seeing death and injury in war has always been high. In this new war of bodies as battlefields, the resistance is immense. There is no way to cast such death and injury as "sacrifice" and make it worth the "cost" when the cost is a cell phone.

Thus it is ever more crucial to stay with the reality of death and also of injury.

Blood

Blood pools on the floor in a picture from Abu Ghraib, bright red and smeared. Next to the pooled blood, an injured prisoner lies, his legs bleeding, especially from the knees. The pooling, smeared blood beside the bleeding knees tells us something of how this prisoner of war was injured—pools of smeared blood and bleeding legs do not lie. Painful injury occurred. That is why Stephen Crane has his main character call war "the red animal" and a "blood-swollen god." The injuring caused by war makes blood flow from the human body. War is bloody.

"The ruthless user of force who shrinks from no amount of bloodshed must gain an advantage if his opponent does not do the same." So Carl von Clausewitz, the German-Prussian soldier and military strategist who died in 1831, writes in the first chapter of his most well-known work, *Vom Kriege* (On War). In other words, the one who is willing to shed the most blood is likely to win a war. Injuring in war may well be measured first by the volume of blood shed and then by the sheer count of the wounded and dead.

Blood colors the battlefield in war; as da Vinci wrote, "let the blood be seen by its color flowing in a sinuous stream from the corpse to the dust." The red blood flows out of the human being as the body is drained of life and becomes the corpse returning to the very field on which battle is waged, the earth.

The original movie *M*A*S*H*, directed by Robert Altman, was a megahit in early 1970. While *M*A*S*H* is supposed to be about a mobile army surgical hospital in the Korean War, it is really a thinly disguised protest about the blood-soaked absurdity of the Vietnam War. And blood is everywhere. Over the mellow guitar sound of a song oddly titled "Suicide Is Painless," helicopters keep unloading bloodied, wounded bodies of soldiers. The operating room scenes are soaked in blood: blood on the patients, on the doctors, on the sheets, on the tables, on the floor. Blood is everywhere. This antiwar film brought home to Americans, already questioning their nation's involvement in Vietnam, the bloodied mess war makes of bodies.

As you work your way through the collection of the photographs, "Mud, Blood and Terror: The Brutality of the Vietnam War Captured in Harrowing Images," the color that leaps out in each scene is the red of the blood, contrasted with the brown, mud-smeared bodies and uniforms and the lush green of the jungle in the background. The photographs were the work of *LIFE* magazine war photographer Larry Burrows as he captured Operation Prairie, the US offensive against the North Vietnamese near the Demilitarized Zone (DMZ) that lasted from August 3 to October 27, 1966.[35]

Color photography was available from the beginning of the twentieth century, but the difficulties of the process meant most war photos were of posed figures and settings. When the technology advanced, so did the merging of the concepts of journalism and photography. Nothing epitomized this merger like the creation of *LIFE* magazine in 1936, and photojournalists created some of the most iconic images ever recorded in covering World War II. It was not until Vietnam, however, that the blood of war came into American homes in "living color" through *LIFE* as well as other journals.

This realism about showing bloodshed in war was actually new in Vietnam. McCullin, who was a photographer covering the Vietnam war for the *Sunday Times* of London, photographed dying American soldiers, helped transport a wounded soldier in a stretcher off the battlefield in Hue, and was himself injured in Cambodia. "I took exactly the same risks that they took," he said. Another Vietnam-era photojournalist, Dirck Halstead, had a similar recollection on war photography in that period.[36]

Vietnam was thus recorded in photographs and films as, indeed, blood-swollen with injury and death. It is no wonder subsequent American administrations shut down such total access to the battlefield by photographers, videographers, and reporters. There is too much blood.

Limbs

A way to imagine war is to stay with the injury and death, no matter how challenging that may be. The number of dead in the Congo may be vast (the International Red Cross now estimates 5.4 million dead[37]) and hidden, but these dead bodies are real.[38] The injuries are vast as well, but they too exist, though on the margins of the societies.

> Just outside a military camp in Katindo, not far from Goma, a group of disabled former soldiers have gathered. Some have amputated limbs, others have lost eyes, and a few have been crippled by shrapnel.
>   These people are collectively known as kajorités, said to be a corruption of the English word casualty. They say that a lack of government assistance for former soldiers is condemning those that have been injured in battle to a life of misery.[39]

Lost limbs are a vivid part of the injuries with which the survivors of war have to deal.

An evocative part of *Guernica* is the soldier lying dead with a severed arm. The reality of death is the reality of war, but dead bodies do get buried. The dead are mourned by their families and friends and by their communities, but then these deaths retreat into memory. The bodies of those who survive war, however, are a living testimony to the ongoing reality of war's identity as injuring. Lost limbs speak volumes of that reality.

In the Congo, there is very little medical treatment for those injured in war. But in the wars in Iraq and Afghanistan, the reverse is true, especially close to the battlefield. Many with catastrophic war injuries are saved by rapid and effective medical treatment.

Baghdad ER is a documentary released by HBO on May 21, 2006. It was filmed at the 86th Combat Support Hospital in the Green Zone in Baghdad, Iraq. The film clearly shows the devastating injuries and death occurring in the Iraq War. After initially seeming to support the project, the army then pulled back. The Army surgeon general took the unusual step of warning military personnel that viewing the documentary could cause post-traumatic stress disorder, while the Secretary of the Army asked HBO to delete some footage from the final cut. HBO's offer to cosponsor a screening of the film at Fort Campbell, Kentucky, where the 86th is based, was turned down by the Pentagon.[40]

A screening of the film at the National Museum of American History was attended mostly by civilians and not the invited military as well. This disappointed the film's producers: "'Maybe people [at the Pentagon] feel the truth will discourage people' from backing the war, Sheila Nevins, president of HBO's documentary unit, said after the invitation-only screening. 'The film certainly tells you what could happen in a war, but it's also about the heroism, courage and dedication of our troops.'"[41]

The documentary is an unflinching look at what happens to bodies in war; in the first two minutes of the film, bloodied, nearly naked bodies on stretchers are carried into the hospital, and then an amputated arm is removed from the operating table and placed in a trash bag. The amputated arm is African American. As it is carried to the trash bag, the viewer of the documentary has a brief glimpse of the injury to the bodies of African Americans in American wars today. African American enlistment in the services has increased significantly and is likely due to the poor economy.[42]

Blood is everywhere, on the bodies of the wounded, mopped from the floors, and cleaned from the tables. Despite the high survival rate of injured soldiers in Iraq (90 percent), death still occurs. At one point, an Army chaplain, reciting last rites for a soldier, calls all the violence "senseless."

While graphic, *Baghdad ER* shows injury as the reality of war. But survival of the injured then becomes an ongoing reality and often a difficult one for veterans as they attempt to cope with disfiguring injury. While more and more, the advances in prosthetic limbs are making it possible for even those who have lost more than one limb to function, their presence in civilian society is a crucial reminder of the reality of war as injuring. It is crucial that society not turn away from those injured from war. This is true especially of the most difficult injury for veterans to present to the society, a disfiguring injury to the face.

Injury to Faces

Perhaps more than any other body part, the human face is most often seen by others. The face is rarely covered, though in the Islamic faith this may not be true for some women. But even a religious obligation to cover the face reveals the importance of the face. The human face is significantly human.

Seeing the injuries to the human face is crucially important in seeing war as injury. Ernst Friedrich's book *Krieg dem Krieg!* (War against War), published in 1924, was a dramatic effort to demonstrate, through photographs, the appalling injury, death, and destruction of World War I and to juxtapose it to the hypocrisy and lies of those who would advocate for war. A particularly compelling section on ruined faces is called "Face of War." The publication of the book, in four languages, created a firestorm of controversy. It was "immediately denounced by the government and by veterans' and other patriotic organizations—in some cities the police raided bookstores, and lawsuits were brought against the public display of the photographs . . . By 1930 *War Against War* had gone through ten editions in Germany and been translated into many languages."[43]

The wars in Iraq and Afghanistan have produced many facial injuries, especially the particular pattern of injuries from improvised explosive devices (IEDs). These injuries can easily be witnessed in survivors of injury in war, and facial injuries are often the most psychologically devastating to survivors of violence.

"I used to look in the mirror at my missing ears, missing nose—do I really want to go outside today?" says Shilo Harris, a 10th Mountain Division staff sergeant who was badly injured and burned in an IED explosion in Iraq in 2007. "I was all bent over, crippled up, I felt exposed."[44]

With so many veterans surviving war, though often with devastating injury, research is being done into how best to reintegrate them into society.[45] But it is equally the case that society needs to be reintegrated to veterans, as the constant desire to keep from really seeing war as injury extends to the constant desire to keep from seeing those whose very bodies carry the scars of war's wounding.

Scars of many kinds, not just facial, are part of the recovery from wounding in war, and veterans who have visible wounds recover better when they are integrated into society and their scars are acknowledged. But this is often difficult when, in the time between wars, focus is taken off the reality of war and a kind of national "amnesia" sets in, allowing the reality, even as poorly seen as it is, to recede from view, paving the way for the next war.

But if it is difficult to get societies to accept those who bear visible injury in war, it is even more difficult to achieve acceptance of the invisible injuries of war that are devastating and extensive.

Post-Traumatic Stress Disorder

Many of the issues covered in this book come together in the history of struggle for the recognition and humane treatment of the mental injuries that result from war. This history replicates the way in which injuring and death in war, in order to be continued by societies, must remain partly if not wholly out of direct view. War, when seen for what it is, inspires resistance. War then is redescribed as "politics by other means" per Clausewitz, or "sacrifice" and "heroism," and thus made acceptable, even sacred.

Psychological injury from war flies in the face of the sanitized "war as politics by other means" description, or the idea that war is about "heroes" sacrificing for a noble cause.

Psychological trauma from war, even when some symptoms were first recognized in the nineteenth century, was first considered men becoming "hysterical." This was horrifying to societies, as the very concept of what it meant to be a "man" was at risk of being overturned. Since the time of the Greeks, hysteria was a term given to the excesses of emotion exclusive to women caused by disturbances of the uterus (from the Greek ὑστέρα "hystera" = uterus).

In World War I, these symptoms were then renamed "Shell Shock." Shell shock was the distinctive injury of that first war of the modern age. The huge artillery shells used in that war were thought to literally concuss soldiers and produce the grave and debilitating psychiatric symptoms that started to fill hospitals. The war poet Siegfried Sassoon, himself a victim, describes the psychological pain of shell shock in his poem "Survivors." He writes of soldiers with "dreams that drip with murder" and their "stammering, disconnected talk."[46]

But what of these symptoms that were occurring in soldiers who had not been concussed by shells? This was then thought to be an immoral attempt to malinger and shirk the duty of a soldier. Some shell-shocked soldiers were shot dead by their own side after being charged with cowardice. *Paths of Glory* is a 1957 American antiwar film by Stanley Kubrick based on the novel by the same name by Humphrey Cobb. It takes place during World War I and stars Kirk Douglas as Colonel Dax, the commanding officer of French soldiers who refused to continue a suicidal attack. Dax attempts to defend them against a charge of cowardice in a court-martial. The venal superior officers demand that some soldiers from each unit be shot for cowardice.

But what was really happening was that "under conditions of unremitting exposure to the horrors of trench warfare, men began to break down in shocking numbers."[47]

When the vast numbers of soldiers suffering from some form of combat neurosis could no longer be denied, it was acknowledged. But treatment focused on how quickly soldiers could be returned to combat.[48] In World War II, this was the approved treatment and considered "successful" if combat personnel exhibiting symptoms could be quickly treated and returned to their units. There was little attention paid to the long-term effects of combat neurosis on the veterans of that war.

It was not until the Vietnam War that sustained attention and research was finally placed on the hidden wounds of war. This was due not to the Veterans Administration but to the Vietnam veterans themselves. "In 1970, while the Vietnam War was at its height, two psychiatrists, Robert Jay Lifton and Chaim Shatan, met with representatives of a new organization called Vietnam Veterans against the War."[49] This was a form of witnessing and action at its most intense. These veterans were organizing against their own war and at the same time creating a movement to treat their own.

"They raised questions," Lifton wrote, "about everyone's version of the socialized warrior and the war system, and exposed their country's counterfeit claim of a just war."[50] The work of the Vietnam Veterans Against the War, along with sympathetic psychiatrists, resulted in the eventual adoption of the term "Post-traumatic stress disorder" or PTSD in the mid-1970s.

Post-traumatic stress disorder is an accepted clinical term today, and those in combat as well as veterans can receive treatment for it. Yet veterans struggle with the negative public perception of PTSD as meaning "ticking time bomb" and fear the diagnosis because of the stigma. "Many service members feel unable to come forward" because of the social disgrace and disapproval still associated with psychological wounds of war. Soldiers "fear being seen as weak or unreliable to their fellow soldiers, or that seeking treatment will negatively affect their career" in the military or once they are discharged. "Unfortunately, veterans who do not seek treatment often turn to substance abuse, or in some cases even suicide, as an escape."[51]

But psychological wounds reveal the central goal of war, the injuring and death that are its reality, and these wounds also reveal that those who experience this reality can be driven to the limits of their minds because of what war is really like, including the War on Women.

Rape and Post-Traumatic Stress Disorder

How much is the extent of the mental damage, specifically for women in the military, a result not only of the violence of the designated battlefield, the area of approved combat, but also of their bodies being made into battlefields in the military itself?

In the past, the photographing, filming, and depicting of injury and death of bodies in war, as well as through art and narrative, were co-opted through the idea of "sacrifice" and translated into the fiction that war is heroic; war was recorded, and films were made about war, because it was deemed a large subject, a worthy subject, especially when recast as "sacrifice." But these records were kept almost exclusively of the appropriately "heroic" subjects of war. It has been a huge struggle to get reports of the sexual assault of women in the military and to get appropriate prosecution and preventive action taken.

Women warriors have mostly been either the exceptional woman hero, often embellished through legend, or mythological figures such as a warrior goddess like Athena. Women actually serving in the armed services—not only in support services such as nursing but also as more immediately engaged in active-duty, combat-related work—is a relatively recent phenomenon in the West, dating from the 1970s.[52]

Along with women serving in the military has come military sexual assault. In the Introduction, the description of a gang rape of a woman who was a brand-new recruit sent to Germany by the US military was compared to the harrowing injuries of the battlefield as described in *All Quiet on the Western Front*.

The cover-ups of the extent of military sexual assault have been extensive, so much so that in 2011, a lawsuit was filed against then Secretary of Defense Gates and his predecessor that alleged the military "created a culture where violence against women was tolerated."[53] This has continued and in fact seems to have gotten worse. The Pentagon released a report in 2013 of estimated sexual assaults in the military from 2012 that shows these attacks are up sharply, up to the rate of 70 per day.[54]

The Service Women's Action Network fact sheet on "Rape, Sexual Assault and Sexual Harassment in the Military" states there have been "25 years of Pentagon studies, task forces, and congressional hearings" and this violence continues to occur at "alarming rates." [55] The military system cannot fix itself from the inside because the culture itself has produced this result. Rape culture in the military is a product of the gender and power relations of military culture.

The personal stories of women who have been raped, often repeatedly, in the military are heartrending stories of injury. These are accounts of being drugged, bruised, cut, improperly treated for the injuries, and punished rather than being helped and their complaints pursued. Myah Bilton-Smith of Vancouver, Washington, said she was raped twice on a Texas Air Force base. It was her mother, who was able to get to her after a week, who documented her external injuries, "a gash in Myah's head and . . . bruises on her body." Bilton-Smith told reporters, "Sometimes I find myself getting really aggressive, getting mad at the people I really shouldn't be made at, crying, hysterically." The reporter wrote, "Those are the symptoms of post-traumatic stress disorder. But the 21-year-old has never been to war."[56]

Actually, Bilton-Smith has been to war: she's been to the War on Women in the military. And she's still there.

Not only women are sexually assaulted in the military, as reports show. Overall, the most recent statistics for the United States translate into almost three rapes every hour, all day long, all night long, every 24 hours. That's combat no matter how you define it.

Weaponizing the Body: War and the War on Women Are Merging

War is vast and complex, as is the War on Women, and there are differences. But today, war and the War on Women are merging. Not only is this seen in the sexual assaults in the military but also in sexual assault itself being a chosen weapon in waging war. Injuring women in war, especially through the rape of civilians, has been part of war for millennia. Now, however, the body, and the bodies of women in particular, are being weaponized and becoming an increasing part of the strategy of war itself.

Rape in war is more and more adopted as actual policy, as a war strategy, to assert the power of one group over another. Wartime rape of civilians, in fact, "produces a relationship of inequality between two kinds of men: those who assert their physical and societal virility by committing the assault and those for whom this same act represents a symbolic castration owing to their inability to protect their wives, sisters or mothers."[57]

This is why there has been such a prolonged struggle to establish that rape is a war crime and to have rape included in the United Nations Convention on Terror and Torture. In 2008, the United Nations adopted Resolution 1820 "U.N. Action against Sexual Violence in Conflict." The resolution recognizes rape as a war tactic and makes rape in war an issue of international peace and security. The resolution demands that parties in armed conflict adopt measures to end sexual violence, punish perpetrators, train troops, and enforce military discipline. Women, the resolution states, should participate directly in all processes to end sexual violence in conflict.

A crucial report on a related United Nations campaign to deal with rape in war as a war crime documents the way in which rape in war, while it has existed for millennia, has now become a "strategic military tactic." In May 2010, the United Nations first appointed special representative for sexual violence began a two-year campaign to begin to challenge this tactic precisely as a war crime, as well as to get help for victims. The struggle has been titanic, with countries banning aid organizations that attempt to provide services to rape victims.[58]

Including rape as a war crime and recognizing that is should be shunned as a tactic of war, not merely considered as crimes committed by individual troops, is an important step. But as the report on the first few years of these efforts shows, the problem is overwhelming in its immensity and the resistance to implementing even the steps to help victims is entrenched. This resistance, in fact, illustrates the extent to which rape is foundational especially to modern war and how the War on Women and war itself have merged in the last decades.

Rape is a particularly intimate form of violence and for that reason more akin to torture than to being killed in war by a bomb or even a bullet. Rape as a tool of war should, in fact, be considered torture, as it is designed to denigrate, humiliate, and ultimately demonstrate total control over the body, mind, and spirit of women. Rape of men in war is an extension of this strategy.

In the fall of 2014, the Senate Intelligence Committee released a report on its more than five years of investigation into what Senator Diane Feinstein, on the floor of the Senate, called "torture" during the Bush administration.[59]

Many Americans were shocked to find out that the extent of the torture and that it included sexualized violence, and threats of sexual violence, against the families of detainees. The CIA used interrogators who "admitted to sexual assault" and practiced rectal feeding and rehydration on at least five detainees without "documented medical necessity." CIA detainees were fed a combination of pureed foods through the rectum. Nasal forced feeding of a prisoner who is on a hunger strike is already legally controversial. Rectal feeding with no medical necessity should be considered rape, as attorney and Cornell law professor Michael C. Dorf argues.

> [I]t is not even clear that it is legal to force-feed prisoners via a nasogastric tube. But at least there's a plausible medical argument for using an IV and/or nasogastric tube if one has decided that forced feeding is appropriate. By contrast, there was no medical reason why the CIA chose rectal feeding and hydration for its prisoners. Instead, the Report concludes, the method was chosen as a means of exercising total control over prisoners.
>
> The CIA used rectal feeding and rectal hydration–rather than some less intrusive method of forced feeding or no forced feeding at all–specifically for the purpose of inflicting pain and humiliation on the prisoners. Put more starkly, in addition to threatening to rape the mothers of some of its prisoners, the CIA used rectal feeding and rectal hydration to anally rape prisoners.[60]

The Senate report shows the torture techniques used were far more brutal than the CIA has ever admitted; in addition to the anal rapes and threats of rape against family members, waterboarding and sleep deprivation went on "in near nonstop fashion for days or weeks at a time." In one facility, a detainee was said to have died of hypothermia after being held "partially nude" and chained to a concrete floor, while at other times, naked prisoners were hooded and dragged up and down corridors while being slapped and punched. Detainees were placed in "ice water 'baths.'"

This is a clear instance of weaponizing the body in a spectacle of power. The Senate report goes to great length to show no actionable intelligence was obtained through torture. Regardless of that, however, torture under all circumstances is a war crime, including rape.

Bodies as Battlefields: The Future of War

Twenty-first-century war, with all its technological sophistication, is being fought more and more specifically on the bodies of civilians, especially the bodies of women and children. Like torture, war is intimately waged on the battlefield of these specific bodies. This means that war and the War on Women are coming to resemble each other more and more.

This is why it is so crucial to understand not only how war is about out-injuring the bodies of the military enemy but why specific aspects of the War on Women are increasingly part of the strategy of war itself. Even when these strategies are made a war crime, like torture has been made a war crime, the strategies are increasing, not decreasing, around the world.

In other words, the War on Women is the future of war.

It is crucial, therefore, both to prevent, reduce, and ultimately to end war, the War on Women must be fully seen and analyzed, and ending the War on Women must become a primary, not peripheral, part of a comprehensive approach to peacemaking. In order to craft a more complex approach to peacemaking in the future, the War on Women must be fully comprehended and the social, political, economic, philosophical, and religious supports for it thoroughly examined, and those aspects that support the War on Women, as well as war, must be rejected and new constructions offered to fuel a comprehensive peace movement.

Actually witnessing the War on Women is the place to start.

2

Injuring in the War on Women

Violence against women is the largest and longest global war.

Susan Thistlethwaite

The War on Women is literally a war, and it is going on all around us, all day and all night, all the time; it is a global war of epidemic proportions, as the World Health Organization data indicate. It is a war fought on the bodies of women, where their bodies are the battlefield, both in terms of violent assault and occupation. Women's bodies, minds, and spirits are the objects of the attempt to occupy them, an occupation that is socially and religiously sanctioned and backed up by the threat of force or through violent attack. It is sanctioned by custom, religion, and often law.

Like war, the War on Women poses a threat to human lives, and thus it is an existential crisis. It is a war where the death of women is common and injury to women all too frequent. But the existential crisis of the War on Women extends beyond immediate death and injury as happens on battlefields in war. It is a struggle for the very lives of women as self-actualizing human beings whose bodies, minds, and spirits belong to them and not to another.

Like war, the global War on Women is about power, but this is power derived not from public spectacle but from being hidden like the "stealth war" in the Congo. The power dynamic in the War on Women comes from the real, but hidden, control of a very specific territory, the bodies of women. This power is supported by a basic ideology, an ideology that has existed in transhistorical and multicultural versions for millennia. This ideology, reduced to its simplest form, is that women's bodies, minds, and spirits are owned by the males in their lives and in their societies.

Whose Is This Body?

The idea that women's bodies, minds, and spirits are at the service not of themselves, but of dominant men, is profoundly supported in many religions and across cultures. In Thailand, when Rita Nakashima Brock and I were researching our book, *Casting Stones: Prostitution and Liberation in Asia and the United States*, a woman who worked in Bangkok with women in prostitution or who were seeking to leave prostitution, asked me this question: "Why are women born into the world owing a debt, and men are born being owed?" This shelter worker's question sums up the puzzling, but all too real, ubiquity of male dominance. While the form of the question she posed is rooted in a Buddhist view, the underlying observation of the perversity of the higher value of males over females is clear.

This volume focuses on a global War on Women. There are other kinds of gender-based wars and these are also important to consider. There is, and has been, a global war on lesbian, gay, bisexual and/or transgender people (LGBT) that is often lethal as well as producing injury. Men who self-identify as straight are also subject to sexual violence as the statistics on sexual assault in the American military makes clear.

Women, and specifically women's bodies as battlefields, are the subject of this examination, however, though "women" is not a group that is unitary by any means. There are significant differences among women, including those of sexual orientation, as well as race, class, national origin, and religious or humanist, non-religious identity. But violence perpetrated on the bodies of women, despite these differences (though sometimes because of them), is a "difference in common" that women have.[1]

One of the achievements of the modern women's movement of the 1960s was the assertion of gender as a political category. The parameters of this assertion were ultimately shown to have been flawed, however, as they followed the fault lines of social and economic hierarchies of race, class, sexual orientation, and national origin. Subsequent work in Womanist, queer, and postcolonial theory has reinvented these categories in indispensable ways. Womanist and queer theory are indispensable to understanding the body and, with postcolonial theory, how the body is made to function in relationship to invading and occupying power before, during, and after violent assault.

Those categories will be employed in this study as the crucial question of "which bodies of women" are the most frequent battlefields in the War on Women and therefore must be kept in constant view. But it is also the case that all women's bodies are at risk of becoming battlefields. No socioeconomic status will protect a woman from domestic violence, no race or ethnicity is proof against rape or battery, there is no "safe" sexual orientation for women, or a nation where the global War on Women, in some form, does not occur.

It is often said that violence against women is "hidden" or "secret," but an unholy surprise is that it can be viewed daily, and that has been true for millennia. It is true that presidents do not send photographers to record the War on Women, but that does not mean the injuries from the War on Women are not visible. The injuries and death of women in the War on Women can be viewed daily in the news media, for example; its very prevalence is an aspect of why it is considered "hidden." The culture of violence against women is so strong because this violence is normalized; violence against women is everywhere but what is sanctioned is calling it into question.

It is possible to break through the normalizing of the War on Women and see the injuries and death as war, but seeing this war, like seeing war in general, means one has to go beyond spectating. The global War on Women can be seen but rarely known for what it is without being engaged in a movement to end this violence. Becoming a witness helps create the conditions where what is right in front of us all the time can be known for what it is.

Witnessing the global War on Women requires connection to, and participation in, the global movement to end violence against women. As a war fought primarily on the bodies of women, women themselves are the key sources of information on the contours of this war; women themselves must primarily be the ones who "map" the injuries and death, and their voices will be privileged as sources. But as a movement, allies can provide important help and are necessary to achieve the political, social, economic, and religious changes required.

"Normalizing" the War on Women

From ancient myths; through the texts of classical and biblical times; in the history of art, literature, and global religions; and through law and culture, the injury and death of women in the War on Women is everywhere described and pictured.

The astonishing volume of this representation, however, does not mean it has functioned, at least until very recently, to provide the witnessing so crucial to resistance. In fact, the reverse has been true. The staggering amount of depiction of violence against women from rape, domestic violence, torture, and death has served to bolster the power dynamic that not only permits it to occur but demands it as an enactment of the very structures on which societies are based.

Women's bodies are frequently displayed as injured and killed in many forms in human history in order to normalize these injuries and then to enforce and police the norms. To actually "see" past what is being normalized, it has to be queered.

To "queer" a subject is to make its very normativity problematic. "It marks not by defining, but by taking up a distance from what is perceived as the normative. The term is deployed in order to mark, and to make, a difference, a divergence."[2]

It is therefore necessary to take up a distance from all this representation of the injuring of women—a position outside the borders of social and religious enforcement—in order to witness it. Queer theory, along with Womanism and feminism, is crucial to displacing the vast amount of injury and death of women from within the power structure of dominance and submission where it has resided and placing it outside. Then injuring women's bodies, even to death, can be seen as beyond the confines of "normal." "Seeing" then becomes not the performance of the customary but of identifying the criminal.

We have to choose, in fact, where we will stand as we look. I have chosen to stand within Euro-Atlantic culture and examine it in regard to its role in the War on Women. The terms of this war set the parameters both for women's bodies as battlefields within Western culture and they also have been powerful in setting the terms for how these cultures engage globally. Increasingly, the model of women's bodies as battlefields is coming to be the model for globalization and the role of war and the War on Women as advancing the interests of global economics.

Rapists as the Shock Troops in the War on Women

Susan Brownmiller has rightly placed rape in the context of a War on Women as she wrote, "men who commit rape have served in effect as front-line masculine shock troops, terrorist guerrillas in the longest battle the world has ever known."[3] Founding myths are routinely rooted in a primal act of violence against women, and these myths travel through history in art and literature and are reinforced over and over again. Walk into any well-known, Western art museum, and you are likely to find representations of the War on Women as a classical theme.

This can be seen, for example, in the Roman legend of the Rape of Lucretia. Roman historian Livy (d. 17 AD) spent 40 years writing his 142-book *History of Rome*. In his work, he repeats this story that connects rape and the Republic.[4] Lucretia, a virtuous Roman woman, married to Lucius Tarquinius Collatinus, is raped by Sextus Tarquinius, the Etruscan king's son. Lucretia subsequently commits suicide, and this was given as the immediate cause of the revolution that overthrew the monarchy and established the Roman Republic.

This classical legend is splashed all over museum walls in the West, represented for all to see. It serves to connect violence against women with the founding of a republic, displacing women from the political to the physical as the public state is founded on their very bodies. It is not enough for these founding myths to be told. They must be told again and again, century after century, to continue to secure the power dynamic that not only permits but also requires a War on Women.

The Death of Lucretia appears over and over in Western art and literature. The use of this legend in Act 2 of Shakespeare's *Titus Andronicus* is especially illustrative. Shakespeare has Lavinia refuse to name rape; she refers to an impending sexual assault as that which "womanhood denies my tongue to tell" and as a "worse-than-killing lust" (2.3.174, 175). This is a representation of rape that carries its own normalizing function within the lines of the play itself. It is the naming of rape that is shameful, not the act.[5]

Another founding Roman myth was the Rape of the Sabine Women. It is an episode in Roman history traditionally dated to 750 BC, in which the first generation of Roman men acquired wives for themselves by kidnapping them from the neighboring Sabine families.

In Renaissance art, the Rape of the Sabine Women was a pretext for depicting extreme poses of bodies in battle scenes with semiclad females in sexually suggestive poses. In the huge sculpture by Giambologna (1579–83), the role of the War on Women as combat with other men is clearly displayed. The sculpture shows a man lifting a protesting woman into the air, while a second man crouches on the ground. The woman is attempting to arch away from her abductor, while the male figure, captured between the abductor's legs, is rendered helpless to assist her. The sculpture, considered a masterpiece, displays two naked men embroiled in a contest over a naked woman in a greater-than-life-size version. It supports the thesis that the War on Women is a contest between men for control of women.

You can trace this theme of the rape of women as a founding social norm of Western culture right up through popular fiction and Hollywood film. *Seven Brides for Seven Brothers* is the Hollywood version. The screenplay is based on a short story, *The Sobbin' Women*, by Stephen Vincent Benét. While cleaned up for Hollywood (the "brides" are chaperoned!), the idea of marriage as a conquest of the female is sufficiently represented. The film was a 1954 Oscar nominee for Best Picture.

The Rape of Tamar (2 Samuel 13:1–22) plays a somewhat similar role as a biblical text that establishes the acceptable boundaries of rape as a social norm in a political context. King David's son Absalom had "a beautiful sister whose name was Tamar" (1); David's son Amnon develops an obsession for Tamar, termed "love" in the text. Amnon tricks Tamar into being alone with him in his bedroom under the guise of taking care of him when he feigned illness (8–14). The obsession reveals itself as hate, and Amnon turns Tamar out instead of marrying her, as custom would have dictated. Tamar does not remain silent; she does go away, but she tears her clothes, puts ashes on her head, and cries aloud (19). Her brother Absalom tells her to be quiet, and she does, remaining "a desolate woman" in his house. But Absalom is not quiet, and he "hated Amnon, because he had raped his sister Tamar" (22b).

Many elements of the tradition of normalizing rape are present in this text in 2 Samuel; obsession is termed "love," it is Tamar who is shamed, and she is told to be quiet. But the contestants in this War on Women are the two brothers of King David, and the struggle is a political struggle fought on and over the body of Tamar as battlefield. Ultimately, Absalom arranges for Amnon to be killed, fixing the idea that the Rape of Tamar is about the conflicted relationships among men—that is, Absalom, Amnon, and their father King David.

The Rape of Tamar is widely represented in Christian iconography of the sixteenth and seventeenth centuries by Dutch and Italian painters as analyzed in an article on the subject for the Society of Biblical Literature by Sara Kipfer. According to Kipfer, the Rape of Tamar "is depicted in no fewer than twenty paintings and probably also in as many copper engravings and woodcuts, among them a whole series of illustrations, such as the ones by Philips Galle, as well as an ink drawing by Rembrandt Harmensz van Rijn."[6]

Her analysis of Antonio Bellucci's painting on the subject is helpful, as she demonstrates how Bellucci plays with perspective and makes the viewer "not only is an observer and voyeur of this act of violence, but also becomes involved as co-rapist." She concludes, of this large collection of paintings on this one biblical text of rape, "the exercise of power and the behavior of the victim are mercilessly and openly depicted."

An issue that is not addressed in the article, however, is why these cultures in this period of time would support a veritable orgy of paintings of rape. The sixteenth and seventeenth centuries in Europe are the Enlightenment, that period of intellectual upheaval in European philosophy, science, religion, and of course, art.

The question of whether the Enlightenment was "good or bad" for women's rights is contested. Since the Enlightenment celebrated the intellect over the body, women as the symbolic carriers of embodiment did not fare well in terms of being included in the "rights of man." But periods of upheaval can have unintended consequences. Certainly, Mary Wollstonecraft demonstrated that in her life and work.

Wollstonecraft (1759–97) was a British Enlightenment philosopher and writer. Her best known work, *A Vindication of the Rights of Women: With Strictures on Political and Moral Subjects* (1792), was an argument that women are not "naturally" inferior to men but only appear to be because they lack education. Building on the central role of reason in the Enlightenment, she suggests that both men and women are rational beings and should participate equally in a social order founded on reason. As she wrote in that work, "I love man as my fellow; but his scepter, real, or usurped, extends not to me, unless the reason of an individual demands my homage; and even then the submission is to reason, and not to man."[7]

One area of contestation, clearly shown by Wollstonecraft in the subtitle to her work, as well as in the book's argument, is the challenge to include women equally in political—that is, public—life. This is why, in my view, the explosion of rape themes occurs in art in this period. Rape and the threat of rape function to create a kind of "no man's land," a policed barrier around the home. Women are threatened with sexual violence if they cross through this zone and venture into the public square.

Rape has always functioned as the ultimate violent barrier to women's public participation. This is despite the fact that, as the Rape of Tamar shows, many rapes are not "stranger danger" but committed by trusted family and friends. It is interesting, as Kipfer points out, that one very talented Baroque painter of the same period, Artemisia Gentileschi (1593–1654), painted many biblical scenes but never painted the Rape of Tamar. Gentileschi had herself been raped by a painter colleague of her father, as court documents showed. But the outpouring of artistic representations of rape on the part of so many male painters may, in fact, be an attempt to put up violent warning signs for women (and for men), as women were taking on roles, or perhaps considering roles, less fixed than in the past.[8]

Painting, in these centuries, was an elite cultural product, given who could afford paintings and who visited galleries and museums. Yet some of these paintings, especially of biblical themes, were also displayed in churches and especially cathedrals. When combined with preaching from these biblical texts, these provided the transmission mechanism for the whole of society, through misogynist preaching. Plays (such as those of Shakespeare) were attended by the working class and elites alike and also served to reinforce the message on the silencing of women about the ubiquity of rape.

The rape of women as portrayed in all these venues also functions as a limiting mechanism for the whole notion of "rights" in relationship to society and politics. Certain individuals—that is, dominant race and class males—have rights but these are not extended to women and to racial and class nondominants.

This can be seen as rape is also made visible in this period as a violent enforcement mechanism in another political and economic practice, the Atlantic slave trade. Slavery was, of course, not new at the time of the Enlightenment. Slavery is as ancient as the Code of Hammurabi and was an integral part of Greek and Roman culture and early Christianity. Slavery in many forms, from indentured servitude to prisoners of war, has been found throughout the world, and rape and battering have been part of its enforcement mechanisms. It is now illegal throughout the world as well, though many are held in industrial, mining, and sex-trade conditions that are slavery.

Yet the Atlantic slave trade was enormous, perhaps eclipsing in size and scope the nature of slavery in prior history. The Atlantic slave trade was helped grow into a huge commercial enterprise by the technological innovations of the Enlightenment that made Atlantic travel feasible, the "discovery" of "new worlds" for economic expansion, and the invention of racism as a means to justify the capture and enslavement of huge numbers of men and women during a period that invented the "rights of man."

The *Rape of the Negro Woman* (1632) by Dutch painter Christiaen van Couwenbergh is a vivid representation of the European construction of whiteness as explicitly achieved through the violent sexual violation of an African woman. The painting features three white men and an African woman. The woman is being held clearly against her will on the lap of a white man sitting on the foot of a bed. Her skin is painted as starkly black, throwing his limbs and torso into a contrasted relief. Another white man, holding a cloth over his genitals, is pointing at the woman and laughing. But his gaze is toward the viewer of the painting, inviting complicity in the rape in a very similar fashion to Antonio Bellucci's *Rape of Tamar*. A third man, in the background, is fully clothed and his hands are raised as if in protest. Is this a servant, helpless to intervene, or is his protest merely a token? It is not clear, but the status of the two naked and nearly naked rapists seems emphasized in their power and privilege over the African woman's body by the one fully clothed. The violent struggle of the African woman to escape being raped is portrayed as an occasion for humor.[9]

The Atlantic slave trade served Euro-Atlantic cultures in their quest for economic dominance. This quest created and maintained a slave system that was as violent as any known in the history of slavery. As is documented in slave narratives, sexual violence and degradation were a daily occurrence in slavery in the United States and in European colonies. The War on Women in slavery was indeed fought on their bodies as battlefields as the Couwenbergh painting illustrates. But paintings like this go further; they are not merely an artistic production, they are one of the primary mechanisms that help create and justify the denigration of African women's bodies.

The social, religious, and economic function of the representation of rape in the Enlightenment period, a period where forces of change were pressing on societies, is mirrored in the twenty-first century in American politics and the images of rape culture, its justifications and even replication in laws that required mandatory, invasive, intravaginal ultrasounds that fit the definition of rape.[10]

The frequent representation of rape in current American culture has been termed a "War on Women" for its virulence.[11] There are aspects of this war that mirror the sixteenth to eighteenth centuries because this twenty-first-century "War on Women" took place within the highly contested American political arena of 2012. As the country's first African American president sought reelection and a more diverse (and increasingly younger) electorate emerged, "change" was perceived as a threat by some, even while it was "hope" to others. Thus this increasingly polarized American political landscape mirrors these earlier centuries in terms of upheaval, and public discourse devolved, specifically into a struggle over the nature of rape.

From forced ultrasounds to questions about "legitimate" versus "illegitimate" rape to all-male panels in the US House of Representatives on contraception, political battle lines were drawn literally on women's bodies.[12]

But there are also aspects that are completely new in this current American cultural context. One crucial example is the filming and posting of videotapes of the rapes of women, as happened in Steubenville, Ohio. Two local football players were arrested, tried, and found guilty of raping a 16-year-old girl and kidnapping her while she was too drunk to resist. The assault, over several hours, was captured on camera phones and posted to the Internet, "like a graphic, public diary."[13] The guilty verdict for the accused football players was met with sympathy for these convicted rapists and not for what the victim had endured both in the assaults and in testifying.[14]

The cultural context of sympathy for the rapists, and condemnation of the young woman raped for being intoxicated, creates the lens through which even these graphic images of sexual assault do not create a demand for an examination of our rape culture. In fact, it creates the opposite, a warning to other women who would report rape. You will receive no sympathy.

It is more likely, in fact, that the horrors of a young woman medical student being gang raped in India will be seen as a "rape culture" in that society, than the rape of a young woman in Ohio will been seen as evidence of "rape culture" in the United States. In that latter case, CNN, with apparently no sense of irony, can publish an article on "Victims blamed in India's rape culture" less than six months after Steubenville.[15]

It is also the case that through the Internet, American rape culture in popular media gets reproduced over and over and also exported globally. In the summer of 2013, an American song and music video went viral that explicitly promoted rape culture. "'Blurred Lines,' Robin Thicke's Summer Anthem, Is Kind of Rapey," wrote Tricia Romano in *The Daily Beast*. "The song is about how a girl really wants crazy wild sex but doesn't say it—positing that age-old problem where men think no means yes into a catchy, hummable song."[16] As Elizabeth Day noted, the video is "eye-poppingly misogynist." It features "women in a state of undress being handled like fleshy mannequins: their hair is played with, their bottoms are slapped, they are ordered to 'get up, get down' and they mutely do as they're told. None of them speaks."[17]

The completely clothed male singers in the music video look directly at the viewer, smiling, making gestures toward the women, inviting the viewer to become a corapist. The visual dynamics, in fact, are strikingly similar to the series of the rape paintings produced in the Enlightenment, and have largely the same goal: establish and police a rape culture to exclude women from being seen as fully human in the public (and private) arenas even as women are increasingly engaged in securing their rights in both spheres.

It is important to recognize how these cultural representations function on both a micro- and macrolevel. Through establishing and securing rape culture, the terms of the engagement of Euro-Atlantic cultures with other cultures around the world is set from that period to this. Thus the liberal "rights" focus of the Enlightenment is undergirded by a justification of violent exploitation of women and nonwhite peoples and is an extension of war and the War on Women taken, finally, to global proportions in the twentieth and twenty-first centuries.

Rape and the War on Women in War

As was noted in the previous chapter, rape has become more and more a strategy of war and is now considered a war crime. The War on Women is fought with other men, especially in war, as women's bodies become a proxy for the "body politic," and the injuring, impregnating, and killing of women is a way to attack the body of a people and grievously injure and even kill it.

Rape, prostitution, as well as other crimes against women during war has been called *War's Dirty Secret*, as the title of a volume edited by Anne Llewellyn Barstow indicates. But again, we need to ask, secret from whom? The violence done to women's bodies during war is there to see if we will only look as witnesses.

The Spanish artist Francisco José de Goya y Lucientes (1746–1828) produced an extraordinary series of prints of the brutal French repression of Spanish rebels against Napoleon in 1808 called *The Disasters of War*.[18] Goya did for artistic representation of war what Remarque did for fiction. Both portray war as completely lacking in heroism or chivalry, and religion is portrayed without mercy. The series is a precursor to Picasso's *Guernica* and indeed to war photography in the modern period.

A perhaps even more remarkable aspect of Goya's prints is the unrelenting focus on the violence against women in war. In *Ni por esas* (And nor do these), a church provides the background, but clearly no protection, for a Spanish mother as she is dragged away by a French soldier. Her baby is left crying on the ground. Set behind them is a soldier who holds a protesting woman. People crouch and slump in shadows, helpless and despairing. In another etching, *No quieren* (They do not want to), Goya shows a woman being assaulted by a soldier as an elderly woman tries to defend her with a dagger.

These prints, shocking as they are, still fall into the interpretive category of the "evils of war." Military strategists have been more or less concerned about "protecting civilians" from violence in war, of which rape is considered one such violence, along with beatings, robbery, and murder. Just War theory, of course, emphasizes the need to protect "noncombatants" from injury or death, and they may not be targeted. From Machiavelli to Clausewitz, these are considered "crimes" and are punishable.[19]

This view does more to mask the ubiquitous nature of rape in war, however, than to actually prevent it. It also serves to turn attention away from women's bodies as battlefield to other ideas of war, such as the rational views of "politics by other means" per Clausewitz. These ideas, as was argued earlier, actually direct attention away from what war is—namely the injuring of bodies.

Sometimes, however, the massive extent of rape in war breaks through this distancing mechanism. The Rape of Nanking is a well-known example from World

War II as a literal description of the mass rapes that took place in 1937 when the Japanese soldiers invaded that city. It is also used as a metaphor for the massacre of about 350,000 civilians, many of them women who had been raped first, as well as 200,000 killed in military prisons. Gradually, however, this astonishing atrocity has receded in public memory.

Sometimes attention to rape in war is given in one place and not in another in the same conflict. The rape and murder of four US churchwomen (1980) in El Salvador was widely reported, but the extent of the rape of Salvadoran women and girls in that violent period has not often been reported or analyzed.

It is also the case at times that rapes in war are documented but then never make it into the historical analyses. The massacre at Mỹ Lai in Vietnam included the rape of approximately 20 women that day 1986, as documented by the Peers Commission investigation in 1970. But the thirtieth-anniversary piece on the massacre written by Seymour M. Hersh, who had won a Pulitzer for his reporting on Mỹ Lai, did not mention the rapes.

While much has been written about the Rwandan genocide of 1994, the extent of the sexual assault that occurred was originally missing from the reports. In March 1995, the *Christian Science Monitor* revealed the hideous extent of the mass rapes. How is it conceivable for so many reporters to have overlooked a quarter of a million rapes? It is possible that almost every Tutsi woman and girl who survived the genocide had been raped.[20] Rape is an intrinsic part of genocide and part of what makes it *"A Problem from Hell"* as Samantha Power writes.[21]

New analyses of the role of violence against women in war are focusing on the gendered power relations at stake in the fact of rape in war. These studies are important.

But what "strategy physicality" adds to this shift is to see that it is the body of the victim, and her (or his) specific physical form, like the capacity for reproduction, that is the location of the War on Women in war. Rape in war shines a laser-like light on the pain of the physical injuring in war that is always felt in the body.

Batterers as the Army of Occupation in the War on Women

I have often said and written that intimate partner batterers are an "army of occupation" in the War on Women because occupying armies use force or the threat of force to keep a defeated enemy subject and compliant with whatever "terms" the conqueror deems appropriate. Batterers have been a permanent army of occupation for most of the centuries of human history around the world. And like an occupation following a war, this has been perfectly legal as the conquerors write the laws.

Wife battering is even more normalized than rape in some ways, as throughout history, rape has mostly been considered a crime, though often a "property" crime committed against men. In the ancient Roman period, wife beating was condoned under the Laws of Chastisement. After the Punic Wars, Roman laws were passed to enable women to sue their husbands for unjustified beatings, but the basic structure of the patriarchal Roman household's *pater familias* is upheld.[22]

This power structure makes it into the New Testament via Ephesians, as "wives are to be subject to their husbands" is a direct import from Roman culture and law of the time.[23]

Domestic assault was frequently represented in medieval and early modern Europe. In a 1582 print edition of the thirteenth-century *Regimen Sanitatis Salernitanum* (Salernitan Regimen of Health), there is a drawing of a man beating a woman with a stick.[24] Woodcuts from the Middle Ages also show domestic violence.[25] In a Medieval theological manual, a man is given permission to "castigate his wife and beat her for correction."[26]

In the Middle Ages, the War on Women in the home was so completely normalized that a medieval court case, brought by a wife because of her husband's physical violence as well as for his failure to give her enough food, had to prove "excessive beating," that is more than the "chastisement" husbands were permitted to do to maintain order in the home. In this case, the accused husband "admitted to the court that 'it is true that he sometimes beat Sitella moderately, with a belt as men do their wives.'"[27] "[A]s men often do their wives" is an almost casual reference that underscores that domestic battery was completely normalized in this period.

The Reformation period, for example, in Geneva, Switzerland, has been extolled as a "paradise for women" as some men were excommunicated for "deadly abuse." The excommunications do not, in fact, contradict the normalization of domestic violence against women thesis but underline it, as the force had to rise to the level of "deadly" for there to be ecclesial court action and not always then.[28]

As the art of the period demonstrates, the issue is control of women. Women are depicted as falling into one of two groups, the "good" women or the "evil" women. Evil women are often portrayed in the nude and in the sway of passion. Restraining the passions of women was one reason often given for the need of husbands to beat their wives. This dualism of good and evil women leaps out from the late engravings called "The Power of Women" by Lucas van Leyden, where "his treatment of erotic nude bodies is aided by gestures and expression that highlight their evil, sinful nature." It was not only in such elite art in the Reformation/Enlightenment period, however, but as cheaper woodcuts became available, poorer peasant women become "the butt of ribald humour and moralizing."[29]

Humor has been an effective social tool to normalize violence against women by belittling and dismissing the real injuries to their bodies. The popular culture *Punch and Judy* shows so beloved in both England and France demonstrate how a quasi-reversal of the roles in the physical battles between "Punch" and his wife "Judy" elicited such laughter. The pun on "Punch" makes clear who does the punching in real life.

Shakespeare's *The Taming of the Shrew* is one of the playwright's comedies, but it takes place inside the prison of women's lives in Elizabethan England. The plot revolves around one woman's attempt to rebel against this system, but she is forced back into it through a series of tricks, humiliation, deprivation of sleep, starvation, and even "accidents." The background of the play is the assumption that the daughter owes obedience to the father and to the husband he selects for her. The comedic aspects would appeal to a wide range of audiences and serve to help sustain battering culture because the comedy comes from the repeated and frustrated attempts of the woman to escape. Modern interpreters, having little understanding of the brutal lives of women, "may see Shrew as a high-spirited comedy about role-playing of game-playing, [but] they suppress the knowledge that men, not only on stage, but off, wrote the play and assigned the roles, chose the game and made the rules."[30]

By the mid-1800s in the US context, courts began repudiating the right of "chastisement" of husbands over wives, and by the end of the nineteenth century, most courts had criminalized it. This does not mean that battering ended, as only wealthy women could afford to bring a court case against their battering husbands, and they faced social ostracism if they did so.[31] The upheavals of the American Civil War in the mid-nineteenth century are precursors to this shift, as the early women's movement in that century came out of the abolitionist movement against slavery. The women-slave analogy was a prominent rhetorical device for early women activists for women's equal rights.[32] With some exceptions, such as the Grimké sisters, this rhetoric was directed exclusively at white, middle-class women's freedoms.

The nineteenth century is a formative period of British colonialism; as a system of cultural hegemony and subordination of many countries and peoples, it extends, in fact, from Elizabethan times to the Victorian period. Domestic violence is a template of the colonialist mentality of dominance and subordination. The Victorian period in particular is a time of tremendous domestic violence against women, but it is also a time when domestic violence in the British bastion of colonialism actually comes to be seen through newspaper reporting and new legislation.

Indeed, the battering of women in nineteenth-century England starts to be sufficiently "seen" that it is joined to a movement to establish legislation prohibiting it. A remarkable piece from the period is an 1856 article by J. W. Kaye, "Outrages on Women," who wrote it in consideration of possible parliamentary penalties for wife abuse. Quoting Dickens's *Bleak House*, and specifically the black eye of the brickmaker's wife, Kaye points out the "public's misreading or failure to read 'the history of the black eye, or the bruised forehead or the lacerated breast.'"[33] These injuries should be plain to see, wrote Kaye, because "outrages upon women have of late years held a distressingly prominent position. It is no exaggeration to say, that scarcely a day passes that does not add one or more to the published cases of this description of this description of offense."[34]

The daily newspapers started to report, and then to sensationalize, the brutal assaults on women in the period. Dickens, who worked as a reporter at the beginning of his career, could not have failed to see these reports that followed the passage of the 1828 "Offenses Against the Person Act," the first nineteenth-century piece of legislation to address domestic violence. Domestic violence fills Dickens's novels, as does the rising cultural anxiety generated by what the society believed were private matters of the home being scrutinized in public.

Newer technologies like newspapers, however, do not guarantee that "seeing" will become "witnessing" in the absence of a movement to change laws. In fact, the reverse can happen as representations of violence against women in a public setting, combined with social upheaval, can set off murderous abuse.

This happened in the period between the late Middle Ages, the Reformation, and the Enlightenment, or from 1480 to 1750. The upheavals of the period were unleashed after the disastrous fourteenth century and the bubonic plague that killed somewhere between 30 to 60 percent of Europe's people. The Thirty Years War, the Enlightenment, and the Reformation challenged social stability and, since social stability and the control of women were so inextricably linked, thousands of women, as well as men, were burned as witches.

Social instability, combined with public representations of women as "evil" and the cause of all that is wrong with a society, continues to be highly correlated with violence against women. In Papua New Guinea, for example, two thirds of women are subject to domestic violence, and about half are victims of rape. In some areas, 100 percent of the women said they had been assaulted. The social instability, often due to the destabilizing effects of globalization, is a crucial factor.[35]

As shown through the work of FotoEvidence, a publishing group "founded to continue the tradition of using photography to draw attention to human rights violations, injustice, oppression and assaults on sovereignty or human dignity wherever they may occur," this violence is extensive, both within the home and in public.[36]

"FotoEvidence" is an example of how some people around the world today are working to turn viewers into witnesses of the staggering amount of violence against women. Thus while Presidents don't send photographers to photograph the War on Women, today many are working to change that in concert with human rights movements.[37] But there is a strong cultural resistance to "seeing" the War on Women when it is not entertainment and not being excused, justified, or eroticized. For example, an advertisement made for television by a British women's group, Women's Aid, on the real danger of domestic violence, was censored by Clearcast.[38] Called "The Cut," this ad shows the actress, Keira Knightly, coming home from shooting a new film to a boyfriend who accuses her of having an affair. He attacks her, beats her, and knocks her down, kicking her repeatedly. In real life, the ad warns, no one yells "Cut!" to stop domestic violence. The ad has been viewed more than a million times on the Internet, but Clearcast deemed it "too shocking" for a television audience. This is frankly ridiculous as the number of shockingly violent television shows has grown exponentially in the last ten years.[39]

Over millennia, the battering of women by their domestic partners has been legalized, justified, normalized, and perpetuated through strong cultural, economic, and religious norms. Despite what progress has been made in identifying domestic battering as wrong and even criminalizing it, resistance runs high to actually witnessing the frequency and severity of battering in the home.

Resistance to witnessing all the forms of violence against women is extremely high. Another thing the forced physicality of rape and torture have in common with many of the injuries to women's bodies as battlefields is the denial or displacement of the violence. But we must witness to these many forms of violence.

Critical Physicality: Mapping the War on Women

Post-Traumatic Stress Disorder

Psychological trauma is a profound and immensely serious injury in the War on Women; there is a case to be made that it is the most widely spread injury in this war. There are several reasons for this, chief among them is the fact that the injuries are most often intimate—that is, they take place at the hands of those who are supposed to be most trusted. Violation by the most trusted person in one's life can cause considerable psychic trauma; psychological well-being requires a framework of trust for a coherent self to be developed and sustained.[40]

Moreover, coherence in one's framework of meaning is jeopardized as the injuries that have been done to women's bodies are often denied, excused, or minimized, or the victim is told she is the one at fault. In addition, unlike the soldier in war who suffers psychological trauma (except in the important case of prisoners), this is a battlefield women very often cannot leave, since it is women's own bodies that are the battlefields themselves. The people threatening them are often not enemies far off but immediate. The rapist is perhaps a family member, friend, coworker, or member of her community, someone she may see frequently. That batterer is her husband or her life-partner. But even when the rapist is an enemy soldier, the shaming and silencing of women who have suffered assault is a source of tremendous psychic trauma.

Judith Herman calls the psychological symptoms of women who have experienced violence the "combat neuroses of the sex war."[41] In the War on Women, the battlefield is everywhere and the threat can be nearly constant. When this fact is combined with denying, minimizing, excusing, and blaming, women often experience what is now called "post-traumatic stress disorder."

Women have always been subject to a War on Women on a battlefield they cannot leave, since it is their own body, and they have exhibited "combat neuroses," or "post-traumatic stress disorder" because of it. For a long time, these symptoms have been misdiagnosed in such a way as to actually exacerbate the trauma, not alleviate it.

In the nineteenth century, in Euro-Atlantic culture, for example, these signs of psychological stress in women who had experienced one or more forms of violence were misattributed to women's weaker mental capacities and their vulnerability to "hysteria." Hysteria was regarded as a medical condition exclusive to women. Hysteria as a term is the Greek cognate of uterus. Plato's dialogue, the *Timaeus*, compares a woman's uterus to a living creature that "gets discontented and angry" and wanders throughout a woman's body where it "closes up the passages of the breath" and causes "all variety of disease."[42] In other words, in this foundational text for Western thought, the idea is that there is a monster inside women that can make them crazy and sick. That monster is their womb.

There has been a prolonged struggle to crawl out from under this kind of psychological barbed wire that imprisons women in a battle fought on their own bodies. In January 1892, for example, the American writer Charlotte Perkins Gilman published a 6,000-word short story called "The Yellow Wallpaper" in *The New*

England Magazine. It is an effort to give voice to the psychological prison created by the way the injuries in the War on Women were denied and the symptoms of that denial misattributed to "hysteria."

It is a work of fiction crafted as a series of journal entries by a young woman who has been imprisoned in a room by her physician husband for a "rest cure" after the birth of their child. She comes to suspect that other women have been imprisoned in the room, and she can see them behind the wallpaper.

> Sometimes I think there are a great many women behind, and sometimes only one, and she crawls around fast, and her crawling shakes it all over. Then in the very bright spots she keeps still, and in the very shady spots she just takes hold of the bars and shakes them hard. And she is all the time trying to climb through. But nobody could climb through that pattern—it strangles so; I think that is why it has so many heads.
>
> They get through, and then the pattern strangles them off and turns them upside down, and makes their eyes white![43]

Does this narrator go mad, or is she finally starting to see the pattern of imprisonment of women's lives?

Charlotte Perkins Gilman is not the only person who saw how women are psychologically traumatized by the war fought on the battlefields of their bodies. Sigmund Freud saw it too, but unlike Gilman, he turned away because the logic of his conclusion, that violence against women and girls was so wide-spread in his society that it was causing the hysteria so many of his colleagues were investigating but profoundly misdiagnosing, was completely unacceptable in his time. Herman writes, "Freud's investigations led the furthest of all into the unrecognized reality of women's lives. His discovery of childhood sexual exploitation at the roots of hysteria crossed the outer limits of social credibility and brought him to a position of total ostracism within his profession."[44]

Today Freud's recanting of his initial findings on hysteria, and his dogmatic insistence that women imagined the sexual abuse done to them, and even desired it, is considered cowardly. But as Herman points out, Freud had no social movement that would support such findings that contradicted everything culture, medicine, and even religion believed about family and society.[45]

But Bertha Pappenheim, a former patient treated for "hysteria" by one of Freud's colleagues, Joseph Breuer, and then abandoned by him, recovered and helped create a women's movement that could sustain the witnessing necessary for women to be believed. Under a pseudonym, she translated Mary Wollstonecraft's *A Vindication of the Rights of Women* into German. She was a lifelong activist for women's and children's rights and safety from exploitation. A colleague wrote of her, "A volcano lived in this woman . . . Her fight against the abuse of women and children was almost a physically felt pain for her."[46]

Yet Gilman or Pappenheim are only certain witnesses to the effort to resist the misdiagnoses of the psychological injuries in the War on Women's bodies. Gilman in particular sees some things but not others, and her work can be interpreted instead, in its racial and cultural biases, to help further the psychological trauma of some women rather than alleviate it. This calls into question its usefulness for building a movement which witnesses rather than covers up violence.

Other witnessing is required and is often missing from the feminist discourse on Gilman's famous essay. Susan Lanser, in a critical study of white feminism's rendering "The Yellow Wallpaper" as a "sacred text," shows how this has valorized it as a lens into a "'female' consciousness" and promoted distortion. It signifies "a somewhat uncomfortable need to isolate and validate a particular female experience, a particular relationship between reader and writer, and a particular notion of subjectivity." In reading and writing about the shape-shifting wallpaper, the reader/feminist writer reads a particular self into it. As such, it reveals the "suppression of difference" in white academic feminism.[47]

It is necessary, according to Lanser, to locate Gilman's text within the "psychic geography" of Anglo-America at the turn of the century. This is a culture "obsessively preoccupied with race as the foundation of culture, a culture desperate to maintain Aryan superiority in the face of massive immigrations from Southern and Eastern Europe, a culture openly anti-Semitic, anti-Asian, anti-Catholic, and Jim Crow."[48]

Thus my interpretation offered earlier of the narrator of "The Yellow Wallpaper" as a voice from within the "prolonged struggle to crawl out from under this kind of psychological barbed wire that imprisons women in a battle fought on their own bodies," is, in fact, wrong in important ways. A different kind of reading illuminates who might be behind the "yellow" wallpaper and why it evokes such horror in the narrator. The wallpaper must be yellow to evoke the fear of the woman/other, the "'yellow woman' who is . . . the feared alien."[49]

Gilman's other writing supports this reading of the fear of color, and its projection by Gilman into a form of gothic threat. For example, in her *The Man-Made World: Or, Our Androcentric Culture*, northern Europeans and Scandinavians are lauded as exempt from patriarchy, and the "unstirred East," "African tribes," or the "Moslem" are examples of "enslaved womanhood." Lanser comments that "the 'progressive and dominant races' Gilman lauds for not 'enslaving' women were at that moment invading and oppressing countries around the world." This seems to present Gilman with no apparent problems, and indeed, Lanser notes per the work of Gayatri Spivak, provides the excuse to "save yellow women from yellow men."[50]

This is the same rationale that led the Bush administration to justify invading Afghanistan to "save" Afghan women.

The "critical physicality" approach to this foundational feminist work shows how crucial it is to make women's differences central and not peripheral; in fact, the very physicality of the approach absolutely requires the centrality of difference. The color of skin is a profound embodiment and matters in the most fundamental way. Conversely, if skin color is not part of the witnessing to end violence against women, then the exclusion of certain women's bodies and the inclusion of others becomes part of the psychological injuring itself.

There is, for example, a thundering "silencing" on the physical violence done to African American women, not only from white culture, but also from within the African American community. The motives of white-dominant culture are perhaps more easily traced; African American women's bodies have been rendered of less value through the history of slavery, through Jim and Jane Crow, and up until the present in our economic apartheid. The roots of this silencing in the African American community go deeply into this same racism, however, with the need to counter the stereotype of the "Black male as rapist," as Patricia Danette Hopkins writes. It is through contending with this form of racism and its threat to their community that Black women in their community also become "de facto unrapeable." She notes how African American women writers such as "Toni Morrison, Alice Walker, and Maya Angelou in their various works give response to the Black male-driven Afro American tradition's call—a call of literary absence and silence."[51] But it does continue.

Here is the commonality in the differences: the silencing of women who have been injured in the War on Women produces further injury. This injury, whether produced by white, male-dominated culture in Euro-Atlantic culture, by white feminists, or by communities of color, is still injury. Witnessing women's bodies as battlefields requires keeping the real body, the specific body in all its contours and colors, in view and not letting our gaze be distracted so that the physical injuries can once again be overlooked or denied for whatever reason.

White women from privileged classes can still be driven mad by white patriarchal culture as it silences and controls them as well. Silencing and denial of injuries turns women's very minds into battlefields. The narrator of "The Yellow Wallpaper," however, may see the difference among women with horror and in so doing will never be able to fully escape.

Freud turned away from the horror of what he had found actually caused "hysteria" in women and girls—namely, the fact that their bodies were battlefields in a war on them. Herman rightly notes that absent a movement to affirm and sustain Freud's findings, it was inevitable that this would occur. But it is also the case that any movement that seeks to witness to the reality of women's bodies as battlefields cannot succeed unless the actual bodies of diverse women are central to the work and each and every one compels concerted action, not action "for or on behalf of," but in complex and multiple alliances that do not collapse all bodies into one abstraction.

We will never build a movement capable of witnessing the full scope of the injuring of women and create a movement to really end it without the presence of all women's physical embodiment.

Bruising

There is clearly considerable pressure on women, from many directions, to "keep the secret" about battering or rape. This is also pressure to hide the injuries. A frequent injury women experience in their bodies is bruising. Many of the posters against domestic violence show women of all races with black eyes.

British makeup artist and YouTube personality Lauren Lake "shocked her 440,000 subscribers when she appeared battered and bruised in one of her online tutorials on make-up tips." Titled "How To Look Your Best The Morning After," Lake appears with a black eye, cuts on her lip and cheek, and bruises around her throat. She goes through a make-up "guide," showing the viewer how to cover up these marks on her face made by a "jealous type of partner." She made the video as part of a UK public service campaign called "Don't Cover It Up" for the anti-domestic violence group Refuge. According to Refuge, "65% of women who suffer domestic violence keep it hidden."[52]

The history of war is represented, and interpreted, by a wide assortment of famous paintings of battlefields, heroics, and highly stylized (for the most part) battlefield injuries. The history of the War on Women has not been absent from classical art, but it has been an art largely designed to normalize the War on Women, not witness it.

Women in Turkey decided to change that. Turkish artist Derya Kılıç presented a photography exhibition called "To Know, To See . . ." in an Istanbul gallery.[53] Viewers of the exhibition were confronted with a series of well-known figures—women painted by the likes of Salvador Dalí, Edvard Munch, Leonardo da Vinci, and Gustav Klimt—each bearing the marks of violence on their faces and bodies.

For example, in the exhibition, eyes in a lovely face framed with a blue-and-gold headdress and with a single teardrop pearl earring gaze out quietly at the viewer, but this face is marred by cuts and bruises on the eyes, cheeks, and chin. The face of the *Girl with a Pearl Earring* is suddenly seen less as placid and more as fixed, even suppressed. "I thought if I used the famous paintings, people could look at my photos and see violence as something that happens to a woman that they 'know,'" Kılıç told *Women's eNews*. "I wanted to show that violence is not just a problem of poor women, and not just today's issue. Violence is an issue for every woman, in every place and in every time period."[54]

"Reported incidents of domestic abuse and violence against women in Turkey increased by more than 66 percent from 2008 to 2011," according to one report. Another study indicates that "upwards of 40 percent of women in Turkey have been victims of domestic violence."[55]

This artist, by taking control over these famous images and showing the lives of perhaps many of these women who posed as models for famous artists or who represent the lives of many other women, is exposing the injuries so that viewers will be startled into viewing and perhaps even witnessing. There are no guarantees this will happen. As Turkish activist Arzu Yay, who volunteers with Mor Çatı Women's Shelter Foundation,[56] cautions, there is also a risk of "aestheticized violence" that can be an unintended consequence of artistic representations of violence against women. This is an aesthetic not unlike media coverage that sensationalizes the most "lurid details" of injuries to women and yet sides with the aggressor.[57]

"The focus on images of the abused also means we end up talking about violence as something that is just physical and separate from us," Yay said. "But violence is also emotional, mental and financial. And it's not just 'other' women who are victims; violence and inequality affects us all."[58]

It is the case that the normalizing of violence against women creates this perfect storm of physical, emotional, mental, and financial injury. But seeing the physical injury is crucial to the "queering" of violence against women. Seeing the injuries within a context of witnessing and support in particular can shift consciousness. In all the bible studies I have had over the years with battered women, the fact of the visible injuries made a difference to helping the group finally claim that these injuries done to them were wrong. Women came to bible study with black eyes, long sleeves, scarfs around their throats, holding themselves stiffly perhaps from bruised ribs. A cuff would fall back, however, and a ring of bruises around a wrist spoke volumes.[59]

Indeed, raising the religious question about normalizing violence against women has been the subject of another creative campaign, this one by "Save the Children India." The Hindu goddesses Lakshmi, Durga, and Saraswati are shown as victims of domestic violence. This campaign showing bruised and battered goddesses went viral. The message that accompanies these images is "Pray that we never see this day. Today, more than 68% of women in India are victims of domestic violence. Tomorrow, it seems like no woman shall be spared. Not even the ones we pray to."[60]

These campaigns are framed with statistics like "40 percent of the women in Turkey," or "68 percent of the women in India," but they are not campaigns based on statistics, they are campaigns based on witnessing the injuries to bodies. The leadership of these artists and activists is in connecting the reality of the bruising to a movement.

Death

Women's bodies are battlefields, and often the wars fought there result in their being injured unto death. The WHO report found that globally, 38 percent of all women who were murdered were murdered by their intimate partners.[61] There is a high correlation among stalking, rape, and murder in the United States.[62]

These deaths are reported in news media, often with lurid details, not as witnessing but as normalizing. Other women should (and do) take note. The War on Women can be fatal. But even if an individual woman survives an assault, there is always the overarching threat of death that characterizes all war.

Women who survive a violent assault often find that a central part of the trauma is that they believe they could have died. Thus they can experience an existential crisis. Mary Pellauer, a Lutheran ethicist, talked about this with me in our chapter "Conversation on Grace and Healing: Perspectives from the Movement to End Violence against Women." Mary said the following:

> First, these traumas are life-threatening experiences. If you are raped, whether with a gun to your head, or by an acquaintance, people very frequently say, 'I thought I was going to die.' And as you know, battered women are painfully aware that maybe this time they survived the assault, but the next time, what if my forehead hits the sharp corner of the dining room table, or the next time I'm pushed down the stairs, what if I break my neck? . . . So these crises contain the whole dimension of the existential quality of death—the realization that this could be my death—a fundamental spiritual crisis.[63]

Often, however, rather than see the life-risk to women and resultant trauma as a "fundamental spiritual crisis" that needs serious address from within Christianity, clergy have been inclined to place the blame and/or the responsibility on women for the abuse. I have counseled abused women who have told me that they first sought out their pastor for help, only to be told to "forgive the beatings, as Christ forgave us from the cross." Such faith responses exacerbate the existential crisis for women rather than helping reduce the risk of injury and death for women.

Dr. Jacquelyn Campbell, nursing professor at Johns Hopkins University and a leader in the field, has worked to develop a "danger assessment tool" to determine the risk of an abused woman being killed by her partner.[64] "Some of the risk factors include past death threats, partner's employment status, and partner's access to a gun."

The epidemic of gun violence in the United States, and the comprehensive failure to get even minimally prudent gun control laws in place, is resulting in more homicides of women in violent relationships. A study from the Johns Hopkins Center for Gun Policy and Research has compiled statistics on intimate partner violence and firearms. "According to federal data collected from police departments, in 2005 approximately 40% of female homicide victims ages 15–50 were killed either by a current or former intimate partner. In over half of these cases (55%), the perpetrator used a gun." The study adds, "More than twice as many women are killed by a husband or intimate acquaintance than are killed by a stranger using a knife, gun or any other means."

While guns are clearly a lethal factor, and there are 20 factors weighed in her assessment tool, Campbell has said unemployment is "'by far the most important demographic' in putting someone at risk to be killed by an intimate partner."[65]

National unemployment rates for minorities are much higher than those for whites. Currently the unemployment rate for African Americans is 13 percent, nearly double that reported for whites. The fact that African American women are much more likely to be killed by their abusive partners is in part related to unemployment. Campbell notes, "Unemployed white men were as likely to kill their partners as unemployed black men, but because the black unemployment rate is higher, we see more deaths of black women."[66] All women's bodies are battlefields, but some women's bodies are more at risk than others including a risk for death.

In addition to guns, as well as race and unemployment, pregnancy is another high risk factor for women being killed. For example, a study published in the March 2005 edition of the *American Journal of Public Health* found that homicide was a leading cause of death among pregnant women in the United States between 1991 and 1999.[67]

Theologian Mary Potter Engel explains this phenomenon, as well as the increase in the battering of pregnant women directed at their bellies, as "contempt for the weak." Women are physically more vulnerable during pregnancy and this is viewed, in the power distortions of patriarchy, with contempt. "This contempt often leads to the abuse of their [men's] power, authority, or force to punish or nullify a vulnerable one."[68]

Power and control are the critical links in the way women's bodies are turned into battlefields.

Disfigurement and Dismemberment

Disfigurement and dismemberment of women's bodies are a way to enforce a life-long "power distortion" by literally etching or carving it into the bodies of women themselves.

Acid attacks on women have been on the rise around the world since the 1960s, though there is significant underreporting. According to a wide-ranging study of acid attacks in a comprehensive report Avon Global Center for Women and Justice called "Combatting Acid Violence in Bangladesh, India and Cambodia," "[a]cid attacks, like other forms of violence against women, are not random or natural phenomenon. Rather they are social phenomena deeply embedded in a gender order that has historically privileged patriarchal control over women, and justified the violence to 'keep women in their places.'"[69]

The physical mapping of injury to women from acid attacks is the stuff of night-mares, and is, indeed, intended so as the majority of the acid attacks are directed at the face to produce lifelong disfigurement and suffering. And it succeeds. If not washed off immediately with water, acid can melt away a victim's skin and flesh going as far as dissolving bones. When thrown at the face, the acid destroys victims' eyes, eyelids, ears, lips, noses, and mouths. In addition to the face, perpetrators aim at the sexual parts of women's bodies such as breasts, buttocks, and vagina. If the victim lives, she must endure surgeries even to keep her alive, and she is subject to infections.[70] Women who survive acid attacks live greatly diminished lives, not only physically, but also economically and culturally.

While acid throwing on women is actually a worldwide form of injury to women, it occurs with greatest frequency in those countries with the lowest forms of gender equality. Acid is also cheap and often readily attainable. Yet acid attacks can be combatted, as Bangladesh is doing through specific legislation and enforcement.[71]

Acid throwing is a common characteristic of the five countries the Thomas Reuters Foundation lists as the most dangerous places to be a woman, along with rape, child marriage, and rampant poverty.[72] Acid throwing may also be on the rise in Western countries. It is difficult to tell, however. In England, for example, separate statistics on acid burnings are not kept. In the United Kingdom, in 2008 a woman named Katie Piper was the "victim of an acid attack orchestrated by her jealous boyfriend." She has had nearly 100 operations and now campaigns against acid attacks. Mohammad Jawad, the plastic surgeon who helped rebuild Katie Piper's face, also works with victims in South Asia. Dr. Jawad says the crime is about trying to destroy someone's identity. "The attacker is saying: 'I don't want to kill her, I am going to do something to distort her.' It's a walking dead situation for the victim and often a grey area in the eyes of the law." He calls it "an extreme form of domestic violence."[73]

Dismemberment is another extreme form of domestic violence, as happened to a woman in Bangladesh whose husband cut off all five fingers on her right hand to prevent her from studying for an advanced degree.[74]

Women's Bodies as Battlefield

Closely mapping the injuries to women's bodies in the War on Women shows how extensive and how brutal this war can be. The injuries overlap with those sustained in war, including torture and execution, but they are not identical. The case is made here that because the War on Women is so systematically hidden, qualified, reframed, reorganized, catalogued, excused, and ultimately authorized, it literally wounds women in their minds as one of the primary injuries they sustain. Post-traumatic stress disorder is a huge injury to women as their bodies are not battle-fields they can leave, except in death, and the death of some women creates an existential crisis for other women.

It is crucial to witness the fact that the specificity of women's bodies matters immensely as the injuries are mapped. Race in particular matters because, while all women can have their bodies turned into battlefields, some bodies are made more available in the racist Euro-Atlantic cultures and in the cultures the West has brutalized through colonialism, neocolonialism, and globalization.

Women themselves participate in covering up their injuries, such as bruises, in the effort to hide the fact that their bodies are battlefields. But there are injuries inflicted on women in disfigurement that are designed to be devastatingly visible and that cannot be hidden. These extreme forms of injury are directed at perma-nently destroying a woman's sense of self and agency as a whole person.

How does this War on Women get conducted every day, all day long, and every night, all night long, and continue to be simultaneously hidden and excused?

One way, for Western culture, has been the role of Western philosophy in this effort.

3

War and the War on Women

Religious and Philosophical Roots

The lord trod upon the hinder part of Ti'amat,
And with his unsparing club he split (her) skull.

Enuma Elish

Females are weaker and colder in nature, and it is necessary to regard the female
status as a deformity, though a natural one.

Aristotle, *On the Generation of Animals*

It is a mere 53 miles from the site of ancient Babylon to Baghdad today. When it comes to the conceptual roots of war and the War on Women, there is also not much distance despite four millennia of history. But this is far from a straight line, historically speaking. The conceptual roots of the relationship of war and women's bodies in the War on Women are in fact vast, and the streams that shape Western thought on these issues, and thus influence Christian theologies on these subjects, are multiple and some are even contradictory.

What is so striking however, when these sources are examined from the perspective of critical physicality, is how much what happens to the bodies of women and bodies in war are intimately and inextricably connected. It may be that we cannot stop warring unless we also cease justifying, excusing, or even mandating women's bodies be used as battlefields in our societies.

Ti'amat: Creation of War as War on the Female Body

Enuma Elish, the Babylonian creation story, is an epic in which a rising young warrior hero, Marduk, creates the world by dismembering the female body of Ti'amat, the First Mother.

The lord trod upon the hinder part of Ti'amat,
And with his unsparing club he split (her) skull.

He cut the arteries of her blood
And caused the north wind to carry (it) to out-of-the-way places.
He split her open like a mussel (?) into two (parts).
Half of her he set in place and formed the sky (therewith) as a roof.
He fixed the crossbar (and posted guards);
He commanded them not to let her waters escape.[1]

The *Enuma Elish* ("When above") takes its name from the opening words. It is dated from Babylon's rise to political supremacy, approximately four millennia ago (2057–1758 BCE).[2] The epic, while dealing with the gods, cosmology, and the creation of the world and human beings, is mainly devoted to politics and war. Much of the epic is about Marduk, his birth, growth, preparation for battle, conquest of Ti'amat, and a lengthy proclamation of his "fifty names."

The goal of this Babylonian epic myth is to establish the claim of Babylon to political and military supremacy in the region through creating a "religio-political-literary" interpretation of reality. This is done brilliantly in the poem. These "Babylonian poets . . . were involved in rethinking the basic values of humankind as understood from their societies' perspectives, what we would call philosophizing or theologizing."[3]

The politicized version draws on myths that are even more ancient, both to claim their power and also to show how the "old gods" are no longer adequate for the current preeminent status of Babylon. The *Enuma Elish* "begins in primordial time"—that is, before the world had actually been created. Water is essential for life and played an enormous role in the Mesopotamian world, situated as it was between the Tigris and the Euphrates rivers. Ancient Babylon was adjacent to the Euphrates; it is not that far from what is now Baghdad. This cradle of civilization, as the region is often called, has also been a cradle of conflict and war, up to this very day.

Apsu, a male god-figure in the epic, is the "sweet-water abyss," and Ti'amat, the female, is the "salt-water abyss." The epic recalls a time when the waters mingled and created divine pairs who begat children and, in an ancient cycle, these god-offspring ruled the universe. But as with most royal families, conflict ensues, and this disturbed the ancient gods, Apsu and Ti'amat. Ti'amat sends her husband, Apsu, to deal with them, but Ea, the god of wisdom, kills Apsu. This is the first cycle of the myth. The second cycle begins when, from within Apsu, Ea sires a "marvelous" son, Marduk. Ti'amat is not at all happy about these developments. She creates monster offspring and the gods are so impressed by this that some join her, including Qingu, whom she makes her new husband and leader of her armies. None of the opposing gods make any headway against her and her armies until the young warrior hero, Marduk, steps up and says he will defeat Ti'amat but only on the condition that if he succeeds, the others gods will make him their king.[4]

Marduk does succeed in a bloody defeat of Ti'amat, using her rage and strength against her. Marduk commanded winds and lightening, and when Ti'amat opened her mouth to devour him,

He drove in the evil wind, in order that (she should) not
(be able) to close her lips.
The ranging winds filled her belly;
Her belly became distended, and she opened wide her
Mouth.
He shot off an arrow, and it tore her interior;
It cut through her inward parts, it split (her) heart.
When he had subdued her, he destroyed her life.[5]

There have been many interpretations of the *Enuma Elish* since the tablets were found and translated in the nineteenth century. It is crucial for this interpretation to have exactly reproduced the bloodying, tearing, splitting, and destroying words used to describe the attack on and ultimate dismemberment of a woman's body. The lines from the epic echo women's accounts of violent rape, the feeling of tearing in the interior, and the splitting of "her inward parts." This is, in fact, an account of a rape/murder.

Like in earlier chapters, the specificity of what happens to Ti'amat's body is essential to understanding something different about this epic. This bloodying, tearing, splitting, and destroying all happens to establish the preeminence of the warrior as ruler. When we turn our attention to what really happens to Ti'amat's body, through the lens of critical physicality, attention also shifts away from abstract "myth making" to structures of politics and gender. A woman's body is the battlefield for the ascendancy of the Babylonian ethos of political and military supremacy. It is striking then how primal this embodied link is: war is primordially about injuring the female body.

As was noted in the previous chapter, there is a difference between "out-injuring" the other party (in Scarry's definition of war as a contest in inflicting pain) and the War on Women. The War on Women is not a war between combatants engaged in mutual injuring, each side struggling to out-injure the other. It is not, then, a war between men and women, where men and women are both duly authorized combatants, it is a war *on women*, where women are categorically more like noncombatants or civilians who are being attacked. The relationship of the rise of a warrior class to the physical defeat of women is crucial.

But the critical physicality of what happens to Ti'amat in the epic, and how war and the warrior class develops in politics, has not been primary, or even acknowledged, even in the most astute of interpreters.

Paul Ricoeur, for example, interprets the primal act of the dismemberment of Ti'amat by Marduk symbolically, and in *The Symbolism of Evil*, calls it a "creative act." This is the kind of act "which distinguishes, separates, measures, and puts in order, is inseparable from the criminal act that puts an end to the life of the oldest gods, inseparable from a deicide inherent in the divine."[6] From this deicide, the killing of the Mother God Ti'amat, Ricoeur extracts a universal connection between creation and destruction. This is the defeat of chaos, according to Ricoeur. Ricoeur also connects the Genesis account of creation with the *Enuma Elish* and equates chaos with evil.

Ricoeur takes this farther, finding that "primordial violence" funds the justification of human violence, as in the establishment of rule by "brute force." There is, in his view, a symbolic origin to war; this keeps violence going, so to speak, as a crucial political tool. Thus, he writes, "[c]reation is a victory of an Enemy older than the creator; that Enemy, immanent in the divine, will be represented in history by all the enemies whom the kind in his turn, as servant of the god, will have as his mission to destroy. Thus Violence is inscribed in the origin of things, in the principle that establishes while it destroys."[7]

What Ricoeur does not draw out, and seems not even to notice, is the long line of connections among the defeat and dismemberment of the female body—the justification for this as the defeat of chaos (also feminized in the myth)—and the origin of war.

Catherine Keller does notice this, however. It is important, in drawing out these connections, to note that this Babylonian epic was "reenacted" every year for centuries, including the laborious reading of the fifty names of Marduk as a religious ritual.[8] Keller references Mircea Eliade, another interpreter of the *Enuma Elish*, who comments on the repeated celebrations of the epic as a passage from "chaos to cosmos." According to Eliade, when the celebrant exclaims, "May he continue to conquer Tiamat and shorten her days!" the "combat the victory and the Creation took place *at that very moment*." But what Keller sees, and Ricoeur and Eliade do not, is that "[a]s the woman-identified powers of 'chaos' will continually recrudesce, they must be repeatedly be killed. The matricide, we begin to realize, constitutes the central act of the heroic life-style." "The combat, the victory, and the Creation" are "the theological psychology of the West. The covert slaughter of the mother is this culture's bond of reenactment."[9]

Ti'amat, the older Mother Goddess, is redefined in the *Enuma Elish* as the source of monstrous beings and thus the source of all chaos. This provides license to the hero to destroy her, giving a cosmic blessing to what is basically the rise of a warrior class to political supremacy and the defeat of older, more female-identified gods and a more agricultural basis to society. We will draw this line out much farther as it reappears in Hebraic, Greek, and Roman sources. It ultimately supports the idea of a Just War, and a "Just War on Women."

The "metapsychology" of the "heroic warrior," in Keller's terms, is an indispensable insight in how myth comes into play in the deep narratives on which war and the War on Women depend for cultural, legal, and of course, religious justification. In the subsequent chapters on the heroic and on the erotic, this will be important. Yet the psychological cannot be emphasized without unstinting focus on the physical. Whatever else war and the War on Women is, it is, at bottom, physical injuring, inflicting pain, and destruction of bodies, human habitat, and the environment. What happens at the level of myth and psychology does not stay at the level of myth and psychology and must be mapped as a physical enterprise.

Yet it is a political enterprise as well and continues to illuminate how the authority structures of Western civilization depend on the destruction of women's bodies. The Rape of Lucretia, as noted in the previous chapter, is a founding myth for Roman civilization.

In sum, in the *Enuma Elish*, the central battle that creates the world, "man," and civilization, is fought on a woman's body. This battle establishes the claim of a war-based political entity, Babylon, to supremacy in a region. These are themes that reappear, though somewhat changed, in the biblical account of creation and in subsequent books in the Hebrew bible.

"Combat Myth"[10]: Creation as a Battle against Chaos

War is supremely chaotic. Yet war is often presented, in both religion and politics, as the opposite of conflict: the attempt to achieve order out of chaos.[11] The overarching cosmology of conflict in the ancient Near East was the restoration of order to a chaotic world. This is clearly illustrated in the ancient Babylonian creation epic.

There are striking similarities between the Babylonian epic and Genesis. In both, there is a divine creator, darkness covering the "deep" (i.e., water), the creation of a firmament above and land beneath, the creation of "man," and resting after the creative act. These are all evidence of the influence of the *Enuma Elish* on Genesis.[12] These similarities have been considered deeply problematic, since the epic was discovered and translated, as they seem to suggest more than some borrowing by the Hebrews from Babylonian sources.

Remnants of the defeat of the primordial Mother are clearly symbolized in the two-fold Genesis creation account. The watery "deep" (Gen. 1:2) is already existent, and the work of creation is pronounced good in the first chapter. Just as the waters of the deep, divided by Elohim (Gen. 1:6–7, 9), recall the fluid world of Ti'amat, so also the snake figure of Eden in Genesis 3 may allude to her serpent-like body. All these factors are continuities with the chaos/nomos conflict presented in the *Enuma Elish* as the defeat of the goddess.

The fundamental idea that creation is the establishment of order over a threatening chaos in an epic battle is often called the "Combat Myth." The basic outline is that a creator deity defeats the archenemy that is "usually depicted as a watery monster or dragon" and the dismembered parts are used to create the whole universe. The "Combat Myth" in Genesis, and its influence on subsequent Jewish and Christian writers, is, according to Batto, a revision of the original "primeval myth first penned by the Yahwist in order to meet new existential faith needs of his community." [13]

What had happened to the Israelites to precipitate an existential crisis of faith and require some dramatic revision of the story of creation? The crisis of faith arises from the significant defeat by Babylon and the subsequent captivity of Israel. This defeat and exile that the Israelite tribes experience gives rise to what is called the "Priestly narrative" in Genesis, where "P" constructs a counter combat myth to that of the Babylonian *Enuma Elish* to deal with how disheartened the Israelites had become by Babylonian captivity.[14] The Priestly Writer had to convince the captured Israelites that Yahweh was the creator and sovereign of all there is and a more powerful warrior deity than the Babylonian Marduk. It is Yahweh the Holy Warrior who would someday rescue his people, as he had done before in the Exodus from Egypt.

The connection between the "Combat Myth" creation narrative of "P" and the idea that Yahweh is Holy Warrior/Creator is plain in Jeremiah.

> Thus has spoken Yahweh,
> Who established the sun a light by day,
> The ordering of moon and stars as light by night,
> Who stills the sea when its waves rage,
> Yahweh of the (heavenly) Armies is his name:
> "If this order could ever fail in my presence
> —Oracle of Yahweh—
>
> Then Israel's seed would also cease
> Form being a people in my presence for all time."
> Thus has spoken Yahweh:
> "If the heavens above could be measured
> Or the underworld's foundations below be fathomed,
> Then I, too, would reject the whole of Israel's seed
> Because of all that they have done."
> —Oracle of Yahweh—

What the Priestly Writer has accomplished in this revision of Genesis as Combat Myth is two-fold: not only one to strengthen the despairing Israelites and give them hope in the future, but also one to make a cosmic theological claim about the power of God, the power of Yahweh, and the need to continually triumph over the forces of chaos as the source of evil in this world. This is done not only by subduing that which symbolizes chaos in the world but literally waging war on it over and over. This chaos, as with Ti'amat, is continually symbolized as female.

War, Disobedience, and the Female Body in the Hebrew Bible

Elaine Scarry emphasizes that the "bodies of women are often used as vehicles to convey the physical manifestation of contemptible physical rebellion and deserved bodily punishment."[15]

Yahweh as Holy Warrior is one of the foundations of the Western concept of Just War theory in particular, because for war to be just, there must be a moral (i.e., divine) authority behind it. But underlying this seemingly lofty role for God's authority in protecting justice, there flows the defeat of Ti'amat and creation out of dismembering femaleness, often pictured as watery, threatening chaos.

There are many Hebrew bible texts that describe the intimate connection of God and Israel's conduct and fate in war. The Exodus experience is a war that Yahweh conducts basically alone. Yahweh is a "man of war" (Exodus 14:3) and the "Lord Supreme of Hosts." "Hosts means 'armies' and this expression which occurs more than two hundred times in the biblical text, should be translated 'supreme leader of armies.'"[16]

It is particularly significant, therefore, that an exilic poet, known as "Deutero-Isaiah," specifically connects the Combat Myth motif with the Exodus in one of the key texts (Isaiah 51:9–11) in the Hebrew bible that establishes Yahweh as Warrior. This passage is often called "ode to Yahweh's arm" and the arm does this by cleaving, splitting, and dominating water conceived as an unruly (*Rahab*) "Sea-dragon."

> Awake! Awake! Robe yourself in Power,
>   O arm of Yahweh.
> Awake as in primordial days,
>   (the) primeval generations.
> Is it not you who cleaves Rahab in pieces,
>   Who pierces the Sea-dragon?
> Is it not you who dries up the Sea,
>   The waters of the great Abyss (*tehom*)
> The one who makes the depths of the Sea a road
>   for the redeemed to pass over?[17]

Just as the Priestly Writer retells creation in Genesis as through the Combat Myth of the defeat of watery chaos, here Isaiah retells the Exodus from Egypt as the Combat Myth of divine rescue through cleaving Rahab, a poetical name for Egypt. In medieval Jewish folklore, Rahab is a mythical sea monster, a dragon of the waters, and the primordial abyss—a water-dragon of chaos and darkness like Ti'amat.[18]

Thus Yahweh's parting of the Red Sea and making "a road for the redeemed to pass over" is recast as "piercing the Sea-dragon." "Piercing" is a rape allusion in the sense, as was previously noted, of the physical experience of rape as women describe it.

Another key issue in understanding the relationship of God and war in these texts that have been revised in light of the catastrophe of the Babylonian captivity is the covenant of Israel and God. The theological purposes of war in biblical war are to serve Yahweh and the ends of Yahweh, and this can be either the martial success of Israel or its defeat. The destruction of Israel, and not only its triumphs in battle, is also interpreted as serving the ends of Yahweh—namely, the punishment of the disobedient Israel. This connects to the larger frame of the threat of chaos (disobedience) and the assertion of order (obedience).

Women and their sexuality play a central role in this paradigm. Women and their sexuality symbolize chaos when they are uncontrolled—that is, not sexually compliant and faithful. Thus they are a logical choice for playing out scenarios of control. When Israel is threatened with defeat in war, for example, the female is very explicitly blamed as the cause of evil and disruption since Israel has been "playing the whore." Drorah Setel has argued that "[T]he emergence of objectified female imagery in Hosea and the other literary prophets can be seen to relate both to the intellectual and psychological disruptions caused by political events."[19] Thus the threatened chaos of political events gets referred, symbolically, to the female body and the way in which the female body *is* the community in Israel.

The function of war is to subdue chaos and to achieve the orderly purpose of obedience to Yahweh. When Israel triumphs, women's bodies can be "enjoyed" as spoils of war, the reward for obedience to Yahweh. The female body, as chaotic and evil, on the other hand, is employed as the symbol of disobedience and evil and thus the cause of defeat.[20]

This might lead one to connect rape as a metaphor to describe war with this Hebraic understanding of the Combat Myth. Rape is frequently employed as a metaphor for war, as in, for example, the Rape of Nanking in World War II where the Japanese Army brutally captured and occupied China's capital city. As with very powerful metaphors, there is an element of actual description as well as an extension of meaning beyond the literal. The mass rape and murder by the Japanese was horrific, but so too were other vicious acts of this conquest. Thus also we hear of the "Rape of Poland" and further violent conquests.

Rape, in my view, actually is not a metaphor that is helpful in understanding the particular role violence against women plays in battle and after in these Hebrew bible texts. Rape in the Hebrew bible is theft of sexual property. The being of women is problematic since, on the one hand, women spoke the same language and shared traditions and values in common with men, but they were not people in a political sense since they could not represent their household. They represented something else: nature, procreation, and the land. This is why sexual violence is so often the way in which images of conquest and domination are framed. In Hosea, for example, this connection between the people of Israel, conceived as a wife who "plays the whore," and sexual and domestic violence on the land itself is made very explicit: ". . . I will strip her naked and expose her as in the day she was born, and make her like a wilderness, and turn her into a parched land . . ." (Hos. 2:3). Sexual violence in war is permitted, though there are rules about conduct toward capturing and raping enemy women and even the offspring of captured women.[21]

The key to understanding women's bodies in the Hebrew bible is their capacity to sexually reproduce. The orderly functioning of the nation, tribe, and family was wholly dependent on the control of women's sexual reproduction. When women's sexuality is out of control—that is, when she "whores"—this is not in prescribed lines either in war or in peace and it is the direct opposite of order; it is chaos.

Chaos is the supreme threat to order and thus evil. Sexual violence against women is conducted both symbolically and actually to assert and maintain this control, whether with war or in the regular conduct of society. The Rape of Tamar (2 Samuel 13:1–22) plays both roles in that this text establishes the acceptable boundaries of rape as a social norm in a political context. Insofar as the triumph of Yahweh as Holy Warrior/Creator needs to be repeated in the continual obedience/disobedience of Israel's relationship to Yahweh, the bodies of women are a frequent literary and actual location for this enactment as women are either good (sexually obedient) or bad and threatening (sexually disobedient).

There are other Hebrew bible themes that are displaced by the Priestly Writer's reframing of Creation as Combat Myth, especially that of Eden. These themes will need to be retrieved and reframed once again, here in the twenty-first century, to critique the deep, even primordial origins of women's bodies as battlefield and to establish a different theory of peace and war.

Greek Thought

War and the War on Women have multiple, overlapping, and even partially contradictory sources. This is certainly the case in moving from the largely ancient Near Eastern sources of the Conflict Myth to the Greek and ultimately Roman conceptions that also structure Christian theological thought and Christian action in war and peace. From the early epics to Greek mythology to Aristotle and Plato, the themes of the hero, the defeat of the monster, and the orderly functioning of the world/cosmos all play a role.

Homeric Epics

Two very important epics, the *Iliad* and the *Odyssey*, date from between the seventh and eighth centuries BCE, and the authorship is attributed to Homer, though these may have multiple authors. The Homeric epics are the foundation for Greek thought.

Perhaps astonishingly, some of the most poignant and trenchant honesty about what war is really like is in the *Iliad*, or, as Simone Weil calls it, "The Poem of Force." Weil's interpretation of the *Iliad* is itself a classic and is clearly influenced by her intimate experience of war, and the struggle against it, in the European experience of two World Wars in a short matter of decades. As a Christian mystic, philosopher, pacifist, and resistance fighter, Weil's work focuses our attention, over the distance of millennia, on the difference between Greek and Roman understandings of force and the Christian appropriation of each.

Weil's monograph begins with these three sentences that demonstrate that in her view, the *Iliad* shows force without pretense it is anything else: "The true hero, the true subject, the center of the *Iliad*, is force. Force employed by man, force that enslaves man, force before which man's flesh shrinks away. In this work at all times, the human spirit is shown as modified by its relation to force, as swept away, blinded, by the very force it imagined it could handle, as deformed by the weight of the force it submits to."[22]

There is a searing tone to Weil's assessment that never becomes brittle, but it is bitter. It is just clear-eyed on the fact mostly that "throughout twenty centuries of Christianity, the Romans and the Hebrews have been admired, read, imitated, both in deed and word; their masterpieces have yielded an appropriate quotation every time anybody had a crime he wanted to justify."[23]

The Greek spirit as seen in the *Iliad* is different in her view, and that difference is the capacity to avoid "self-deception" that is present in the Greeks and mostly absent from the Hebrews and the Romans. This Greek spirit was "transmitted from the *Iliad* to the Gospels by way of the tragic poets, but this never jumped the borders of Greek civilization; once Greece was destroyed nothing remained of this spirit but pale reflections."

Her reflection on the *Iliad* is not that dissimilar to the view of force of Elaine Scarry.

Weil defines force as that which turns anyone subjected to it into a thing or, at worst, into a corpse. Force is not just dangerous to the victim of force but also to the one who wields it. Force intoxicates, and it numbs both reason and pity. Even the one who uses force becomes a thing.

Love and justice do not make much of an appearance in the epic or in Weil's thought on it. Heroes from both sides do not escape tragedy, and that serves as a kind of universal compassion for the human condition that in Weil's view rarely appears in Western thought, beyond Greek tragedy, the Gospels, Shakespeare and a very few others.

It is crucial to consider, however, how Weil's own experience as a woman in war-torn Europe, and the trauma of her own experience, influences her interpretation of this epic poem. It is a commentary on living with a conscience during a massive world war as much as it is a commentary on Greek thought. What is crucial to take away from the narrative is Weil's own refusal to look away from the tragic dimensions of war and injustice. In Weil's view, the use of force is deforming to all. There is no such thing, in Weil's view, as a Just War concept in the *Iliad* as that idea comes to be established in Western thought through Plato, Aristotle, Augustine, and Aquinas. Homer's depictions of battle are very realistic, and the victory at the very end is not a cause for celebration as the somber costs are counted. Rarely do any philosophers want to show the real injury, death, and costs of war. Otherwise, many would refuse to fight.

The *Iliad*, and Weil's interpretation of it, are far from the whole of Greek thought, especially when it comes to women's bodies and war. The *Iliad* demonstrates, in fact, that the male actors are the sum and substance of the "human." Women weep and moan and mourn the lost husbands, fathers, and sons, but they are not the central human actors in the drama of force.

But in the *Iliad*, force is drama and human beings and gods are subject to the whims of a capricious fate. That was far too disorderly for Plato. In addition, when it came to actual bodies and actual battlefields, Plato placed all that action far, far offstage in his work.

Plato: No Body, No Battlefield

Plato's *Timaeus* can seem similar to the *Enuma Elish* as it intends to explain the origin, existence, and meaning of the universe. It is a creation narrative in the sense that Plato observes a beautiful, wonderful order in the universe, and from this, he deduces it must be the handiwork of a divine Craftsman ("Demiurge," *dêmiourgos*, 28a6), who, imitating an unchanging and eternal model, imposes mathematical order on a preexistent chaos to generate the ordered universe (*kosmos*). Thus there is a hint of the chaos/nomos struggle, but astonishingly, Plato does not as much defeat threatening female chaos but rather submerges it very thoroughly.

A key problem for Plato, as seen in the *Timaeus*, is that however beautiful the universe appears, it is a copy; it is not the timeless and eternal forms themselves.

How can the Craftsman even imitate that which is invisible, intangible, and non-spatial? Thus Plato introduces a concept that, he admits, is hard to describe, since it is a totally characterless subject that temporarily, in its various parts, gets considered in several ways.

This is the receptacle—an enduring substratum—apparently neutral in itself but temporarily taking on various characterizations. However, it is anything but neutral in its philosophical and cultural effects when it comes to the War on Women and war itself. According to Judith Butler, in her aptly named work *Bodies That Matter*, writing on this specific Platonic text, "[T]here is a disjunction between a materiality which is feminine and formless and, hence, without a body, and bodies which are formed through—but not of—that feminine materiality."[24] As was noted in Chapter 2, Plato compares a woman's uterus to a living creature that "gets discontented and angry" and wanders throughout a woman's body where it "closes up the passages of the breath" and causes "all variety of disease" unless it becomes filled with an actual, masculine "essence."[25] Some of the chaotic feminine as threat can be seen in this latter passage.

Plato's discourses on materiality, and the feminine and female bodies in particular, play a key role in directing our attention away from actual bodies. Plato was, of course, unable to completely do away with physical existence, but our attention is directed toward eternal forms. But it gets worse.

Female metaphors and pronouns abound in describing the receptacle, this characterless subject; it is a kind of "nurse" that is "the universal nature which receives all bodies." Yet while receiving all things, "she [sic] never departs at all from her own nature, and never in any way, or at any time, assumes a form like that of any of the things which enter into her." In other words, she receives "impressions" and thus seems different at different times. "But the forms which enter into and go out of her are the likenesses of real existences modeled after their patterns in wonderful and inexplicable manner." (50d2–4, 51a4–5) In other words, "she" is not real, only the forms that "enter into and go out of her" are real. While the sexual connotation of "into . . . her" is barely hidden, we need to ask if there is a kind of sexual violence implied as well. The "receptacle" is so formless, there seems no way for "her" to consent, so can it be an implication of rape?

One thing we can definitely derive from this section in Plato is that "she" has no power. But then, this can fit contemporary feminist analyses of the social construction of rape in a "context of intersecting power inequalities" and "gender as a primary locus of subordination." As Deborah Turekheimer writes in her article "Sex Without Consent" in the *Yale Law Journal*, the fact that in history, "women's sexuality has been variously denied, controlled, and harnessed" means that focusing on consent in cases of rape can mislead. Rather, she argues, "[R]ape is the negation of women as sexual subjects."[26]

This is precisely what Plato's metaphysics sets up for Western culture, the absolute negation of the female as subject or agent. "She" has no agency, but is merely astonishingly formless and passive, not even what we might think of as materiality at all. "She" has no power and as Butler reminds us, "'[m]ateriality' designates a certain effect of power or, rather is power in its formative or constituting effects."[27]

Is this just female bodies that are rendered so formless and passive? What then of bodies maimed and killed in war? Butler confronts us exactly at this point. She challenges us to ask, "How can we legitimate claims of bodily injury if we put into question the materiality of the body?"[28] Thus it is important to note that a legacy from Plato is, effectively, if the body does not matter, then the battlefield itself will not matter.

It is crucial to recognize how this Platonic paradigm in Western philosophy works in regard to critical race theory as well. Womanist theologian Kelly Brown Douglas starts her consideration of the "complexity of Christianity's role in the white attack on the black body as well as its continued role in issues of racial, gender, and sexual injustice" with the influence of a "Platonized tradition" which "advanced antagonistic dualistic paradigms and a demonization of the flesh/body." Plato's specific influence was in the area of the "attack on the black body."[29]

#BlackLivesMatter was a Twitter meme (a series of posts to Twitter with that hashtag) created in 2012 after the murder in Florida of Trayvon Martin, an unarmed 17-year-old African American teenager, and his murderer, George Zimmerman, was acquitted for his crime. It was Martin who was relentlessly attacked posthumously in the media. The website www.blacklivesmatter.com explains that #BlackLivesMatter is "[r]ooted in the experiences of Black people in this country who actively resist our de-humanization." This is a new movement, the website explains, that is deliberately and widely gender inclusive and goes beyond earlier movements that kept "straight cis Black men in the front of the movement while our sisters, queer and trans and disabled folk take up roles in the background or not at all. Black Lives Matter affirms the lives of Black queer and trans folks, disabled folks, black-undocumented folks, folks with records, women and all Black lives along the gender spectrum."[30] This critical physicality is crucial to identifying exactly what the legacy of Platonic dualism has been in turning certain bodies into battlefields.

This new movement and its choice of "matter" in its new media activism is precisely what Kelly Brown Douglas is arguing has to be countered in the Platonic legacy. There can be no claims to the offense of bodily injury if the materiality of the body, especially certain specific bodies, does not even exist. Those bodies, then, do not matter at all, and so that is what has to be specifically resisted.

Plato on War

Plato writes less about war and peace than one might think, considering he wrote the dialogues during the Peloponnesian War. Plato knows war but considers the end of war must be the establishment of peace in terms of orderly civic virtue. The justification for war is to establish peace and civic order. This is a concept that will profoundly influence the development of Just War theory.

The goal of Plato's *Republic* is to develop the ideally just city. As long as some cities are not fully just, however, the ideal city will have to be prepared for war and, in the *Republic*, be very prepared to not only defend itself but also to spread justice. But war itself must not be known. Plato forbids young people, in the *Republic*, to read the Homeric epics. Homer's depictions of battle are just too graphic, and the victory at the very end is costly, probably too costly. That is scarcely the idea of war as establishing peace. Perhaps it is Plato's view, then, that actual war not be known by the young, as it is they who would have to fight.

War itself, it hardly needs be said, makes no actual appearance in the *Republic*. Considerable attention is paid to the training of soldiers but not to their death or injury in battle. Much has been made of women being included in book V as soldiers or rulers, but since Plato considers women weaker in every area of life, it would seem this is at best a supportive or, even more narrowly, a reproductive role. What matters is that military training is a substantial part of what we would call a good or even ideal city.

Plato is therefore also influential in integrating a "warrior class" into the very fabric of what he considers an ideal society and thus making militarism foundational for civilization itself. Politics and war are thus joined, but at the level of theory.

This is war in the abstract, war not unlike that described by Clausewitz as politics by other means. Combined with Plato's views on role of the "receptacle" in the formation of the universe, war is known solely as an abstract theory of justice and politics rather than the practice of out-injuring the bodies of enemies. This abstraction about war is a strong legacy from Plato.

It is this very characterless femaleness of materiality that provides Plato, and his philosophical heirs, a way to very effectively hide the injuring of bodies, especially of women's bodies, while simultaneously arguing that war or even violence are justified. If you have no bodies that matter, then how can you know what battlefields are really like? Injured bodies, dead bodies, from war and the War on Women simply sink out of sight into the formless, femaleness of the material.

Aristotle: Bodies Matter, but Not as Much as You Might Think

Aristotle was Plato's student, but as is well-known, he rejected his teacher's core theory of forms. For Aristotle, abstract entities cannot exist independently of the objects themselves, and the forms simply cannot explain the *existence* of particular objects. For Aristotle, the universe lies between two poles, matter without form on the one hand, and form without matter on the other. Movement is what takes form to matter but with a purpose.

This led Aristotle to focus closely on the material world, but for the purpose of bodies as battlefields, and the War on Women, this does not help as much as one might think. Surely careful attention to the material would be a step forward in the focus on injuring the body, but the form/matter union in Aristotle still privileges certain bodies over others because the principle of form is more advanced in some than in others. That is, there are some bodies that matter and some bodies that do not.

For Aristotle, the soul is the form of the body. In *On the Soul*, he says, "The body is the subject or matter, not what is attributed to it. Hence the soul must be a substance in the sense of the form of a natural body having life potentially within it. But substance is actuality, and thus soul is the actuality of a body" and never the other way around.[31] The body is not body in itself but body where the purpose has been installed, so to speak.

Feminist critiques of Aristotle have often centered on his biological views of women's deformed nature, as well as his assertion in his *Metaphysics*, that women are linked to matter and men to reason. It is also the case that the soul is warmer and the body colder.

According to Aristotle in *The Generation of Animals*, woman is the beginning of the category of monster. "Females are weaker and colder in nature, and it is necessary to regard the female status as a deformity, though a natural one."[32] As Catherine Keller explains, the monstrous originality of females is in Aristotle's thought because, in biological terms, the soul provides "heat" and thus the "colder" female creatures have less soul.

The male substance is also dry, while woman and ovum are wet. Already, "she seems fishy, akin to sea monsters, indeed to the sea itself." In procreation, the female provides only the body, and the male provides the soul. Thus a female child is a kind of deformity in herself, a monstrous creation. The male provides the form, so when a woman gives birth to a daughter, she is giving birth to a deformity—that is, a monster.[33] Astonishingly, these Aristotelian ideas on women's coldness as well as human deformity were given credence up through the Middle Ages.[34]

The assumption of normative links between maleness and form (superior) and femaleness and matter (inferior) translates into women's inferiority in his ethical and political works, as "it is clear that the rule of soul over the body, and of the mind and the rational element is natural and expedient . . . the male is by nature superior, and the female inferior; the one rules, and the other is ruled; this principle of necessity extends to all mankind."[35] This provides what we might call a biologically based defense of the use of force when extrapolated from the capture of slaves in war.

The argument on force comes in the same section as the "natural and expedient" rule of the male over the female, the hierarchy of force is established as natural and right when it comes to women, though it must be subject to some notions of "justice" when it comes to war. This will have enormous consequences in the influence of Aristotle on Aquinas and on the development of Just War theory and its thundering silence on violence against women.

Aristotle defends slavery "by nature" and thus argues it is "an institution both expedient and just." Yet a contrary argument can be made, he allows, because when it comes to those conquered in war, they become slaves when they were not before. This rather is the law, "a sort of agreement under which the things conquered in war are said to belong to their conquerors." Is this "monstrous," since it is plainly not "natural"?

Force, when used by virtue for the good, is not monstrous because "in a certain manner *virtue when it obtains resources has in fact very great power to use force, and the stronger party always possesses superiority in something that is good*, so that it is thought that force cannot be devoid of goodness, but that the dispute is merely about the justice of the matter." The "justice of the matter" can vary and can be a convention rather than a condition of nature when it comes to slavery; this is demonstrated by the various conditions of slaves, either when slave by nature or by capture in war.

But when it comes to women, there is no condition under which their inferiority is anything but natural, as "the male is by nature superior, and the female inferior; the one rules, and the other is ruled; this principle of necessity extends to all mankind." Some conventions about masters and rule can thus be applied in war but none at all in the household and about the condition of women.

The War on Women did not exist for Aristotle either in his cosmology or his politics. Any violence done to women as the inferior who must be ruled would be, by virtue of the good power bestowed on men, just. This view is plainly carried forward in Western culture as justifying violence against women as "rule" for a very long time. Aristotle's views on slavery are also profoundly influential in establishing the superiority of some; clearly this undergirds white supremacy in the West.

When it comes to more conventional notions of war, however, it must be said that Aristotle did contend, in the *Nicomachean Ethics*, that "we . . . make war that we may live in peace."[36]

Greek thought comes close to understanding war in the Homeric epics where force is the only real actor, and the rest are caught in a tragedy somehow not of their own making. Plato and Aristotle both try to control war and make it into a political instrument, each from their own perspectives. There is no effort, in any of these ancient sources, to see violence done to women's bodies as a problem in itself, nor violence done to those who are not "superior." Where such acts are deemed a wrong, it is a wrong against a male hierarchy. War is mostly taking place "offstage," except for the *Iliad* where it is frustratingly center stage. The War on Women makes no appearance.

Yet it must be said that the Greeks attempted to find a way to limit, if not eliminate, war. The same cannot be said for the Romans.

Roman War and Peace

> The Romans are the robbers of the world. After denuding the land, they rifle the sea. They are rapacious toward the rich and domineering toward the poor, satiated neither by the East nor by the West. Pillage, massacre and plunder they grace with the name of empire and where they make a desert, they call it peace.
>
> Tacitus, *Agricola*[37]

In *Agricola*, the account by Roman historian Tacitus of the life of his famous father-in-law, Roman General Gnaeus Julius Agricola, the corruption and tyranny of the Roman Empire as unleashed on the liberty of the native Britons is recounted. The rapaciousness of the Roman thirst for conquest is disguised as the *Pax Romana*, a parody of peace, for "where they make a desert, they call it peace."

Simone Weil says of the Romans that they "saw their country as the nation chosen by destiny to be the mistress of the world . . . Strangers, enemies, conquered peoples, subjects, slaves, were objects of contempt to the Romans; and the Romans had no epics, no tragedies. In Rome gladiatorial fights took the place of tragedy."[38]

Greeks who had been conquered by the Roman war machine wondered, "What manner of men are the Romans?" The viciousness of the Roman drive to conquer seemed to them to be especially corrupt. Was this, the Greeks pondered, because the Romans had actually founded their nation on violence against women? Are they then men of "base blood" who, in order to obtain wives, "seized them by violence?"[39]

The Roman paradigm of conquest that brought about "civilization" in terms of laws and infrastructure along with colonial control and a denuding of the local economies is profoundly formative, along with the Combat Myth and the thought of Plato and Aristotle, for what eventually become the Christian ideas of war and peace. Peace in the Roman model, as Tacitus observes, is not the presence of justice and the means to live, as the Hebrew bible describes *shalom*, and it is not even the absence of war, as the Roman idea of *Pax Romana* would contend. It is the presence of war by other means. It is power and control.

Mapping the Physical

War and the War on Women have this physical dimension in common: injuring, inflicting pain, and fatal destruction happen to bodies. There are many other dimensions, as is clear from this analysis. There are psychological, philosophical, religious, political, and economic factors that characterize war and the War on Women. But what these latter characteristics have in common themselves is that they funnel attention away from the injuring and destruction of bodies.

Whether the cosmic female body is splayed open for dismemberment as in the *Enuma Elish* or whether the physical simply sinks out of sight, taking injury and death with it, there are many mechanisms with a surprisingly common purpose: injury and death in war and the War on Women must be justified, or even better, not seen and therefore not needing justification at all. Some lives simply don't "matter."

Very often, these kinds of philosophies and theologies service political and economic functions. Chaos or disobedience are deemed supremely threatening at the cosmological level and must be subdued. Female bodies are frequently the "vehicles," per Scarry, to "convey the physical manifestation of contemptible physical rebellion and deserved bodily punishment." Often, this is literally taking place on the bodies of women through rape and battering. But it is also taking place on the bodies of those deemed more material, as they are nondominant races.

The suppression of chaos, or the command of obedience, literally on the bodies, is theorized at the political and economic level, creating and sustaining ruling and warrior classes. This cannot be accomplished in Western culture, however, without the strong support of Christian sources and their theological interpretations that justify war, hierarchy, and the War on Women.

4

War and the War on Women

Christian Theological Sources

I saw a woman sit upon a scarlet colored beast, full of names of blasphemy, having
  seven heads and ten horns . . .
And upon her forehead was a name written, Mystery, Babylon The Great, The
  Mother Of Harlots And Abominations Of The Earth.
And I saw the woman drunk with the blood of the saints, and with the blood of
  the martyrs of Jesus: and when I saw her, I wondered with great admiration.

Revelation 17:3b, 5, 6

It takes a lot of philosophical and theological effort to justify war. As Plato clearly
realized, if war is really shown in the all its bloody, violent injury and death, as
it was in the *Iliad*, the young would not fight.

The madness and chaos of actual war exposes the fiction that war is a virtuous
pursuit of peace and justice. Thus to justify war, the threatening chaos of war itself
must first be defeated but without an admission of the true nature of war. Since
the chaotic, threatening nature of war cannot be directly named and tamed, it
must be referred elsewhere and dealt with there. The chaos of war is philosophically and theologically referred to the bodies of women, and there it is defeated,
over and over.

Critical physicality helps expose this strategy of referral of the chaos of war on
to women's bodies and, in so doing, helps defeat its effectiveness. When we map
what really happens to the body in war and connect that to what happens to the
female body in the War on Women, we can better witness what is going on. We
can refuse to turn away from what is actually happening to bodies, refuse to ignore
this real pain and suffering, and refuse to deny that it has meaning in and for itself.
Then, and only then, do we get a glimpse into why it is that Western culture thinks
war will save us from chaos and therefore why the War on Women is justified.

Revelation to John: Defeating the Female Body as Babylon (Rome)

The idea of war and conflict is raised to extraordinary levels of imagination and violence in the New Testament Revelation to John. While the conquest, defeat, and dismemberment of Ti'amat is brutal in its descriptions of battle on a woman's body, that description pales beside the vivid, hate-filled, and violent defeat of Babylon (AKA Rome); in the text, this is the "great whore who is seated on many waters" (Rev. 17:1).

John draws on many of the Combat Myth renderings in the Hebrew bible, not only the Priestly Writer in Genesis, but also Isaiah, Jeremiah, Ezekiel, and Daniel as they had reinterpreted the Babylonian War of 600 years earlier. The Revelation to John is the application of the Combat Myth to Jesus of Nazareth and a substantial reframing of Jesus's message as one of war, not of peace, and of conquest rather than the "love your enemies and bless those who persecute you" of the Sermon on the Mount.

The author of Revelation is called John, typically called John of Patmos, a small island off the coast of Turkey. Early tradition held that John was banished to Patmos by the Romans, and as Revelation 1:9 confirms, John considers himself a brother "in tribulation" for "the word of God." Banishment was a common Roman punishment used for many offenses, including prophecy. As Adela Yarborough Collins notes, "Prophecy with political implications, like that expressed by John in the book of Revelation, would have been perceived as a threat to Roman political power and order."[1]

John is writing in the turbulent late first century and claims to have received visions and prophecies while on the island of Patmos. These are visions churning with apocalyptic imagery, but they are nevertheless political. I believe there is a good case to be made that the mythological images and the numerology so characteristic of Revelation are, in fact, a form of code so that the explicit connection to the hoped-for political and economic destruction of Rome and all it stood for would be less obvious to the uninitiated.

The Revelation to John is certainly war literature. War had broken out in Jerusalem in 66 CE when Jewish groups attempted to expel the Romans from occupying Judea. The Romans not only quelled the rebellion, but they also sent 60,000 troops and laid siege to Jerusalem, where the Jewish groups were holding out. They starved the inhabitants, eventually defeated them, cruelly executed the survivors, and burned the Temple to the ground.

The brutal physicality of Roman soldiers, not only the method of torture by crucifixion for execution the Romans routinely used, but also the torture of flogging leading up to crucifixion, was legendary. It was one of the sources of the particular kind of power exercised by Rome. This was on display in full force when putting down the Jewish armed insurrection that included the Roman destruction of the Temple, as the Jewish historian Josephus describes: "*They [the Jewish insurrectionists] were accordingly scourged and subjected to torture of every description, before being killed, and then crucified opposite the walls ... five hundred or sometimes more being captured daily ... The soldiers out of rage and hatred amused themselves by nailing their prisoners in different postures; and so great was their number, that space could not be found for the crosses nor crosses for the bodies.*"[2]

John, on Patmos, understands himself and the other followers of Jesus to be in a brutal war, and he is not wrong about that. Not only has the Kingdom vision of Jesus of Nazareth, a community of those who ate and drank together and who cared for the poor and gave compassion to their enemies, failed to arrive, what has come is the worst of war and the scattering of the Jesus movement. Jesus and then Peter had been crucified, and Paul of Tarsus had been whipped and beheaded. Jesus's own brother James was either beaten or stoned to death near the Temple in Jerusalem.

This is war, a war on everything the followers of Jesus believed. John contains some of the most vivid imagery of war of any literature—the four horsemen of the Apocalypse.

The white horse and rider come first and they are conquest. Jesus may have been sacrificed like the innocent Pascal Lamb, but the vision of the white horse in John reveals the paradox that this time, as Jesus returns, he is coming "conquering, and to conquer."

The second horse is bright red, the red of blood that flows in war, the color of the blood that must have flowed like a red river as 500 or more were flogged and crucified each day in the final war. War *is* "the red animal," according to Stephen Crane, and this biblical red animal "was permitted to take peace from the earth, so that people would slaughter one another."

Starvation follows war, and that is the black horse; the rider of the black horse holds scales that measure the inflated prices of food in times of conflict, as much as "a quart of wheat for a day's pay." And finally, Death rides out, pale green, and Hades follows: "they were given authority over a fourth of the earth, to kill with sword, famine, and pestilence, and by the wild animals of the earth" (Rev. 6:1–8).

While it is important, in understanding war, to stay with the body, it is also crucial to see how the extremes of physical suffering can sometimes only be captured in images so vivid it shocks the hearer into witnessing. Thus, from Crane's "red animal" to John's horsemen of the apocalypse, the spasmodic violence of war can be evoked.

Perhaps John himself, but certainly many of the other remaining followers of Jesus, saw and experienced this flowing blood, starvation, and death in many forms in the brutal repression by Rome following the insurrection in 66 CE. But in John's vision, this is no longer taking place on earth. In Revelation, this war is taking place in *heaven*. This is where Rome will get payback for all its crimes and be crushed. But the central image for this is the body of a woman (Revelation 17).

John sees the "great whore" sitting on a "scarlet colored beast." She is garbed in purple and scarlet and covered in jewels. She is covered in royal colors but holds in her hand "a golden cup full of abominations and filthiness of her fornication." She is labeled, named on her forehead, "Babylon the Great, The Mother of Harlots and Abominations of the Earth."

But so many images combine to tell the reader that this is Rome: blood-spilling, rapacious, war-like, torturing Rome. This is clear as the woman sits on "seven hills," the seven hills of Rome. The woman is "drunk with the blood of the saints, and with the blood of the martyrs of Jesus." This could be a reference to Nero who was rumored to light his garden with flaming torches made up of the Christians he had ordered arrested or to the unspeakably violent death of Christians in the Coliseum.

In John's vision, however, Rome does not win in the end. The judgment of cosmic war is coming for Rome, coming brutally. The battlefield will be on the body of a woman—this whore—who will be made "desolate and naked, and [the beast] shall eat her flesh and burn her with fire." This brutal sexual assault and murder is paired with other sexual imagery, a pregnant woman who is "clothed with the sun, with the moon under her feet and on her head a crown of twelve stars" (Rev. 12:1). This is certainly Israel, as the number 12 would indicate and as the desired reproductive life of the community that "good" women represent. This mirrors the dualism on gender in ancient Israel that divides women into the controlled reproductive vehicle or the threatening chaos that must be brutally subdued and/ or destroyed.

In Revelation, the images of war lead to the final triumph over violence so that the "river of life" can be restored; these images are incredibly rich and dense and can be inspiring as well as disturbing. New Testament professor Barbara Rossing, in her book *The Rapture Exposed: The Message of Hope in the Book of Revelation*,[3] has argued therefore that the Christian fundamentalist idea of the "Rapture," a popular interpretation of this text that is often used to support war as God's judgment, is a profound distortion. According to Rossing, that "Rapture" interpretation is based on a psychology of fear and destruction. Instead, Revelation offers a vision of God's healing love for the world, a love that is designed to lead people to God's beloved community.

While it is helpful to have a study like Rossing's to confront the worst of the war-making uses of Revelation, it is crucial, for the purposes of this argument, to recognize what trauma theory reveals about Revelation. From the Babylonian captivity to the brutal destruction of the Temple, and the massacre and exile of so many Jewish people, the terror of war is the backdrop of these texts. These texts are not only wartime literature but they are also texts of trauma.

As Judith Herman describes it, "At the moment of trauma, the victim is rendered helpless by overwhelming force." Left untreated, traumatized people tend to "relive the moment of trauma." Adults and children do this, and can recreate the moment over and over, "either in literal or in disguised form." The fantasy can take the form of imagining a different outcome—that is, where the one terrorizing the victim or victims is defeated rather than being triumphant, as John of Patmos reimagines Rome being cosmically and decisively defeated for all time. Freud first conceptualized this as an effort to regain control over the traumatic event, but that explanation was not complete. Freud realized this did not capture "the 'daemonic' quality of reenactment."[4] The biblical book of Revelation, however, clearly captures the "daemonic" quality of trauma reenactment from the first verse.

A deeply "daemonic" quality of Conflict Myth is that it has to be reenacted over and over, thus keeping the trauma alive and the desire for revenge strong. Conflict Myth refers trauma from one generation to the next, from one century to the next, literally from one millennium to the next. War is not ended because war becomes reenacted in unresolved trauma.

Trauma theory is critical to understanding what happens to bodies, minds, and spirits in war and the War on Women as was described in Chapters 1 and 2. The good news is also that there is a way out psychologically, socially, and ultimately religiously to heal from trauma and that is not to try to escape into fantasy but actually to face the trauma not as imagined but as real, to know it in the body and for there to be a communal, witnessing response. Since the "core experiences" of trauma are "disempowerment and disconnection from others," Herman argues that recovery "is based on the empowerment of the survivor and the creation of new connections."[5] John's visions promise recovery but after history. Can recovery in heaven help the survivor now?

Whether John's visions help the survivor of war, his anguish is the anguish of the one crushed by unjust rule and by the grotesque violence of war. John writes from the margins. He can recognize the bloodletting that is war all too well.

Augustine and Aquinas, however, do not write from the margins of empire and from under its heel but rather from the center of power. This changes their theology of war and of violence against women. An order has taken hold of the world. Their theory is that order is God's order. The cosmic threat posed by an all-consuming Babylon (Rome) is subdued. But neither of these theologians think societies are safe from the lurking threat of chaos.

Augustine and the Body Politic

Augustine of Hippo, the great theologian and early architect of Just War theory, was an African and knew the deep sense of wrong of the conquered. Yet he was also a Roman citizen, a Latin-speaking heir to the Christianizing Empire.

Scarcely a generation before Augustine was born, the Roman Emperor Constantine the Great made Christianity the dominant religion of the Roman Empire. While persecution had waned prior to Constantine, it was within living memory of some. Thus the adoption of Christianity by a Roman emperor would have seemed like evidence that God's kingdom was finally coming into being. This was the Roman Empire Augustine knew for many years, the Empire that had not only stopped persecuting Christians but that had accepted Christ. Was that a miracle?

The sack of Rome by the barbarian Alaric and his army in 410, when Augustine was more than 50 years old, would have therefore been shocking. How could this happen when the Empire had accepted Christ? While Augustine was not in Rome when this atrocity occurred but instead 1,000 miles away in Hippo, in North Africa (current Annaba, Algeria), it still must have been traumatizing to his world that such a thing could happen. What shock waves must have rippled around the Mediterranean region; mighty Rome could be successfully attacked by barbarians. Augustine began writing his magnum opus, *Civitate Dei* (City of God), almost immediately after word of the sack of Rome reached Hippo. He wrote to make sense of this event in light of God's plans for human salvation.

Pagans and Christians were each blaming the other for the disaster. Pagans said Rome was successfully attacked because Romans had abandoned the old Roman gods. This was insupportable for Augustine, and he begins his work with an impassioned defense of Christianity over against the pagan claims. For Augustine, however, the issue is far deeper than blame or exoneration of Christians or even the Christian God. There is a profound theological question that he thinks must be answered. Clearly it is right to worship the God revealed in Jesus Christ, so then why did God allow this catastrophic event to happen?

Augustine hardly ignores the pagan gibes, however, and he engages in a highly polemical treatment of Roman history to show how inglorious the history of the "Glory that is Rome" really was. Rome, he contends, was founded on fratricide, the abduction of the Sabine women, as well as the brutality of the Roman games and the extensive poverty in the empire. Those who would blame Christianity for Rome's fall do not know the ignominious history of Rome.

But while Augustine does argue that the sexual violence against the Sabine women was part of the proof of Rome's degeneracy, he has a larger, profoundly theological argument against Rome. Augustine's view is that there is a divine providence that governs history and that history is from the beginning of time and is even now playing out with the ultimate consummation of God's plans assured. This view is more Hebraic than Greek; as described by Weil, the Hebrews have no Greek sense of the tragic because "it was their God who exalted them and they retained their superior position just as long as they obeyed Him."[6]

Augustine's understanding of divine providence means history should be seen as an unfolding of God's plan from creation to apocalypse. But then how to account for such a jolting event as the sack of Rome in God's plan? Augustine sees history not as linear but as a struggle between the City of God and the Earthly City, moving on toward a final resolution in the eschaton. In this schema, Rome is Babylon, the earthly city, even the City of the Devil, in contrast to Jerusalem, the City of God and now the Holy Church. According to Augustine, Rome is the second Babylon, and Babylon is the first Rome. "One empire took the place of another." So Rome is not innocent and is certainly not the City of God even though now the Christian God is worshiped there. Jerusalem, in a universal sense, is the heavenly city. Israel lost its citizenship in the history of the City of God after the Babylonian captivity. After the coming of Christ, the City of God (Jerusalem) is no longer the exclusive province of the Jews but rather becomes universal. History is dynamic and complex. Human beings are obstinate and rebel against God over and over, but there is continual movement toward salvation by God's work.

Make no mistake, Augustine is also influenced by Rome and certainly the Christian theology that comes after him is enormously influenced by Roman imperial power. Augustine believes it is part of God's plan that the Roman Empire has accepted Christianity, but that does not make Rome the City of God. The struggle with paganism in Augustine's time means Rome has to be the new Babylon, even as the City of God is a perfect, universalized Jerusalem.

The focus in Augustine's work is on divine providence. This means his concern with Rome's treatment of women, for example in the rape of the Sabine women, is not at the forefront of his thinking. It is merely illustrative of other theological points. The fratricide and rape in Rome's founding is proof that Rome is indeed the continuation of the empire, Babylon.

War, on the other hand, does not belong to Babylon but to God and God's purposes. War is an instrument of divine purpose. This is not a view of war from the point of view of the victims of war, despite the shocking development of the sack of Rome, but from ruling power justified by God.

Augustine: Lust and War

For Augustine, there is more than one war in human life. There is the war without: the wars between nations. There is also the war within: the war with sexual drives and the struggle with lust as part of the condition in which human beings find themselves caught because of original sin.

The war within and the war without result from original sin: the sin of Adam and Eve that resulted in their being cast out of the Garden of Eden. The war within—the war with lust—can, in some ways, be construed in the thought of Augustine as the more difficult and intransient struggle. Original sin is actually transmitted through the semen to each succeeding generation of human beings. The semen itself is not sinful; what is sinful is the lust which drives the sex act where there is a physical reenactment of the original disobedience. This is not a sin of the body, however, but a sin of the soul as "it was not the corruptible flesh that made the soul sinful, but the sinful soul that made the flesh corruptible" (14.3). The "lustful excitement of the organs of generation" take over the will—that is, "moves the whole man" (14.16). Thus lust occurs apart from, and even against the will of, a man's body, and this is shown by the fact that everyone "considers sexual desire shameful" (14.17).

Normally, Augustine's views on sexuality and war are not treated together. But to understand the complex origins of women's bodies as battlefield and how this ultimately influences Christian understandings of Just War theory, these must be kept together. In an Augustinian sense, conflict in the self, like conflict in the city, is a clear sign of sin, especially the sin of disobedience. This is clearly seen in how Augustine condemns both "passion" for injuring in war and having "lust" in war. By that, he does not mean sexual lust, but the "lust for power." Thus he says in *Contra Faustum* (xxii, 74), "The passion for inflicting harm, the cruel thirst for vengeance, an unpacific and relentless spirit, the fever of revolt, the lust of power, and such like things, all these are rightly condemned in war." In other words, for Augustine, the chief moral risk in war is that you will enjoy it, even as in the sex act.[7]

If there had been no original sin, no disobedience by Adam in the Garden of Eden, then for Augustine, institutions of society, both familial and political, would have looked like the paterfamilias of the best of Roman society. Yet this hierarchical order in the family, in particular with father ruling over mother, children, and slaves, is foundational for domestic violence not only in the Greco-Roman world but also in later European societies and areas where these ideas are imported via

European colonial expansion such as the United States. It is also foundational for Augustine's influential Just War theory, and it is what ties these concepts together.

If Adam had not fallen from grace, then there would also have been no war. In Augustine's view, the fact that war exists means it must have some part in God's providential plan. All God's acts are just, and so war, as terrible as it is, must serve God's purposes. This is true even if the terrible suffering in war obscures the divine purposes. The two cities are mixed, the earthly city and the heavenly city, and waging war and engaging in violence are not as yet overcome. All avoidance of war, under these conditions, is impossible and so the righteous must cope as best they can.

While the "wise man will wage just wars," war is still horrible in Augustine's view, and when waged out of the "lust for power" and the "passion for inflicting harm," it is sin. The wise man laments "the necessity of just wars." On the one hand, "if they were not just he would not wage them," and it is entirely due to the "wrong-doing of the opposing party." On the other hand, one "thinks with pain on all these great evils, so horrible, so ruthless" and has to "acknowledge that this is misery." But it is not the misery per se that renders a war unjust but actually the inflaming of the passions in desire to injure and lust after power.[8]

Augustine believes Christians can wage war in peaceful ways to attain the end of peace,[9] even as the father in the family can physically chastise women, children, and slaves to maintain order and obedience. This is the major flaw in his thinking about war and peace that there is a way to use violence that is "peaceful." This is more clearly seen, in fact, in the home than on the battlefield when we add the argument of this work, that women's bodies are battlefields. Can a husband "peacefully" beat his wife and children?

The lens of women's bodies as battlefield allows more witnessing in regard to the thought of Augustine. Augustine must be challenged exactly on this battlefield, the battlefield of the bodies of the weaker and more vulnerable in the home. Then it becomes clearer that causing pain and harm, even risking killing, cannot, even to establish order, be called "peace."

There are parts of Augustine's reflections that can eventually be useful in considering what is deeply, theologically wrong about both war and the War on Women and that provide a critique of Augustine's own thought. Let us indeed posit that it is the "passions" that tempt one to sin, not only in war but also in violence against women in war, and that they are the passions to lust after power and control.

In the specific case of violence against women in war and the brutal violence of rape, Augustine shows that he is not just wrong, but he is profoundly wrong. Because Augustine must find the outworking of God's providence in war, even the brutal act of rape in war is subjected to this conviction of God's providence. This leads Augustine to the disreputable position that what is ultimately wrong about sexual assault in war is that the victim of rape will enjoy it.

Augustine devotes part of book I of the *City of God* to the rape of "consecrated and other Christian virgins" in the barbarian invasions. He passes quickly over the "pain" that "may be inflicted" but focuses in on the "lust gratified on the body of another." He concludes that the act of rape brings shame to the one raped "lest that act which could not be suffered without some sensual pleasure, should be believed to have been committed also with some ascent of the will."[10] For these consecrated virgins, it is not the "integrity" of the members of the body that matter, it is the integrity of the soul. "The sanctity of the soul remains even when the body is violated."[11]

The body/soul dualism that carries through Augustine's work, an inheritance of Platonism, directs Western Christian thought away from what happens to the body in war and away from what happens to the bodies of women when treated violently—that is, the "pain"—and toward what is supposed to be happening in the soul. Examining what is happening in the soul, not in the body, is what is consummately important in his work. For Augustine, reason rules, and thus the spirit is supposed to command the body, and when the body is unruly (i.e., feeling passion or lust), this is sinful. If we live "after the flesh" and not "after the spirit," then we will be ruled by the passions and bodily pleasure and be engaging in sin.[12]

When you couple this body/soul dualism with Augustine's view of divine providence, then, in the case of the consecrated virgins who have been raped, even though they felt pain, there must be something of God's plan in it. "By what judgment of God," Augustine presents, "the enemy was permitted to indulge his lust on the bodies of continent Christians." Those Christian women who were raped, Augustine argues, may yet have "had some lurking infirmity which might have betrayed them into a proud and contemptuous bearing" so that their "humiliation" in rape and in the taking of the city was to teach them "humility."[13]

So much of what rape victims and victims of war suffer is that their actual experiences, what has happened to them in their bodies, are totally ignored and even dismissed. This horror is based, in part, on this Augustinian legacy. As Mary Pellauer points out, what drives us to sometimes be "blind with tears" over these "misbegotten theological ideas" in this section of the *City of God* is the ceaseless repetition of what "*Augustine had done* to the consecrated virgins: *he hadn't listened.*"[14] Even worse, the extended legacy of Augustine's view is that victims of sexual or domestic violence, even the victims of war, are often blamed for their own victimization.

Listening is a central part of witnessing, it is not turning away from women's bodies as battlefields and from battlefields in war but paying close attention to the physical experience and understanding war from that topography of pain. The human being is one body and soul together and what happens to the body is of consummate importance.

According to Chris Hedges, seminary graduate, war correspondent, and social critic, if we really witnessed what happens to bodies and spirits in war, we would know why war is unjustifiable. "If we really saw war, what war does to young minds and bodies, it would be impossible to embrace the myth of war. If we had to stand over the mangled corpses of schoolchildren killed in Afghanistan and listen to the wails of their parents, we would not be able to repeat clichés we use to justify war."[15] In Hedges own work, however, this witnessing of what happens to bodies in war itself may not be enough to have us stop repeating the weak justifications of war. He argues in his ground-breaking *War Is a Force That Gives Us Meaning* that war (and I would add, the War on Women) is a kind of Augustinian perversion of lust, an addiction to power and inflicting harm. "The rush of battle is a potent and often lethal addiction, for war is a drug, one I ingested for many years."[16]

Augustine is right, therefore, that there is indeed a perverted passion in war and the War on Women. Where Augustine is wrong is that the injury and death in war must be part of God's providence. This leads to his frankly impossible notion that somehow a war that is justified in its authorization and intention somehow can split off the lust for war from the conduct of some wars. Augustine sees, per-haps because of the shocking nature of the sack of Rome, that war is sinful. But the combination of his views of divine providence and the dualism of body and spirit prevents him from being consistent about his own insights about what is sinful about war. He glimpses what is corrupt and cruel about war, and even the War on Women, but he loses that insight when he tries to rescue absolute divine providence from the realities of injury and death.

Aquinas: Ruthless Efficiency

Thomas Aquinas, the "Angelic Doctor" and saint, does not write from under the heel of empire, as did John of Patmos, or from the first centuries of a Christianity adopted by empire, as did Augustine, but decisively from the center, religiously, politically, and economically. Aquinas was born in a castle (though a minor one), and this well-educated and well-connected "Father of the Church" lived during the time of the "medieval synthesis," a combination of political and ecclesial power that worked to control large parts of Europe. The decades of Aquinas's life over-lapped with the most of the last decades of the Crusades. This was an expansion-ist time in terms of political power, and yet it was also all about to unravel. But that did not happen during the lifetime of Aquinas. His worldview was distinctly formed by a Christianity that had effectively merged with political power, not a Christianity tortured and trampled by empire nor a Christianity threatened by barbarians.

Like Aristotle, Aquinas holds that Plato's concept of universal ideas existing in a nonphysical or noncorporeal realm is wrong. Yet unlike Aristotle, he does not think sensory experience alone can account for ideas. But the influence of Aris-totle on Aquinas is vast, especially in the relentless pursuit of the "great chain of being"—Aristotle's classification of animals from the highest to the lowest. What Aquinas did with Aristotle's chain was add angels and then God at the very top.

The soul is over the body (*Summa Contra Gentiles*, book II, chapter 68), and "naturally," men over women (*Summa Theologiae*, 37). Immediately following the gender hierarchy is the ruling hierarchy, with one exception, Christians can-not be ruled by nonbelievers (On Kingship; *Summa Theologiae*, 38), but he adds another Christian element, saying that Christians cannot be ruled by nonbeliev-ers (*Summa Theologiae*, 62), but they still must obey secular (Christian) rulers (*Summa Theologiae*, 76).

Hierarchy is itself natural, and was part of God's plan even before the Fall (*Summa Theologiae*, 38). This rigid, hierarchical chain is also causal and leads from God as first cause through all secondary causes, linking existence in a reasonable, orderly fashion to the creator. While Aquinas frequently quotes the works of Augustine, the tension at the center of Augustine's theology, the stress and strain of a City of God in vivid contest with an earthly city as both move toward Armageddon, is absent. Instead, there is this inexorable march of reason that governs all.

This is political through and through. The Great Chain of Being is really a "Great Chain of Ruling" and a justification of "natural rulers" (*Summa Contra Gentiles*, book III, chapter 81) who possess superior intellect and hence are best able to rule. It is ruthlessly efficient and drives attention up the chain and away from what is happening to the body, especially the bodies of women.

Aquinas takes over some of the biologically based misogyny of Aristotle, yet not entirely. In regard to women's individual nature, she is "defective and misbegotten, for the active force in the male seed tends to the production of a perfect likeness in the masculine sex; while the production of woman comes from defect in the active force or from some material indisposition, or even from some external influence; such as that of a south wind, which is moist, as the Philosopher observes (*De Gener. Animal.*, iv, 2)." This defective nature results in women's subjection to men in all things, in the governance of the home and in the governance of society. But in the chain of being, on the other hand, women are not misbegotten, because they are "included in nature's intention as directed to the work of generation" and the "general intention of nature depends on God, Who is the universal Author of nature." In other words, God does not author anything "misbegotten," and "God formed not only the male but also the female."

This sounds like a step forward in terms of valuing women, but this is a narrow valuation, confined to procreation. This leads Aquinas into ranking rape as not nearly as sinful as, for example, masturbation or homosexuality, because rape of a female by a male is "unlawful" but it is not against nature; masturbation or homosexuality, on the other hand, are considered against nature (Question 154, Article 12).

Even worse, from the point of view of critical physicality, is the conclusion that the violence done to women's bodies, and by extrapolation, violence done to bodies in war, is not the worst offense in a fairly lengthy list of offenses. Instead, violence done to the ordering of nature, which is from "God himself," is the worst. Thus "sins contrary to nature, whereby the very order of nature is violated, is an injury done to God, the Author of nature." Aquinas then quotes Augustine from the *Confessions* (iii, 8): "Those foul offenses that are against nature should be everywhere and at all times detested and punished, such as were those of the people of Sodom . . . For even that very intercourse which should be between God and us is violated, when that same nature, of which He is the Author, is polluted by the perversity of lust."

The words in the example seem similar, but the framework is different. Augustine thinks with the body, even when he comes to the conclusion that consecrated virgins who had been raped perhaps secretly enjoyed it. Aquinas does not think with the body, but from such a divine distance that what the bodies of raped women do or do not feel in a war is of absolutely no consequence. For Aquinas, lust of any sort is not the perversity. What is perverse in his system is the violation of the hierarchy of nature and of the order of rule.

Aquinas: No Lust, Just Logic

It would seem, as Aquinas starts out in his polemical fashion in the section "Of War" in the *Summa Theologiae* (Question 40), that it is "always sinful" to wage war because "punishment is not inflicted except for sin." After a reference to Augustine and to the fact that Jesus did not "forbid soldiering," Aquinas gets to the real business of ordering war: the question of "can war be just" is answered first by the authority of the ruler: "In order for a war to be just, three things are necessary. First the authority of the sovereign by whose command the war is to be waged." It is up to the sovereign, not individuals, in "defending the common weal against external enemies." Second, "a just cause is required, namely, that those who are attacked, should be attacked because they deserve it on account of some fault"— that is, some punishment is being meted out for unjust behavior. And crucially, there must be a "rightful intention" to advance the good, and avoid evil.

The latter, Aquinas notes, are meting out punishment, citing Augustine, in "kindly severity" because it is actually a benefit to those who have done wrong to be punished, otherwise they will be in the awful position of being happy in their sin.

War is not always like that, however, even Aquinas has to acknowledge. War can be declared by a rightful authority and for a just cause and still be "rendered unlawful through a wicked intention." Here Aquinas quotes Augustine's observant words about the "passion for inflicting harm, the cruel thirst for vengeance, an unpacific and relentless spirit, the fever of revolt, the lust of power . . ."

Even all of this description, however, remains at the level of intentionality, not at the level of commission. What Aquinas does not see is that in war, there is not only a "passion for inflicting harm" but there is also actual, physical harm. There is not only a "cruel thirst for vengeance" but there are also actual cruelties enacted on the bodies of enemies, whether combatants or not. The combatants feel fever and lust, not only in the spirit but also in the act of assault that is relentless and which can grievously harm or destroy bodies. We need to have Aquinas account for the status of those bodies.

Aquinas: Philosophical Rendition

In the Great Chain of Being, where God is the first cause, how is it that when human beings are gutted, slaughtered, and are dying "from the sword" on battlefields, God is not the author of that mass injury and death? One way, as demonstrated earlier, is to claim the authority is rightly given from God to rulers, to posit the ruler has a just cause to punish those who threaten the state, and to note that the war is pursued with the intention to punish sin and bring about peace. But in war, that is not always so, as both Augustine and Aquinas acknowledge. How exactly can the passion, cruelty, and harm occur? In other words, where does evil come from in the system?

Aquinas, having chained up being, does have a problem with causality when it comes to evil. He believes he has solved this by the use of secondary causes. In the case of war, when killing and maiming is authorized by a right authority and conducted to establish peace and for reasons of justice, there is, in the logic of Aquinas, actually no problem with evil since it has been avoided. But even Aquinas knows that war includes "slaying or plundering" that does not serve the ends of peace and justice. While his preference is not to attend to what is "inordinate"— that is, not serving God's justice and the ends of peace—he knows it happens, though he acknowledges it only reluctantly. When pressed, Aquinas would say that these are the result of secondary causes and not to be attributed to God.

For Aquinas, the physical slaughtering, the plundering, and the raping, whether in war or in society, are effectively sent to the rendition sites of secondary causes. Philosophical rendition, like the post-9/11 CIA practice of what is called "extraordinary rendition" of terrorist suspects, is a way to hide the bodies. In the case of the CIA, suspected terrorists were captured, some in broad daylight off the street, and secretly flown to other countries to be interrogated and tortured in "black sites" as described in detail in the Open Society's report, *Globalizing Torture: CIA Secret Detention and Extraordinary Rendition*.[17] Enormous effort has gone into hiding these bodies from sight, even up until today.

Whether in "philosophical rendition" or in "extraordinary rendition," the bodies of those injured, raped, tortured, maimed, and killed are actually, however, not out of sight, and they should not be out of mind. Somebody is a witness, like those interviewed for the Open Society's report. It is clear from the fact that Aquinas lists rape as a sin in his magnum opus that rape occurred, even if the system he constructs discounts it in the hierarchy of sins; it is still a sin and it did and does happen. "Slaying and plundering" did occur in war, and somebody knew it. There are always witnesses, no matter how attenuated the circumstances may be and no matter how hard we try, philosophically and theologically, to look the other way.

John, Augustine, Aquinas, and Twenty-First-Century War

It can sometimes seem like twenty-first-century war planners are taking their cues directly from the book of Revelation. "The first angel blew his trumpet, and there came hail and fire, mixed with blood, and they were hurled to the earth; and a third of the earth was burned up." (Rev. 8:7a) This is exactly what it must have seemed like to the inhabitants of Baghdad on March 21, 2003, when the United States and its allies launched a massive aerial assault on Iraq. Within an hour of the beginning of the attack, tremendous explosions rocked the Iraqi capital from the hundreds of targets hit. A CNN video shows the huge extent of the fire hurled to the earth; the buildings and the earth around them are burning.[18] Blood flowed from the killed and injured.

This bombing campaign was called "shock and awe"; it was designed to traumatize and induce fear in Iraqi leaders.[19] Shock and awe is an actual military doctrine, otherwise known as "rapid dominance."[20] Overwhelming power is used in a spectacular display of force to "paralyze the enemy's perception of the battlefield" and cause them to lose the will to fight.

Except, of course, the Iraqis did not lose the will to fight. Shock and awe was a complete failure as a war strategy, a ghastly miscalculation that cost at least half a million lives and three trillion dollars.[21,22] And that is only if Iraq, after more than a decade, does not continue to spiral downward into chaos, engulfed in regional conflicts.

Women's bodies are an imaginary battlefield for John of Patmos, but the bodies of women and children were (and continue to be) an actual battlefield in Iraq due to the effects not only of the aerial bombardment and the fighting but also of the lasting effects of some of the weapons used. Dr. Samira Al-Alaani, a pediatrician at Fallujah General Hospital, treats and researches birth defects brought on by the Iraq war. Depleted uranium (DU) is among the toxic munitions used by the American military in Iraq, and it is known to lead to cancer and genetic defects among those exposed to it. Scientific studies "strongly suggest that DU can interfere with the pre-natal development of a fetus."[23]

Women's very wombs have become an ongoing battlefield in Iraq through exposure to toxins in these weapons; in fact, women's wombs, children's bodies, and indeed all civilian bodies are potentially a place where the Iraq War continues because the exposure continues, since many of these sites have not been cleaned up by the United States.

Confronted with deformed children born to women exposed to these weapons, as well as with the bodies of the tortured, the maimed, and the dead, is it possible to say, "The Iraq War was a Just War?" Many people did argue, in the fall of 2002 and using the criteria of Just War developed by Augustine and Aquinas, that the authority, the cause, and the intention was just in attacking a country that had not attacked us. These same Iraq-War apologists claimed the war could be conducted "proportionately"—that is, protecting noncombatants—and it would have a good outcome. They were not correct on any of those points. Yet the war rolled on for nearly a decade.

Neither "God's purposes" in war nor philosophical rendition are sufficient to get people into war and to keep war going over time. War needs ever more rationales, as it can burn through many philosophical and theological justifications quite rapidly as bodies pile up and injuries, including the raped and tortured and the bodies of deformed children, can no longer be hidden.

If you really want to keep war going, what you need are heroes.

5

The Heroic Fictions of War

In war, truth is the first casualty.

Aeschylus, fifth century BCE

Blowing Smoke in the "Fog of War"

The concept of the "heroic" in war is a fiction created precisely to hide the nature of war and to obscure the reality of the battlefield, the injury and destruction to bodies and societies, with a smoke machine to create a "fog of war."[1] Individuals can perform acts of incredible self-sacrifice in war and even give their lives for the sake of what they believe they are fighting for. Those individuals are not the subject of the critique in this chapter. The heroic fiction of war is something else; it is a counternarrative that is designed and orchestrated over and over again to specifically and systematically hide the truth about war.

"Blowing smoke" at battlefields is well illustrated by the actions of the US military in regard to Daniel "Pat" Tillman who was shot and killed in Afghanistan on April 22, 2004.

By the spring of 2004, neither the wars in Iraq nor Afghanistan were going well, and the idea that these wars had been a terrible mistake, and/or were being bungled, was spreading. The horrific images from Abu Ghraib prison in Iraq had just been published by CBS News and *The New Yorker*, along with stories of the staggering amount of torture and suffering that had been inflicted on prisoners. Iraq was spiraling into civil war, and the Afghan War, as a 2010 massive exposure of documents on the Afghan War from January 2004 to December 2009 by Wikileaks has demonstrated, was chaotic and brutally violent. Per the assessment of what the Wikileaks document dump on Afghanistan showed, the *Guardian* summarized, "US intelligence records reveal civilian killings, 'friendly fire' deaths and shadowy special forces."[2]

A "hero," a larger-than-life figure who represented "everything we were fighting for" was clearly needed to counter the stream of devastating news out the Afghan and Iraq wars. The death of "Pat" Tillman must have seemed tailor-made to be the heroic story of American war efforts in the region. Tillman had given up a multimillion-dollar professional football contract to enlist in the US Army in 2002, following the attacks of September 11, 2001. He served in both Iraq and Afghanistan. Tillman joined the army rangers and served in several combat tours before being killed in the mountains of Afghanistan. Tillman's very genuine commitment to service made him an ideal candidate for the status of war hero.

The problem was, the "heroic" narrative about Tillman's death in charging enemy fire was not true. Tillman was not engaged in combat at the time he was shot, and he was not killed by the enemy. He was most likely killed by "friendly fire," yet some books on his death even speculate it could have been deliberate.[3]

The Tillman family has spent years trying to get the truth about their son's death; they were initially told he had "died a hero," his mother recalls, and he was awarded a Silver Star, given to the family by President Bush. Pat Tillman was apparently nothing like the G.I. Joe action figure the military tried to make him out to be. He was a critical thinker about the very wars in which he was engaged.[4]

Mary Tillman thinks the story of her son's heroism was invented because the wars were going so badly. "The Abu Ghraib prison scandal was breaking at that time. Things were in an uproar in Fallujah. There were more casualties in the month of April 2004," Mary Tillman said in an interview. "It would just look bad to have their most high-profile soldier killed by their own troops." In fact, despite her trenchant critique of a "lust to fight" that defines the battlefield in war, she does not blame those who may have shot her son accidentally.[5] She does want those higher up to be held more accountable than has been the case so far. The army, however, has insisted it did not try to deceive anyone in the Tillman case.

In the introduction to his book on Pat Tillman's "odyssey" in these wars, author Jon Krakauer tries to explain the collision between what "warring societies" want people to believe about war, and the harsh reality of "friendly fire": "Inevitably, warring societies portray their campaigns as virtuous struggles, and present their fallen warriors as heroes who made the ultimate sacrifice for a noble cause. But death by so-called friendly fire, which is an inescapable aspect of armed conflict in the modern era, doesn't conform to this mythic narrative. It strips away war's heroic veneer to reveal what lies beneath. It's an unsettling reminder that barbarism, senseless violence, and random death are commonplace even in the most 'just' and 'honorable' of wars."[6]

Krakauer, however, ducks the question of whether there is even such a thing as a "just" and "honorable" war, a question that apparently Pat Tillman himself was considering. Perhaps there is no such thing as a war that is "just," and lying about what war is like is an inevitable part of concealing the truth of what battlefields in war are always like. Mary Tillman and St. Augustine may indeed have it right. There is a "lust to fight" and carnage follows.

The "Cult of the Hero" Is War Propaganda

Skirmishes between tribes in hunter/gatherer societies were not war; war was invented along with civilization. War is defined as a state of armed conflict between different nations or states or between groups within a state. Thus there needs to be a "nation-state" to provide the civilizational matrix out of which war as a conflict between states can arise.

War is not "natural" but a human invention that goes hand in hand with the creation of the city-state and the nation.

The cult of the hero develops along with the development of civilization as more complex political organizations need cohesion to bind people to a network of relationship beyond family and tribe. As was the case in the Babylonian creation epic, this hero can be a divine or semidivine figure like Marduk whose defeat of Ti'amat justifies Babylonian political and military dominance; in Greece, the cult of the hero develops in epic narratives as well and supports the development of the polis or political organization. The Greek hero can be a divine being, like Marduk, or a mortal who is elevated to divine status after having done a great deed, or the hero can be a warrior who is willing to die and who, through the cult of the hero, will live on in the memory of his descendants and his society.

The cult of the hero in Greece functioned in both a political and a religious sense, just as it did in Babylon. It sets the pattern for how the cult of the hero becomes the kind of war propaganda necessary for the legitimation of the state. The god-figure hero and the divinized, triumphant human warrior both function in this way.

Serbian ethnographer Lada Stevanović has done research on the cult of the hero in ancient Greece, comparing it to the role of war propaganda in the former Yugoslavia in order to examine the "powerful mechanism of this national ideology" of the hero and its ability to "mobilize citizens for war."[7] She draws on archeological sources that reveal traces of the development of the hero cult in post-Homeric times, beginning in the tenth century but especially popular in the last quarter of the eighth century. The graves of ancient heroes were "discovered" and made into sanctuaries around the same time as "the appearing and development of the polis (city-state) in the 8th ct. Thus it is possible to claim that the introduction of this cult was the result of change in the social life and new political organization."[8]

A new state religion developed around the cult of the hero, and private funerals were turned into public events. Fewer individual graves are found from around this time, Stevanović notes, as monumental tombs as sanctuary sites replaced them. The hero was praised and eulogized at the public funeral in order to create a "common political ideal." Laws were introduced to govern how these public events were to be conducted, and the laws were often "aimed at limiting and controlling women's behavior at the funerals" and even limiting the number of women relatives who could attend at all. The laws also governed how one could speak of the dead.[9]

Thus the telling of the heroic tale, the deeds of the hero in battle, is what is being governed; the presence of too many weeping women relatives surely would have diminished the triumphal nature of the public hero funeral and would have marred the heroic narrative with reminders of pain and loss. There is, in this ancient Greek history, an eerie echo of the approved "telling of the tale" of the heroism of Pat Tillman and the role Tillman's mother actually comes to play in finding out exactly what happened to her son in war.

It is no wonder that legally protecting the "telling of the tale" is so critical; in fact, it becomes one of the key ways the human warrior becomes semidivine. Thus, in the *Iliad*, Hector (immediately before his death) wishes to die a "heroic" death and thus be remembered forever: "Nay, but not without a struggle let me die, neither ingloriously, but in the working of some great deed for the hearing of men that are yet to be" (22, 304–5).

This is the Greek concept of the "beautiful death," a "death that existed in Greek public discourse." It applied solely to "the death of a warrior, preferably young one, on the battlefield."[10] That was not the only Greek view of death, however. Aristotle represented the nonpublic, ordinary view of death, which was that death was horrible. Aristotle flatly said, "Death is the most terrible of all things, for it is the end."[11] The idea that "death is the end" throws the "beautiful death" that was recounted in epic poetry into great relief. The heroic is the only way to achieve immortality. Those who die in bed, and not on the battlefield, are subject to ordinary death that is horrible and is the end.

But to die in battle! The heroic death gives the promise of immortality, and as Stevanović saw in both the Greek past and in the much more recent drive to create Serbian war propaganda, it also serves to "mobilize people and make them eager both to die and to kill. The main prize of the heroic death is promise of eternal glory." She quotes the famous Greek orator and general, Pericles, from a speech at a public funeral of Athenian soldiers, after a *failed* expedition during the Peloponnesian War. There is, in fact, no more urgent time to give a speech on the "promise" of immorality in battle than when your side has lost a battle because that is when the citizenry most need to be rallied again to the cause.[12]

From the Peloponnesian War through the wars in Iraq and Afghanistan, the heroic ideal of sacrifice combined with the eternality of memory is a common way in Euro-Atlantic culture to justify, even sacralize, massive amounts of suffering, injury, and death on battlefields. The idea of heroic sacrifice in war turns your attention away from the pain, suffering, and death and toward an abstract ideal that in actual fact does not exist. It is important to emphasize again that this is not to say that individuals have not and cannot exhibit tremendous self-sacrifice in war, but that personal heroism is not the same as the cult of the hero as war propaganda. In fact, it is the argument of this book that personal suffering and self-sacrifice should not be obscured in favor of a political agenda.

Strategic physicality, as an analytical lens, therefore, focuses our attention on what is actually happening to bodies on battlefields in war and is the antithesis of the cult of the hero as propaganda. Strategic physicality leads us to witnessing, and has as one of its engines the resistance to mechanisms that obscure, distract, reframe, obfuscate, and distort what happens to bodies in war, as well as in the War on Women.

The cult of the hero is a way societies consolidate their citizenry around the concept of war-making, and motivate them to urge their young men (and young women) to go onto battlefields where they are likely to be maimed or killed. The creation of "heroic myth" is a tried and true way this deception about what war is actually like takes place.

Myth, Fiction, and Critical Physicality

Joseph Campbell was an American writer and lecturer, best known for his work in comparative mythology and religion. Influenced by the work of Carl Jung and Jung's theories of the human psyche, Campbell developed the concept of "mono-myth," meaning one myth. This is a "grand narrative" idea that regards all myths as variations of a single story regardless of their culture of origin or time of creation. The absolutely central pattern, for Campbell, was "the hero's journey" and was first described in his work *The Hero with a Thousand Faces*.[13]

"Monomyth" is antithetical to critical physicality; it may be fair to say it is the polar opposite of critical physicality. Critical physicality is not unitary; instead, critical physicality embraces difference, including those of sexual orientation, race, class, national origin, and religious or humanist (nonreligious) identity. Critical physicality also takes into account cultural dominance, especially colonial and neocolonial domination, and does not attempt to homogenize culture for the sake of a "monomyth." Critical physicality begins with specific bodies in pain and demands that these bodies be "witnessed" as part of a historical movement to end violence. As employed in this book, this witnessing is from a stance within Euro-Atlantic culture in order to examine it in regard to its role in the war and the War on Women. The terms of this war set the parameters both for women's bodies as battlefields within Western culture, but they also have been powerful in setting the terms for how these cultures engage globally in warring.

For monomyth, however, none of these specificities of race, gender, sexual orientation, or national origin are relevant or even interesting. Body itself is irrelevant except as it is symbolized in the unconscious. Western culture and its capacity to project itself on the world in terms of dominance is especially visible in the concept of monomyth. Monomyth, in fact, is a large part of this Western self-projection and it is a projection that is predatory toward other peoples and cultures, taking their history and culture and using them while at the same time having contempt for them. There is no better way to illustrate this combination of predation and contempt than with Campbell's own words from the first pages of *The Hero with a Thousand Faces*: "Whether we listen with aloof amusement to the dreamlike mumbo jumbo of some red-eyed witch doctor of the Congo, or read with cultivated rapture thin translations from the sonnets of the mystic Lao-tse, or now and again crack the hard nutshell of an argument of Aquinas, or catch suddenly the shining meaning of a bizarre Eskimo fairy tale, it will be always the one, shape-shifting yet marvelously constant story that we find . . ."[14]

The "cultivated" eye of the Western reader is contemptuously contrasted to the African "mumbo jumbo of some red-eyed witch doctor" or with the "bizarre" and infantilized (fairytale) Eskimo. "We"—that is, this imagined Western observer—are entertained by the culture of others, while finding the roots of our own culture in Aquinas difficult and complex. There is "shape-shifting" going on, but the shape-shifting is imposed and not actually present. The heroes of others are forced into the Western "monomyth" despite the many meanings they may carry in the culture of origin.

Campbell's work makes it not only acceptable but actually intellectually necessary for Western culture to "shop" the world, looking for ideas to employ. And the heroic ideal is "made to order" for those who would consolidate their civilization in order to justify wars of colonial and neocolonial expansion. The mythic is a way to falsify the meaning of colonial war by providing a fictionalized justification.

Marks of the Heroic: Defeating the Female

According to Campbell, one of the chief marks of the hero is defeating and mastering the female. This is because, for the hero to "*soar to the immaculate ether beyond, he can't be ruled by the world/goddess, he has to defeat the world (the female), or the world, the body, and woman above all, become the symbols no longer of victory but of defeat . . . No longer can the hero rest in innocence with the goddess of the flesh; for she is become the queen of sin.*"[15]

This description by Campbell is not a "monomyth," despite the fact that he argues that it is; it is a very accurate description of what Western thought has contributed both to the heroic justification of war and to justifying the War on Women. Far from being a cultural universal, it is a very specific mythology that arises from Greco-Roman culture as well as Semitic culture. Many of these themes, especially the defeat and mastery of the female and the female as world and body, are eventually incorporated into Christianity and its understandings of war and peace, and violence against women, and via these sources, into the formation of Western views, some of which get exported around the world.

One thing Campbell is demonstrating in the previous quotation is that there can be no heroes without monsters to slay. The Greeks tended to identify women with nature, especially nature as that which existed beyond the boundaries of orderly civilization. So many monsters in Greek mythology are female, and the drama of the myth is the male defeat of the monstrous female. This is often the defining moment of a hero, and in Greek mythology, the monstrous female plays an outsized role. Thus Medusa, Scylla and Charybdis, and the Harpies and the Furies, for example, are all Greek myths of the chaotic threat of femaleness that has to be conquered and destroyed, often cut apart, by the male hero.

All the hero has to do is kill the monstrous, chaotic female to accomplish an escape from finitude and "oblivion" in death into immortality. The monstrous female in philosophy and in mythology creates a fertile ground, in both a literal and figurative sense, for the defeat of chaos and, of course, the justification for war.[16]

This very specific understanding of the defeat of the female and the world as female gets carried along, as was noted earlier, and becomes formative for Christianity, and especially for Christian saints, where in fact the defeat of the female as erotic, bodily temptation, is so central to that cult.

But this is not a smooth journey in the history of ideas, and there are moments where, like in the *Iliad*, the tragic makes an appearance and the whole framework of heroic death is partially called into question. It is from these sources that alternative cultural roots that support the witnessing of war and the War on Women, not its justification, will be found.

The Great Temporal Defeat: Death and Tragedy

Beowulf, the masterpiece of early English literature, composed sometime toward the end of the first millennium CE, is best known as a heroic narrative. It tells the "once upon a time" story of a Scandinavian prince named Beowulf who defeats two monsters and who is vanquished by a third. It has been widely regarded as steeped in warrior culture where the hero is obligated, by an ancient code, to seek glory on the battlefield or die trying.

There are some astonishingly scary monsters in the poem; for example, there is Grendel, who comes by night to slay those hiding in fear in their barricaded houses; there is Grendel's mother, who drags her victims underwater; and finally, there is the 50-foot dragon, whose greed for treasure is unbounded and who kills with fire.[17]

Interpretations of this foundational classic of Western literature abound, and the poem itself has been imposed on generations of English literature students to read and interpret, often badly. One of the most intriguing was offered in a 1936 speech on *Beowulf* by J. R. R. Tolkien, the author best known for his own fiction. It's not about the monsters or even killing monsters, Tolkien contends, even as archaic elements of monsters are employed. "Defeat is the theme." Death wins and death will always breach the citadel of the human body. "Triumph over the foes of man's precarious fortress is over, and we approach slowly and reluctantly the inevitable victory of death." Death is the main foe in *Beowulf*, according to Tolkien, and the monsters are but symptoms.

Beowulf, viewed in Tolkien's speech, is "*a man, and that for him and many is sufficient tragedy.*" This is not the usual "buck you up so you will go fight well" kind of tale of heroism. It is far more like the *Iliad* in that respect. According to Tolkien, "Beowulf's author is concerned primarily with *man on earth*, rehandling in a new perspective an ancient theme: that man, each man and all men, and all their works shall die." This means the great heralding of deeds in the past is cast into an awful relief; seen in the light of the tragedy of the human condition, what do even such tremendous deeds as slaying all these monsters actually accomplish? At the end of *Beowulf*, the conflict that is coming will be not with monsters but with other peoples, and "bad blood" on bad blood will fuel wars.

But in the meanwhile, and ignored in Tolkien's interpretation of the tragic sense of life conveyed in Beowulf's ultimate death by the dragon, is how even in a poem of such human complexity, the theme of heroes defeating the monstrous female still gets carried along and yet earns no notice even from this astute critic.

Grendel's mother is a "swamp-thing from hell" (1518) who lives in the watery depths of a lake (1495). It is not hard to see the remnants of the defeat of the primordial Mother as was clearly symbolized in the two-fold Genesis creation account and also in the Babylonian epic. Recall that the fundamental idea is that creation is the establishment of order over a threatening chaos in an epic battle.

This is the Combat Myth. The basic outline is the defeat of an enemy that is "usually depicted as a watery monster or dragon." It is widely remarked that *Beowulf* draws far more on the Hebrew bible than the Christian scriptures, and it is clear that the defeat of the monsters who threaten social chaos in *Beowulf* are influenced by that Combat Myth as seen in the Hebrew bible.

There is a double dose in *Beowulf* of these Combat Myth themes, both a watery monster and a dragon. Grendel's mother is a monster, a "tarn-hag" who has "terrible strength" (1519). Grendel's mother is getting the upper hand in the fight with Beowulf, and then he finds a sword in her lair from the "days of the giants." Then the "hero, hard-pressed and enraged, took a firm hold of the hilt and swung the blade in an arc, a resolute blow that bit deep into her neck-bone and severed it entirely, toppling the doomed house of her flesh; she fell to the floor. The sword dripped blood, the swordsman was elated" (1559–69). Beowulf then proceeds to find Grendel's body and cut off his head as well. He takes that battle trophy back to the hall and proudly displays Grendel's head: "Grendel's head was hauled by the hair, dragged across the floor where the people were drinking" (1647–48).

Beowulf credits both the weapon of the giants and God for his success in defeating these monsters (1657). Tolkien observes there is a blending of Norse and Christian materials in *Beowulf*. But there is a twist to the regular heroic tale. Beowulf cannot overcome the dragon; nevertheless, it is not the dragon that finally defeats Beowulf, it is time and a world hostile to human existence.

Tolkien's insight into the tragedy of the human condition as represented in this poem helps us see how extraordinary it is. It contradicts what is so customary in the Western cult of the hero—that is, normally the hero slays the dragon. This is pretty much a must, as the Disney Company fully well knows. Heroes slay dragons. Dragons are depicted as both female and male, but it is telling in American culture that very often it is famous actresses who play dragons. Susan Sarandon played a dragon in *Enchanted*, and the hero kills her. Angelina Jolie played both Grendel's revengeful mother in the film version of *Beowulf* and then "fires up her dragon" in *Maleficent*. That film shows her ruling over a swampy dominion, rather like that of Grendel's mother, so "instead of one knight vs. one dragon, we see all the forces of Maleficent's shadowy, swamp-like army clashing with the warriors defending the king's realm."[18] There is also a metaphorical rape scene in *Maleficent*, where Maleficent is betrayed and broken by someone she thought she could trust. As writer Hayley Krischer comments, "Rape has so permeated our culture that it ended up in a Disney movie."[19]

This is more "backstory" than we normally get on dragons, but it serves to make the point that heroes are justified in whatever they do to defeat the monstrous female.

But there is a difference in *Beowulf*. Beowulf does not slay the dragon, the dragon defeats him. What kind of hero does this make Beowulf, that at the key moment of hero-making, the absolutely essential hero-slays-dragon climax, he fails to do so (though a younger hero rises up)? Moreover, Beowulf does not fail because of some Aristotelian tragic flaw that keeps him from killing the dragon. He's a great warrior and king, but he's just old. Death wins.

Beowulf is a poem situated between the old and new religions, between a pagan past and the new Christianity, and it is a profound work that turns on heroic myth, while also challenging it through the existential crisis of human existence. By contrast, in Tolkien's own work, the existential angst is missing; death doesn't win, though there are some unlikely heroes.

As influential as *Beowulf* may be to English literature students, it is actually Tolkien, through his enormously popular books about Middle Earth, who is the far more culturally influential figure today. Tolkien's own dragon, Smaug, derives from the Old English *smeag* (of or pertaining to a worm) and is a very scary dragon. In chapter 12 of *The Hobbit*, Smaug boasts of his prowess to the "Thief in the Shadows"—that is, the Hobbit Bilbo Baggins. "I kill where I wish and none dare resist." But Bilbo spies a weakness in Smaug's armor, and eventually this allows Bard the Bowman to kill him. But Bard the Bowman is not one of the main heroes of the books. It is a more classical Combat Myth motif, the vicious defeat of a female monster, the great spider Shelob, that establishes the hero credentials of one of Tolkien's main characters, the Hobbit Samwise Gamgee.

Shelob was a ravenous predator who fed on orcs, men, elves, and dwarves alike. Frodo, the "ringbearer" of the *Lord of the Rings*, and his great friend, Samwise Gamgee, encounter her in her den in their quest to destroy the One Ring. Frodo is paralyzed by a sting from Shelob, and Sam fights the spider. The fight is described in remarkably vivid terms of disgust for her parts, and it is clearly a vicious, if not fatal, sexual assault where Shelob herself is said to have helped cause her own rape and injury.

> Great horns she had, and behind her short stalk-like neck was her huge swollen body, a vast bloated bag, swaying and sagging between her legs; its great bulk was black, blotched with livid marks, but the belly underneath was pale and luminous and gave forth a stench . . . Sam sprang in, inside the arches of her legs . . . he slashed the bright elven-blade across her with desperate strength . . . She yielded to the stroke, then heaved up the great bag of her belly high above Sam's head. Poison frothed and bubbled from the wound. Now splaying her legs she drove her huge bulk down on him again. Too soon. For Sam still stood upon his feet, and dropping his own sword, with both hands he held the elven point upwards . . . and so Shelob, with the driving force of her own cruel will, with strength greater than any warrior's hand, thrust herself upon a bitter spike. Deep, deep it pricked, as Sam was crushed slowly to the ground.[20]

Tolkien creates a classic rape and near-murder scene to establish the hero credentials of the unlikely Hobbit hero, Samwise. The scene shows utter contempt for the bloated female body, crossed with "livid marks" like a woman's belly with the stretch marks of pregnancy, and efficiently establishes the monstrous female. Sam jumps between her legs and goes to drive the "elven point" into her. Her own bulk causes her to be pierced with a "bitter spike." She is penetrated and, in that penetration, grievously wounded.

Tolkien's dragon may be more dragon than that of *Beowulf*, but the tragic sense of life that somewhat redeems the Combat Myth of that poem is absent in Tolkien's own work. In the scene between Samwise and Shelob, in fact, all the elements of the rape and murder of the female as chaotic monster are present and help advance the heroic credentials of a Hobbit.

Beowulf, in fact, is far more "Christian" than the twentieth-century Middle Earth narratives. The Christian God, for example, at least took an interest in the outcome of the fight between Beowulf and Grendel's mother, though it also took a giant's sword to kill her. There is no God recognizable from the Christian narratives in Tolkien's fiction; this fictional place called "Middle Earth" stays on earth.

Yet Tolkien himself emphasizes both that *Beowulf* represents "*man on earth*" and also that is "[a] theme no Christian need despise." Exactly so, but what happens, in fact, is that some Christians do end up despising "man on earth" and, as Simone Weil argues, the tragic sense of life all but disappears in the Christian west until the modern period.

Christ and the Culture of the Hero in the Early Middle Ages

In the early Middle Ages, a poem called "The Dream of the Rood" portrays Jesus Christ as "the young hero" and "the warrior." The existential angst of *Beowulf* is completely absent. This warrior Christ boldly confronts and defeats sin. Upholding honor through warrior culture was highly valued in the Middle Ages, and this culture is given a divine source in the poem.

> Then the young hero (who was God Almighty)
> Got ready, resolute and strong in heart.
> . . . the warrior embraced [the cross].[21]

Rather than Jesus being subject to Roman military authority, arrested, tried, convicted, and executed, this poet shows a Jesus who is vigorously preparing for combat rather than being lead passively to the cross. Where the Bible states, "they [the Roman soldiers] stripped him,"[22] the poet writes "the young warrior, God our Savior, valiantly stripped before the battle."[23] Later, the poet suggests that Christ actually initiates the battle for human redemption.

> He climbed onto the lofty gallows-tree,
> Bold in the sight of many watching men,
> When He intended to redeem mankind.
> . . . the warrior embraced [the cross].[24]

Christ as the confident hero, "The Dream of the Rood" combines both the "brave deeds" of the warrior with the divine hero.

Anselm (1033–1109), a medieval theologian and philosopher as well as Archbishop of Canterbury, is best known for what is called his "ontological argument" for the existence of God. His work *Cur Deus Homo* (Why God Became a Human Being) has been very influential in the development of Christian theologies on the atonement—that is, on how sinful human beings can be reconciled to God. Anselm attempts to show that the debt incurred by human beings due to their sin can only be discharged by one who could, in fact, be worthy to pay a debt to divinity. Human beings on their own cannot pay this debt, but since it is a debt owed to God, it would have to be discharged by "one who was both fully divine and fully human." Anselm presents this case as a "rational argument," but it is in fact similarly steeped in the honor culture of the period. Anselm does not identify Christ as the warrior/hero per se, but the implication is there.

Like "The Dream of the Rood," *Cur Deus Homo* ignores the life and ministry of Jesus of Nazareth. Instead, the governing concepts are those of feudal society: the punishment, obedience, honor, and order. In his work *The Nonviolent Atonement*, J. Denny Weaver argues Anselm's view is derived both from the medieval penitential system and "the image of the feudal lord who gave protection to his vassals but also exacted penalties for offenses against his honor."[25]

What has come to be called the "penal theory of the atonement"—that is, the work of Christ in reconciling sinful humanity and God by paying the honor penalty—is steeped in warrior culture. The image of Christ in the Middle Ages is often that of a triumphant warrior, and the central act of salvation is a victorious battle of good over evil. War itself is taken into the fundamental drama of Christian revelation and is not a "necessary evil," but in fact, a "necessary good." This pivot in Christian theology where Christ becomes the warrior is foundational for understanding war in the Western tradition.

Hero Worship and War in the Twentieth Century

The heroic has not survived the twentieth century unchanged, but it has survived as it has been reinvented over and over again in the throes of the staggering number of wars in that space of a hundred years. The heroic dimensions of "Christian culture" inherited from the Middle Ages were crucial in the justifications for the "Great War"—that is, World War I—but as the sheer carnage of modern, industrialized war was revealed, these ideas faltered.

That was not the case in 1914. After the assassination of Archduke Ferdinand, Europe plunged into war with astonishing speed, and Christian theological ideas helped justify the near-spasmodic outbreak of violence. The English poet laureate Robert Bridges fueled the war propaganda with explicitly Christian theological themes of good versus evil and heroic "honour" versus the "careless." His poem, "Wake Up, England," was published in *The Times* on August 8, 1914. These verses serve to illustrate the atonement theology of suffering and shedding blood leading to "Beauty" and "Salvation" and to dishonor peacemakers. The poem is addressed to those who would make peace instead of war, blaming and shaming them, and casting them as working contrary to the will of God for salvation and that through blood and suffering the "careless" peacemaker can be cleansed and saved.[26]

Christian theologians were not far behind the poet laureate in connecting the themes of war making with heroic sacrifice and even with Christian devotion. Canon J. H. Skrine of Merton College Oxford wrote, "War is not murder . . . War is sacrifice. The fighting and killing are not of the essence of it, but are the accidents, though the inseparable accidents; and even these, in the wide modern fields where a soldier rarely in his own sight sheds any blood on his own, where he lies on the battle sward not to inflict death but to endure it—even these are mainly purged of savagery and transfigured into devotion. War is not murder but sacrifice which is the soul of Christianity."[27]

The transfiguration of "devotion" evokes the transfiguration of Jesus, where scripture records he became radiant on a mountain (Matt. 17:1–9, Mark 9:2–8, Luke 9:28–36). Christian theology often interprets these texts as a miraculous moment where human nature meets God, and the temporal meets the eternal with Jesus as the connecting bridge between heaven and earth. Instead, in this Christian theologian's view, it is *war*, not Jesus, that becomes the meeting place of heaven and earth and the central act of salvation. War replaces the person and work of Jesus Christ in these theologies.

But as *All Quiet on the Western Front* showed, the unrelenting carnage of the first industrialized war destroyed so many of the heroic delusions about war with its unrelenting portrait of men locked in trench warfare over a destroyed landscape. The battlefield as the gore-filled, body-destroying wasteland was the "open belly" of Europe, not its salvation. The warriors were not heroes, they were literally "slippery lumps of flesh" bleeding into the mined landscape.

But war itself persisted, and Christian justification of war in Western culture met again on the battlefield in the 1940s. The Germanic ideals of war as heroic reached a screeching crescendo in the theology of the Third Reich, but they were also present in some of the Just War thinking of the allies who fought against Hitler.

Theologies and philosophies of the hero were crucial for the Third Reich. Hitler had *Thus Spoke Zarathustra*, a 1883 work by the philosopher Friedrich Nietzsche, issued to every soldier in the German army. In the novel, Nietzsche had his character Zarathustra propose what he called the *Übermensch*, a "superman" or "superhuman," as a goal for humanity. Nietzsche clearly disagreed with many things he had Zarathustra say, but for Hitler's race-ideology, this concept was adapted to mean a German superman whose superiority destined him to conquer and rule.

In *Christian Theologians and the Bible in Nazi Germany*, religion professor Susannah Heschel examines how the Nazis redefined Jesus as an Aryan and Christianity as a religion at war with Judaism. A Nazified Christianity needed to posit a Jesus who was the savior of the Aryans. Politics, theology, racial ideology, and political ambition came together, as in the Middle Ages, to alter Christian theology and biblical interpretation to emphasize war making as central. Not unlike "The Dream of the Rood," these theologians muted the crucifixion and emphasized the resurrection within the race-ideology of the Third Reich.

The record of German atrocities in World War II continues to be compiled, and the genocide against Jews as well as other groups such as homosexuals, the disabled, and racial/ethnic minorities is, beyond question, one of the great crimes against humanity. Violence against women was central to the German ideology of "superman," both in terms of the Holocaust and also against conquered populations. Even now, however, focusing on sexual violence in the Holocaust continues to be controversial as women tell their stories.[28] Russian violence against women in the conquest of Berlin has also been documented. The Japanese, allies of the

Germans, also committed atrocities especially in regard to the capture and use of the Korean "comfort women." These are perhaps better known because of political efforts to demand apology and reparations, but a memorial to such women is very controversial.[29]

By contrast, World War II for the allied nations, and especially in the United States, is often referred to as "the last good war." This world war as the good war is a cornerstone of the twentieth century support for Just War thinking. It is most often cast as the ultimate parable of good and evil, and even today, American political and religious conservatives routinely critique liberals and progressives as "Nazis" and feminist thinkers as "feminazis." Dwight Eisenhower, supreme wartime commander of American forces in Europe, and later US president for eight years, went further however and called the fight against Nazi Germany "the Great Crusade." But he is scarcely alone in allying American participation in this huge conflict with the aims of God; from Republican to Democrat, this is a staple.

Idolizing World War II as an unambiguously good war means it has taken generations for the violence against local populations, and especially the violence against women by American soldiers during World War II, to come to light, and even that is still muted.

Recently, however, the thousands of rapes committed by American soldiers during World War II, and especially in France, have begun to be documented and analyzed. In *What Soldiers Do: Sex and the American GI in World War II France*, Mary Louis Roberts of the University of Wisconsin has debunked the myth of the good war as always good. In total, it is estimated that some 14,000 women were raped by American GIs in Western Europe from 1942 to 1944. A few (152) were tried, of whom 29 were hanged. But these statistics do not get at the argument of Roberts's book. She contends that there was an "erotic adventure" aspect to the military expedition that was explicitly "sold" to American GIs by their command.[30]

How do we reconcile this history of rape by US soldiers in World War II with the ideology that World War II was a Just War? This is not to decry the bravery and skill of individual American GIs in the war. Certainly, the fact that rape was punished, even if only a few, indicates that it could be said that rape is a violation of Just War theory in its principle to protect noncombatants. In the next chapter, however, this part of the history of World War II will be engaged further in the discussion of the erotic aspect of violence against women. Is "Just War" sufficiently opposed to sexual violence, or is there the more troubling question of whether what is "justified" in war includes the conquest of the female at its heart?

Vietnam and the Antihero

Unlike World War II and the heroic GI images, Vietnam began an antihero period in American warfare, as was noted earlier in regard to the film and the television series *M*A*S*H*.

Robert Jay Lifton, a psycho-historian who has worked extensively with Vietnam veterans, writes about the crisis for the GIs who fought in Vietnam. What happens is the purposes put forward for the US involvement in that war "are directly contradicted by the overwhelming evidence a GI encounters that *he* is the outside invader, that the government he has come to defend is justly hated by the people he has come to help, and that he, the American helper, is hated . . . most of all."[31] In short, he is not a hero, he is a violent intruder. This identity became insupportable for those who believed serving in the military is service to their country.

One of the other differences about Vietnam that began to erode the idea of the American warrior there as a hero, accomplishing a "redemptive" task through the judicious use of violence, was the "body count." The success of the American mission, as acknowledged by General Maxwell Taylor, was the number of dead bodies. "We are looking for these people and destroying them at the greatest rate that has ever taken place in the history of the struggle."[32] The deeply corrosive moral shift was to identify the enemy as the enemy only after he or she had been killed. "If it's dead, it's VC."

This is strategic physicality in its clearest form. War is genuinely trying to out-injure the other side, but it is normally better hidden from the soldiers and the public. Vietnam laid that bare and it was traumatic for the American soldier who fought in Vietnam and for the American public.

This became very clear in the massacre at Mỹ Lai. For many Americans, the image of the American GI as a heroic warrior was tarnished beyond repair as the details of that massacre became publically known. This was not the universal response, however. Despite the overwhelming evidence presented at the trial of Lt. Calley, the leader of the group that committed the atrocity, after he was found guilty, more than 100,000 telegrams and letters were sent to President Nixon in favor of Calley. In a pro-Calley rally in a stadium in Columbus, Georgia, Reverend Michael Lord used explicitly Christological language to describe the lieutenant and defend him. The reverend said, "There was a crucifixion 2,000 years ago for a man named Jesus Christ. I don't think we need another crucifixion of a man named Rusty Calley."[33]

LIFE magazine's December 5, 1969, issue contained graphic images of the atrocity. As was noted earlier, Vietnam was extensively photographed and without a lot of censorship. Letters to the editor about that issue of *LIFE*, however, "revealed that people often objected to the pictures of the event rather than to the event itself."[34] In other words, when confronted with the opportunity to witness the carnage and cruelty that often is war, people vastly prefer not to look because really looking, bearing witness, would require giving up the heroic comforting stereotype of "our boys" and their bravery.

Americans have still not come to terms with Vietnam, and "kicking the Vietnam syndrome" was crucial to overcoming American reluctance to attack Afghanistan and Iraq. But there have been strong artistic efforts to show the utter destruction of the myths of war that was Vietnam.

Apocalypse Now by Francis Ford Coppola was originally considered a major disappointment, compromised in part because of its incoherent violence. With 25 years of retrospect, however, its status has climbed to that of a flawed masterpiece.[35] Coppola used violence to express what could not be understood—namely, the Vietnam war itself. The violence in *Apocalypse Now* to some extent succeeded in breaking through the emotional censorship that Americans had imposed on themselves for the only war this country has "lost." But it was only temporary.

Mel Gibson's Heroic Jesus: A Theology of War Propaganda

Scarcely two months before "Pat" Tillman was killed, filmmaker Mel Gibson released his controversial film *The Passion of the Christ* about the death and resurrection of Jesus of Nazareth. I have argued this is a war movie.[36] Gibson recasts the Christian accounts of the life, death, and resurrection of Jesus of Nazareth not only as a war on sin but as a War on Women who symbolize evil in the person of Satan and a snake.

It is crucial to bring the theology of that film into conversation with what was happening in the wars in Iraq and Afghanistan. Instead of "Mission Accomplished," an insurgency had developed in Iraq. The CIA had been forced to admit there were no weapons of mass destruction. Resources were diverted from Afghanistan to Iraq, and the Afghan gains were starting to erode.

A Christian, heroic salvation narrative about war emerged in this powerful Gibson film as a direct rebuke of the antihero views of war post-Vietnam and the liberal and liberation biblical interpretations of the life, death, and resurrection of Jesus of Nazareth. Instead, Gibson returns, with astonishing visual economy, to the Jesus-as-warrior theme of the Middle Ages.

In the first scene of "Passion," Satan appears to Jesus when he prays in the Garden of Gethsemane. Gethsemane is portrayed more like a smoke-filled, primeval forest than a garden, and blue light, thick fog, and jumpy camera work cue the viewer that nothing good will happen here. We see Jesus, agonizing in prayer. The camera pans to Jesus's face and we see our next big visual clue: this is a strong, good-looking, American, white guy. In the Hollywood visual lexicon, good-looking, American, and white usually code "morally good." Thus even if we (somehow!) did not know the Christian "back story," we would know as consumers of Hollywood images that we have just met the movie's hero.

But then, a black-cowled figure appears in front of a prostrate, praying Jesus. The eyebrowless face under the cowl, deathly pale, is feminized rather than explicitly feminine. (In his interview with ABC's Diane Sawyer, Gibson did refer to Satan as "she," only shifting, when sharply questioned by Sawyer, to the pronouns "he, it.") The horror-movie quality of the film is ratcheted up when a maggot appears in the figure's nose. Down the devil's black, slimy robe the camera glides until our view rests on its hem, and we see a snake slither out from under its (her?) robe. Now we know which garden we are really, religiously in: not Gethsemane, but Eden. In Eden, Satan found its opportunity through a woman and came in the form of a snake. Now the Satan-female-snake slithers menacingly toward the hero and rears its head as if to strike.

With one strong, decisive movement, Jesus stomps the snake to death. The character of Jesus as mythic hero, defeating the female in the form of a snake, is established with astonishing economy. The male is stronger than the female; the hero is stronger than evil. Jesus has come to kill sin.

The heroic Jesus of *Passion* evokes the warrior Jesus of "The Dream of the Rood" all through the film and especially in his death and resurrection. Despite the fact that when the Gospels record Jesus as speaking immediately after the resurrection, his first words are of reassurance, "Do not be afraid" (Matt. 28:10); in sharp contrast, we have Gibson's take on the resurrection, perhaps the most offensive scene in the *Passion*. A shaft of light appears on a stone, and a fluttering, clearly empty shroud deflates on the tomb's stone slab to the beat of martial drums straight out of the Scottish hills of Gibson's heroic film *Braveheart.* Boom, boom, boom go the drums. A grim and pale-faced Jesus, unscathed despite the lengthy torture inflicted on him, sits up with a look of quiet anger on his face.

This is war, not peace, and confrontation, not resurrection, as the triumph of life over death.

This resurrection scene in fact makes no sense without the extraordinary amount of violence visited on Jesus by the Romans. The flogging and scourging go on for nearly 40 minutes. Then Jesus is beaten repeatedly before and after his presentation to the crowd. Thorns gouge his head. He is beaten, shoved, and kicked all the way through the city and up the hill to Golgotha. The nails are pounded in. The cross is raised and dropped. His torment is excruciating and excruciatingly portrayed. And then, after a brief pause, Gibson gives us his martial resurrection.

The attraction of grand myths of the heroic in a battle between good and evil is that this mythology tempts us to focus away from actual violence and its destruction of bodies and gaze instead on some larger, salvific theme. In *Passion*, the risen heroic Jesus returns to punish evil and especially those who wronged him. This is a distraction from the Gospel accounts and a deliberate mythologizing of Jesus as warrior.

In other words, the life, death, and resurrection of Jesus of Nazareth are turned into a glorified battlefield.

And that is its purpose.

The Heroic Avatar: Heroes in Comics, Movies, and Video Games

The hero evolves dramatically in the late twentieth and early twenty-first centuries along with the advent of greater and greater technological representation, as in films and videogames, and through the comic-book genre. But there is a strong continuity with the heroic themes of the past, especially the conquest of the female. Yes, Wonder Woman exists, but female comic heroes are numbered by their absence. It's true that female characters are present in comics, but most often as victims. *The New Republic* quoted *Kick-Ass* creator Mark Millar defending his comic book depictions of rape and sexual violence by saying "I don't really think it matters."[37] There was a huge backlash, of course, but that does not change the fact that there are an enormously disproportionate number of female characters in comics who are "killed, maimed, raped or stripped of their powers for the sake of advancing a male character's plot."

The staggering amount of violence against women in comics was labeled the "women in refrigerators" syndrome by Gail Simone, and it is tracked by her website Women in Refrigerators, created in 1999.[38] The website features a list of female comic-book characters that have been injured, killed, or disempowered as a plot device within superhero comic books. Commentary seeks to analyze why these plot devices are used disproportionately on female characters.

In short, violence against women defines the comic-book hero as much as it did Marduk. It is also a staple of video games as a compilation of the most extreme of violence against women in video games, made for a university course, reveals. This video compilation is extremely violent with many depictions of rape as well as mutilation, so caution is advised in viewing it.[39] Remember that video games are player driven, unlike comics that are pictorial narratives. That means, rather like the paintings of the Rape of Tamar that invited the viewer to be part of the violence, these video games are inviting extreme violence against women in conquest scenarios.

Violence against women is not much in evidence, however, in what is a defining cultural moment on the heroic in a technological future—that is, in George Lucas's *Star Wars*. The phrase "Use the force, Luke," as Obi-Wan Kenobi, Jedi knight and mentor to young Luke Skywalker, says to the hero-in-training in the first of the trilogy of films, has entered our cultural lexicon.

The first *Star Wars* film had a strong female character, Princess Leia. Granted, she was a princess, a standard female trope, but Princess Leia was no slouch in picking up a blaster, nor did she back off from leadership of the team of heroic resisters. This strong female character was subtly muted in the next two films, most symbolically by being dressed in a skimpy slave girl costume in *The Empire Strikes Back*.

Instead in *Star Wars*, the arch-villain is black—the menacing Darth Vader. Vader, a tall, sinister figure, voiced by famed African American actor James Earl Jones, revealed another aspect of the Western hero/villain motif. The white guy is the hero, and the racialized figure is the embodiment of evil. Like Mel Gibson's Jesus, a Western hero needs to be a white guy even as he helps himself to the heroic in other cultures.

George Lucas defends himself against critics who see the plot as predictable and even trite by claiming it is an "epic myth" per Joseph Campbell and his idea of the heroic "monomyth." Campbell returned the compliment, praising Lucas in an interview with Bill Moyers, for the films and their use of mythological themes from many cultures and periods. With the triumphant *Star Wars* theme playing in the background, Moyers asks Campbell, "Does a movie like *Star Wars* fill some of that need for the spiritual adventure for the hero?" "It's perfect," Campbell enthusiastically replies. Campbell continues, "George Lucas was using standard mythological figures," including the model of the "Japanese sword master." "That's real Japanese stuff," he enthused. Campbell's and Lucas's assumption is that Japanese culture is theirs to appropriate as they wish.

The comic-book, movie, and video-game genre is vast but surprisingly coherent when it comes to the construction of the heroic for Western culture as the dominant-race male hero who often demonstrates his heroism through conquest of the female.

Heroes, Robots, and Drones

The future of war is clearly biocybernetic, with drones and robots becoming the "warriors," and war itself—the bloody battlefield—becoming ever more remote and hidden behind machines while, at the same time, it is being fought on the bodies of women and other vulnerable civilians as strategy. But this is relentlessly hidden.

Drone strikes are popular because they seem effective in reducing the threat of terrorism without loss of American lives and without the cost of "boots on the ground." This is an incredibly dangerous moral position to take. Bodies are still being blown up on battlefields; it's just not American bodies any more. Civilians in bombed areas are being killed, despite the much-vaunted idea that drones are so "targeted" in their killing of militants that civilian deaths are minimal. A March 2011 drone strike killed at least 38 civilians in Pakistan.[40] A Pakistani tribal elder, Malik Faridullah, described the result of the so-called precision bombing: "There were no bodies, only body parts—hands, legs and eyes scattered around. I could not recognize anyone. People carried away the body parts in shopping bags and clothing or with bits of wood, whatever they could find."[41]

It is difficult even for those who want war mythologies of the hero to find "heroism" in flying remote aircraft over villagers and launching missiles at them, a point made by two former military members in their objection to a new award, announced in 2013, for the Distinguished Warfare Medal for drone pilots and "cyberwarriors." What really seemed to gall these combat vets was that the medal would rank above both the Purple Heart and the Bronze Star, given for wounds sustained in battle. "In other words, a drone pilot flying a mission from an armchair in Nevada might be afforded greater recognition than a rifleman wounded in a combat zone." They regarded this as "ridiculous" because "[t]hose on the front lines require real courage because they face real danger" of being physically wounded, not just risking that a monitor that would "go fuzzy." A "Nintendo" medal should not be elevated, they contended, "above those awarded for true heroism and sacrifice." The award was ultimately cancelled.[42]

But these veterans of combat said they continued to be alarmed because "[o]ur most senior leaders in the Pentagon, civilian and military alike, increasingly understand warfare through the literal lens of a drone camera."

That much certainly seems true. On the other hand, recent research shows that this is a dangerous distortion of what is really happening to people involved in conducting drone warfare. Drone operators, it appears, are subject to mental harm from conducting "Nintendo" combat in this way. Wounds to the mind are real wounds, in fact.

The debate over whether there are "heroes" in drone warfare is enormously revealing of both the need for the heroic narrative to justify war and what happens when that narrative is lost. The purposes of war become even more vague, and killing is made to seem "safe" and "easy." It gives too much power to those who want the United States to engage in killing. The ability to kill without risk of American lives promotes enormous moral risk. Augustine pointed out this exact issue when he argued the lustful love of power was the chief moral risk of using violence.

Fictionalized Heroes

On real battlefields, physical human beings like "Pat" Tillman don't get up and fight again when the game reboots. Tillman, like many others before and after him, suffered and died from wounds sustained in war. And like many others before and after him, his real sacrifice has been obscured, even insulted, by the attempts to use this tragic death to support the heroic myth of war.

Christian theology has often been bought into heroic myth to lend support for violent retribution in a presumed battle between good and evil. The person and work of Jesus Christ have been used to support, even demand, this interpretation and then recruited to justify war.

The Western paradigm of the hero frequently includes the conquest of the female, and this cannot be considered an occasional "lapse" for the heroic or for the nature of war. War itself includes, at its core, the injuring of bodies that includes, both symbolically and actually, the wounding and killing of women and girls. Myths of the heroic from other cultures and periods are appropriated to shore up the Western myth of the hero.

Why does this so endure in Western culture, and why is this injuring, especially to the bodies of women and girls, not seen for the grievous harm that it is?

One reason may very well be, as can be seen quite graphically in the YouTube video on violence against women in video games, that violence against women is eroticized.

6

The Erotic Fictions of the War on Women

What pornography is really about, ultimately, isn't sex but death.

Susan Sontag, "The Pornographic Imagination"

Force has "the ability to turn a human being into a thing while he is still alive."

Simone Weil, "The Iliad, or The Poem of Force"

Eroticized violence in fiction, whether in films or novels, is treacherous because it promotes the idea that women desire to be treated violently. Violence against women then becomes part of the very construction of the nature of love and desire in societies, orchestrating the eroticizing of bodily pain itself and deadening the impulses to compassion and empathy.

Fiction in the War on Women

The Story of O is the English title of a postwar (1954) novel by author Anne Desclos who used the pen name Pauline Réage for its publication. Desclos was a French journalist and novelist who used the name Dominique Aury in her professional life. The author did not reveal herself as the author of *The Story of O* for 40 years after the initial publication.

The main character, called only O, is a French fashion photographer who, for no reason that is ever given, passively assents to being blindfolded, chained, whipped, raped, sodomized, branded, and humiliated. The novel's sparse, even clinical prose moves relentlessly on through this torture, until, at the end, the final lines dispassionately note that O was then abandoned by her last "lover," and she asks his permission to die, which was granted.[1]

The Story of O has flashes of artistic merit, particularly in the first dozen or so furious pages. The first edition had a beautiful cover and a laudatory preface by Jean Paulhan, the older, male lover of Aury to whom she claims she had first written what became the book as a series of "love letters."

In his preface, Paulhan argues that for women, "happiness is slavery." Women in their truest nature crave domination; that the character of O is empowered by confessing her desire; and that, in truth, slaves love their masters, would suffer in their absence, and have no wish to achieve independence. Indeed, as one reviewer noted, the more O is brutalized, the more "perfectly feminine" she becomes.[2] Love, torture, and annihilation are intertwined, so that one can conclude, in reading this novel, that the only way to be "perfectly feminine" is to be dead. "She [O] did not wish to die, but if torture was the price she had to pay to keep her lover's love, then she only hoped he was pleased that she had endured it."

Beginning in the late 1970s, feminists began to take on the pornography industry and a screening of the film based on *The Story of O* in San Francisco was their target. Women against Violence in Pornography and Media (WAVPM) was a feminist antipornography group founded in San Francisco in 1977 after the Women's Centers Conference on Violence against Women. Founding members included Laura Lederer, Lynn Campbell, Diana Russell, Kathleen Barry, and Susan Griffin, all well-known activists and writers in the movement to end violence against women. Forty members protested the film carrying signs that said, "Who Says Pain is Erotic?" and chanting, "The Story of O has got to go!" Susan Griffin pointed out that *The Story of O* was largely about overpowering and silencing women, since the heroine in the story was instructed by her Master not to speak at all.[3]

Eroticized violence against women in a compelling narrative such as *The Story of O* is more dangerous because it promotes the idea that women desire to be treated violently in a way that is more fascinating than cruder versions. Yet there is much more to the critical treatment of eroticized violence against women that needs examination.

This Violence That Is Not One

Protest against *The Story of O* in the feminist antipornography movement was not without controversy among women.

Some lesbian groups objected that the antipornography feminists were rejecting all pornography. Some in their movement enjoyed, used, and even produced pornography and did not want to be harassed as part of further suppression of sadomasochistic (S and M) materials. The social location of the antipornography feminists, as more elite, mainstream, white women blinded them to what women on more radical sexual margins might experience as a result of their campaign. Increased criminalization of pornography would, given the homophobia of US society, fall disproportionately on lesbians and sexual minorities as vulnerable people.

Women of color also protested WAVPM's tactics in portraying African American women and that their "educational materials, like the slide-shows, were criticized for failing to explain how racism contributed to stereotypical portrayals of women of color in pornography, such as black women shown in chains."[4] In other words, the founders of WAVPM conflated all violence against women, trading on race to construct gender outrage and action to end pornography without including actual strategies to confront and end racism. Their views and the views of lesbians on pornography, especially their social location vis-à-vis social policy changes, were ignored.

Judith Butler observes "[h]ow quickly a critical encounter becomes misconstrued as a war."[5] These critical reactions by some lesbians and women of color to the antipornography movement did not result in substantively changed practices by WAVPM at the time. Instead, what changed is that a gulf widened among women. This is one area critical physicality seeks to confront. The "war" that results from a failure to change practice due to critical encounter becomes a war among women rather than a deeper and more complex engagement with the forces that coconspire to normalize physical violence against women.

On the one hand, there is no question that pornography is a way violence against women is normalized through the socialization of men who use it. A large body of social-science research shows that "high pornography consumption added significantly to the prediction of sexual aggression." Men who internalize the "rape myth" that women actually "want it" through the consumption of pornography are more likely to commit sexual offenses.[6]

On the other hand, the issue is not just whether this happens but how to craft multiple resistance strategies. The multiple effects of eroticizing violence against women need multiple and different strategies to change them; one thing a movement that seeks to counter these effects does not need is some women deciding for others what their response needs to be. That kind of hegemonic attitude by some women can just end up facilitating the dominant culture and its mechanisms of control. The dominant culture is well able to reframe every challenge to its hegemony by blaming vulnerable people, and unless conscious resistance to that is part of every step of movement building, it will happen again and again. It does happen, again and again.

What is being examined in this chapter then is not the erotic or the pornographic per se but what should be called the "erotics of normalization of violence." Violence is normalized in Western culture, and a primary way that happens is through economic and political power that projects and protects an image of the superiority of white, male, heterosexual economic elites. This is how violence becomes normalized, even becomes desirable, as a form of repression. This is why there is so much eroticized violence in both the police and the military.[7] The erotics of the normalization of violence are the construction and deployment of desire through many cultural mechanisms. One important mechanism in this regard is religion and the religious inheritance of the West.

Religious metaphors abound in *The Story of O* and they are not at all subtle. O, when she is being abused by a group whom she cannot see, is bent over. "Then they let her rock back a bit, as nuns are wont to do." "She [O] considered herself fortunate to count enough in his [Rene's] eyes for him to derive pleasure from offending her, as believers give thanks to God for humbling them."

These and many other religious references invite the reader of this text to recognize the inherited sexual guilt and shame from Western Christianity in regard to sexuality and sexual appetite. Part of the erotic in the text is violating not only sexual "taboos" but also religious ones. This feeds on itself in *The Story of O* because the very religious and sexual taboos that the reader is invited to transgress are the foundations of what makes the novel erotic—that is, the obliteration of women's agency through sexualized violence. Without the deeply perverse Western cultural and religious inheritances on sex and violence, the novel would have little transgressive power and hence not titillate.

This is a prime example of the devastating consequences that are derived from problematized sexuality as inherited through Christian theology. As sexual pleasure is projected through pornographic violence against women, a violence that women are fantastically shown to enjoy, the physical bodies of actual women are put more at risk of violence as a vast amount of social-science literature demonstrates. Thus *The Story of O*, both as text and as film, is many things in theory, but one thing it is, at the level of physicality, is an enabler of risk of injury to some women's bodies.

The context out of which *The Story of O* was produced however, as one of both war and colonial conquest, is also relevant to this analysis of how and why the War on Women is eroticized.

The Erotic, War, and Colonialism

Another aspect of *The Story of O* that I believe is crucial to consider is that it is an immediate product of postwar France. Both the author of *The Story of O*, and her married lover, Jean Paulhan, met and started their relationship while doing work for the French Resistance. Yet despite the Resistance, the Germans exercised brutal control over French citizens, and they were forced to submit to the Germans and their occupation. Is there an interpretation of *The Story of O* that includes the sublimation of their guilt at seeming to have "given in" to the Germans in the occupation and whatever the Germans made them do regarding racially discriminatory laws against the populations, running Jewish concentration camps, cooperating with deportations of Jews, and persecuting the "unfit," including homosexuals? This context can also help us to understand the lesbianism in the text that is a strong part of the narrative. Dominique Aury, née Desclos, was actively bisexual in her life.[8] Was this also a part of Aury's resistance to the German occupation?

Racism was a political construction in France, not only during the German occupation, but also for centuries of French colonialism, and is another important source of analysis of how the erotic functions in this novel. For example, the voyeuristic stance in which the reader is cast includes not only eroticizing the violence against O as a woman but also racializing the sexual "slavery" to which O is subjected. O's clothing is white, and there are frequent contrast references to her white skin, a white skin "which seemed even whiter" against backgrounds specifically described as black, such as "black fur." The red welts O receives from the repeated whippings are described as red against her white skin.

The French experience of domination and submission is not confined to being occupied by the Germans. In fact, France was most often the occupier and the suppressor. It had engaged in colonial expansion for centuries. In the nineteenth and twentieth centuries, France was the second-largest colonial empire after the

British Empire. France's colonial dominance in these centuries was chiefly in North and West Africa and in Southeast Asia. The French justification for colonial conquest was highly racialized and sacralized. In 1884, a leading French proponent of colonial conquest, Jules Ferry, declared, "The higher races have a right over the lower races, they have a duty to civilize the inferior races." French Catholicism was heavily recruited to help justify this effort and missionize the colonized.

The French participated vigorously in the Atlantic slave trade and enslaved four times as many Africans as Americans did. French slavery was considered very brutal, and the French continued the slave trade long after the rest of Europe had prohibited it.[9]

Perversely, the French held romanticized and eroticized attitudes toward colonized and enslaved races, particularly the African. This can be seen very vividly in the paintings of Henri Rousseau.

Rousseau (1844–1910) was a French postimpressionist painter in the Naïve or Primitive manner. The period in which he painted was one of rapacious and violent colonial conquest by the French, including vast parts of Africa. Rousseau perfectly captured the erotic desire of this conquest. He often painted fantastic jungles with exotic animals and racially ambiguous, often female figures. Yet these images frightened Rousseau, so much so that he said when he painted "fantastic subjects, he had to open the window, so much was he overcome with fear."[10] The erotics of the normalization of violence usually include a strong element of fear of the other in order to provide justification for the desired exploitation.

Rousseau's painting, *War*, is truly frightening for the viewer as it constructs the violence of war making. This painting projects the violence of colonial conquest onto a terrifying figure of another racially ambiguous woman with feral hair streaming out behind her, even as the untamed mane and tail of the black horse she rides also streaks out, and the two barrel through the center of the painting. She is described as a "terrifying woman, with bared teeth and wild hair, [who] rides on horseback across a barren landscape littered with corpses."[11] The corpses are white, some of them bleeding from severed limbs. Red clouds dominate the sky. War is portrayed as perpetrated by an out-of-control, all-purpose native woman, and she leaves only white male corpses. This is the fantastical inversion of French colonial conquest; when the painting is seen in this light, it defines the dangerous sexual and racial erotic in the colonial imagination.

When we consider the total context of the so-called eroticism of *The Story of O* from the context of how violence against women and the violence of war become normalized, our interpretation can change. So much of what drives this violence is never seen. It may seem farfetched to ask questions about the French experience of German occupation and their colonial history in analyzing a famous "erotic" French novel, but is that simply because the effects of war and the effects of colonial conquest are not seen as relevant to what we call erotic?

It is very important to consider that the possible relationship between this erotic novel and its creation immediately following the most devastating war ever experienced in Europe and to France itself, as a deeply racist, colonial power and why it is never commented upon. The sex is very distracting, but then again, is that not a big part of the erotic, to stimulate desire and at the same time suppress the kind of consciousness that leads to resistance?

One thing this interpretation can yield, however, is how the domination and submission themes in *The Story of O* as the erotic are a template for how Western culture constructs violence and then also distracts us from forming complex resistance strategies against them. That is how the "normalization" of violence against women works.

Critical physicality seeks to be a "disrupter" of the normalization of violence and to expose the multiple engines that powerfully connect violence and desire and then use them to justify injuring bodies. The construction of the erotic normalizes physical violence by making it both seductive and lethal. The many powers that drive eroticizing the War on Women and war itself in a specifically Western construct must be exposed and confronted even with all the internal contradictions that entails. If this does not occur, then movement building will continually be sabotaged, and the bodies of women, girls, and vulnerable men will be injured and killed with impunity. Indeed, they will be justified and sometimes even enjoyed. Eroticizing violence against women and eroticizing war is a delivery system for multiple forms of power, particularly geopolitical, economic power.

The erotic is "very powerful," as Audre Lorde, Womanist, civil rights activist, and poet, points out in "The Uses of the Erotic: The Erotic as Power." The very word *erotic*, she notes, "comes from the Greek word *eros* and is the personification of love in all its aspects—born of Chaos, and personifying creative power and harmony." This is the power of feeling what we feel, not only physically, but also mentally and spiritually. To sabotage erotic power, especially as exercised by women, Lorde argues, it must be corrupted or distorted and made into the obscene or pornographic in order to control and to keep women "docile, loyal, and obedient." To reclaim it means we have to reject "a european-american male tradition."[12]

To reject that "european-american male tradition," we have to know it in-depth and also explore what forces within it might be deployed to subvert its eroticized normalization of violence against women and the violence of war.

Cupid's Lethal Arrow: Eros and Violence

Eros is the Greek god of love from which we get the term "erotic," Cupid is his Roman counterpart whose name means "desire." Cupid is often portrayed as a youth or even a young boy armed with a bow and arrow. The bow and arrow are supposed to represent how being consumed with uncontrollable desire can wound. It is important to consider that the bow and arrow are one of the earliest projectile weapons and were a crucial part of war for millennia. To see Cupid in contemporary terms, he should be holding a gun to make the point clearer that erotic desire is physically dangerous. The Roman poet Ovid (43 BCE–17 CE) makes this clear when he portrays Venus's son as having "fierce anger" that he unleashes with his bow, deliberately causing suffering.[13]

Ancient mythology also frequently equates desire and sexual violence and sometimes sexual violence perpetrated by a god. Zeus, for example, sees a Phoenician princess, tricks her by changing into the form of a bull, and kidnaps her. According to Ovid, Europa is one of the "loves of Jove"—that is, Zeus.[14] What that actually means, of course, is that she is one of a series of women who have the misfortune to be loved by a god and who are abducted and sexually assaulted as a result.[15]

Some modern mythologists such as Joseph Campbell find these "familiar images" from myths that "portray the rape of a moral—or 'relatively moral'— virgin by a deity" harmless when it comes to the actual physical violence committed against any particular woman. They are wrong. The Western construct of normalized violence against women is built on such foundational myths of rape of women by gods, such as Zeus's abduction of Europa and also of Leda, as well as Hades's rape of Persephone, Apollo's pursuit of Daphne, and so forth. These myths, as has been previously shown, are then replicated in art and literature and repeated over and over so they make rape both visible and invisible.

Campbell conveniently rolls all these myths of divine sexual violence on the bodies of women into one abstraction. "They are all the same event, just as the heroes are in an ultimate sense always one, Campbell's 'hero with a thousand faces.'" That is, the rapes, over and over, "simply dramatize the will of consciousness, portrayed with male power, imposed upon poignant natural frailty."[16] There is perhaps no better definition of patriarchy than this equation of the will with "male power" dominating nature conceived as female. Myths, art, and modern mythologists all coconspire to keep the foundations of normalized violence against women strong.

Patriarchal domination gets identified as "love" in the West over and over through repetition and display. The Rape of Europa was one of the most popular classical subjects for Renaissance paintings. The renaissance painter Guido Reni did a version commissioned by King Władisław of Poland, shortly before 1640. In this highly romantic version, Cupid gets included, drawing his bow to shoot the arrow of love at Europa. The British National Gallery notes that although this "dark subject" was popular in the paintings of the European Renaissance, in Reni's version, "Europa is shown at the moment when her disquiet at being abducted begins to turn to love."[17] Sexual violence is OK, apparently, as long as you include Cupid in the scene and the abduction and rape is reframed as love.

Violence against women is hidden by being portrayed everywhere, and paintings of the Rape of Europa solidify the relationship between eros and violence against women. As A. W. Eaton notes in an article titled "Where Ethics and Aesthetics Meet: Titian's Rape of Europa," while this painting by Titian (1559–62) is "often touted as the greatest Italian Renaissance painting hanging in an American collection," it has "an overlooked dark side, namely, that it eroticized rape." Eaton makes a case that art criticism should contain the ethical dimension. The way the aesthetics "works" in the painting—that is, the sensual textures and coloring, and not just the subject itself—help create the ethical issues.[18] The reproduction of the erotic fiction of violence against women does not just happen. As these myths travel, in effect, they are not the "same thing" over and over again as the mythologists would have us believe, they are remade over and over again in order to reproduce the acceptability, even desirability, of eroticizing the War on Women and branding it as love.

Make Love Not War: Views in Greek Philosophy

Platonic philosophy takes a much different view compared to the myths of the eroticizing of violence against women as love; instead, Plato privileges love or eros as a complex of desire and affiliation without reference to war. For Plato "he who loves the beautiful is called a lover because he partakes of it." (*Phaedrus*, 249E) It is normally held that in the Platonic world of Forms or Ideas, it is the ideal of beauty, not any particular beautiful person, who is the object of desire. This gives rise to the general notion that when one says he or she is in a "Platonic" relationship, that means it is not a sexual relationship.

Not quite.

In Plato's various dialogues, the *Lysis*, the *Phaedrus*, and especially the *Symposium*, Socrates is shown to be one who "loves beautiful boys and philosophical discussions" (203b6–4a3). You cannot read these dialogues without the backstory, of which Plato is all too aware. Socrates, as a lover of boys, is in potential conflict with the Athenian social institution, that of *paiderastis*, that regulated sexual intercourse between an older Athenian male (*erastês*) and a teenage boy (*erômenos*, *pais*), through which the latter was supposed to learn virtue. In 399 BCE, Socrates was found guilty of corrupting the young men of Athens and was condemned to death.

The effect on Plato is palpable in his works, turning very many of them into defenses—not always uncritical—of Socrates, and an argument for how the erotic love of beauty and the virtue of friendship are far more important than the physical expressions of this love.[19]

In the *Symposium*, the love stories are predominantly about the older male lover and a beloved boy. They are passionate love stories, even when presented as comedy. These are really not theories about love and certainly do not discount the physical attractions of the beloved. But they are written to present love as the ideal of friendship and tutelage for virtue as the highest ideal with a backdrop of the criminalization of the erotic as powerful sexual desire, as Socrates found out, and Plato rightly would fear.

The *Symposium* dialogue deals with this by splitting Aphrodite, and therefore love, in two. The elder Aphrodite is the goddess who is the "daughter of Uranus," and she has no mother and in her birth, "the female has no part." Thus this love is heavenly, the love of the soul. The "common" Aphrodite is the daughter of Zeus and Dione and this love is "of the body rather than of the soul." This splitting becomes necessary to continue the illusion that the love of a young man is for the good of his soul, for virtue and has nothing to do with physical, carnal love such as characterizes the female, embodied, common form of love.

But the sheer physicality that runs through these arguments makes this ridiculous. There are blatantly physical images (pack asses, for example!) that undermine the distinction. It really is a dualism, and the dualism is made explicit by Socrates when he claims to be quoting Diotima, a "wise woman of Mantinea." But Diotima is not a real person, "she" is a device to describe love as the intermediary between dichotomies like poverty and plenty, ugliness and beauty, and lover and beloved. Diotima says at 204b that it is obvious even to a child that love is between wise and ignorant; it is the relationship between wise and ignorant. She presents love as the intermediary between mortality and immortality at 206d–e, where she notes that it brings men and women together to procreate so that they may survive their own mortality. While Diotima does call the union of men and women a divine thing, her comments themselves and the fact that she is absent from the dialogue with her views supplied by a male, serve to underline that the position attributed to her is a defense of hierarchical dualism. Rosemary Radford Ruether, feminist liberation theologian, has long maintained that a dualistic view of reality, rooted in Platonism, is a primary source for the alienation from the body, community, and the earth that is so destructive.[20]

The origins of the splitting of the body and eros, and the dualism that gets projected onto women and women's bodies, is revealed by this examination to be far more social than philosophical. If Socrates had not been criminalized, how differently might these Platonic dialogues present the issues surrounding love and the physical? If Greek society had been less rigidly patriarchal, and Diotima had been an actual philosopher at the feast, how much of women's full physical and spiritual nature might have made it into the legacy of Western philosophy?

But as it is, there are social conditions that help create alienation from the body and sexuality in which philosophy then becomes complicit. The erotic as much hides as reveals the physical dimensions of desire and, even worse, becomes available for recruitment into an aggressive desire that can become violent. Mythology contributes its own corruptions of eros when even divinities engage in violent sexual conquest.

Hebrew Bible: Lust and War

Sexual violence against women in both the Hebrew bible and the New Testament book of Revelation are so intimately connected with war and political conflict that it is difficult to talk about the "War on Women" and not talk about "war" from the start.

In the Hebrew bible, Yahweh (God) is a "man of war" (Exodus 15:3) and there is such a thing as wars that Yahweh pursues himself (defeating Pharaoh's army in Exodus being a prime case in point). Thus the question should be asked: Is Yahweh ultimately the author of the violence against women in these texts, a kind of Zeus but at one remove? Furthermore, as texts that normalize violence against women, and the violence against war, are these eroticized?

As was discussed in Chapter 2, the Rape of Tamar is a biblical text that establishes the acceptable boundaries of rape as a social norm in a political context. But it is also the case in that text that the eroticization of violence plays a huge role. Amnon's erotic desire for his seemingly unattainable sister, Tamar, "And desired her Amnon, son of David" (13:1), sets the violence in motion. Both the fact that Tamar is unattainable, and that she is a virgin, turns his desire to "violent yearning" and "lust-sickness" per Trible.[21] Eros and violence become completely entwined in this text. Amnon rapes Tamar (13:12) and immediately the true face of the eroticization of violence is revealed: "Then Amnon hated her a great hatred indeed. Truly, greater was the hatred with which he hated her than the desire with which he desired her" (13:15a).

In that sequence, however, the author of 2 Samuel has it wrong. The desire that is erotic violence is hatred and it is from the start. The perversion of desire does not become hatred, it is hatred. At the root of the eroticization of violence, as this text profoundly shows us through its misunderstanding of what happened with Amnon and Tamar, is the hatred of women. But like much of the violence against women in the Hebrew bible, this sexual violence is done to Tamar, but it is not ultimately about Tamar. The sexual violence is actually about the political turmoil in the House of David, kind of a "Game of Thrones" like the popular and very violent fantasy television series.

It should be noted parenthetically that *Game of Thrones* has included numerous episodes of sexual violence. One of the most controversial and one that bears a resemblance to the Rape of Tamar is when, in Season Four, a noblewoman is raped by her brother, though she has been in an incestuous relationship with him. Rape is even more graphic in the comic-book version of *Game of Thrones*, where the comic novel "graphically depicts, by the fourth page, a barbarian preparing to rape a nude woman after conquering her village."[22]

Game of Thrones fairly well represents the "Texts of Terror" in the Hebrew bible as the political and sexual violence go hand in hand. Judges 19:1–30 is a text that Phyllis Trible calls "The Extravagance of Violence" against an unnamed woman, a "concubine" who is betrayed, tortured, murdered, and ultimately dismembered. The story appears toward the end of the book of Judges, a time when "god seldom appeared, and chaos reigned among the Israelite tribes."[23]

The last three chapters of Judges (19–21) contain not only violent sexual crimes and war crimes but also the authorization for these crimes supposedly in response to laws of hospitality and even divine command.

Judges 19:1–30 is the story of an unnamed woman concubine from Bethlehem who "becomes angry" with her master, a Levite, and she "went away from him to her father's house in Judah" (19:2). The Levite follows her and basically engages in a lot of "male bonding" in the absence of the woman whose fate was in question.[24] Finally, the Levite determines to leave, even though it is very late and clearly a dangerous time to travel. They cannot make it to his home in a single day and they try to find hospitality; finally, he thinks, they have found it with an old man in Gibeah. But "men of the city" who are wicked came and "started pounding on the door." They demand that the old man deliver his male guest "so that we may have intercourse with him." The old man is horrified at "this vile thing" and so, instead, *he offers his virgin daughter and the concubine to them.* "Ravish them and do whatever you want to them; but against his man do not do such a vile thing" (Judges 19:22–24).

The "vile thing" is not raping women. Instead, the "vile thing" is raping a male and a guest. The laws of hospitality do not extend to women and girls. But even so, the men intent on raping the Levite wouldn't listen to the old man, so the Levite himself takes his concubine and shoves her out the door. The sequence sounds like there was a pack of wolves at the door, as they fell on the woman like so much meat thrown out to them. "They wantonly raped her, and abused her all through the night until the morning," and then they let her go. She crawled to the house and fell down at the door.

The text does not lavish pornographic details on the rape and torture of the concubine. This does not, as Trible so well indicates, diminish the "extravagance of violence," it "discloses" it as the horribly injured woman crawls toward what should have been safety, and she is met with further callousness. Is her master, who has traveled so far to try to get her back, at all concerned with what has happened to her? Apparently not, as he just goes to the door, sees her fallen down "with her hands on the threshold. 'Get up,' he said to her, 'we are going.' But there was no answer"(19:27–28). He puts her on his donkey, and even then, the reader still does not know if she is dead or alive. When he gets home, he took a knife and "grasping his concubine he cut her into twelve pieces, limb by limb, and sent her throughout all the territory of Israel" (19:29).

The concubine's body belongs to her master, and he is upset at *his* loss, not the suffering the concubine endured in being raped and tortured for hours; whether he murders her or she died from her injuries is unimportant in the text. What is important is this "offense" that becomes a pretext for one of the most appalling sequences in the history of war, a gigantic outpouring of violence against the Benjaminites in revenge for killing the Levite's concubine. Thousands and thousands of men fight and are killed, especially on the Israelite side.

It is only when God takes over that the Benjaminites are defeated. "The LORD defeated Benjamin before Israel; and the Israelites destroyed twenty-five thousand one hundred men of Benjamin that day, all of them armed" (20:35). Only 600 men survive, and this would mean one of the tribes would be wiped out if they cannot get wives and reproduce. An oath complicates matters, since the Israelites have vowed not to give their daughters in marriage to Benjaminites (21:1). So they attack "the derelict town of Jabesh-Gilead, murdering all the inhabitants except four hundred young virgins" (21:10–12).[25] But 400 young virgins are not enough for 600 men, so they abduct 200 "young women of Shiloah" when they "come out to dance the dances" during a festival of the LORD (21:19–23).

Six hundred young women have been abducted and raped because one man has used his own concubine to save himself. This mass abduction and rape has been made "necessary" not just because of an oath but because the Israelites committed a massacre when they put "to the sword—the city, the people, the animals, and all that remained." And then they set fire to the whole (20:48).

That is in fact the pornographic connection between this horrifying rape, torture, and murder of an unnamed concubine and the spasm of violence that breaks out against the Benjaminites. Are we then to conclude this was authorized by God?

New Testament: The Rapture

The New Testament Revelation to John contains brutal, hate-filled imagery of the violent defeat of Babylon (AKA Rome) as noted in Chapter 4. This imagery is profoundly eroticized as the "great whore who is seated on many waters" (Rev. 17:1).

It is also war literature that has influenced the erotic normalization of war and the War on Women up to this century.

The background of the Revelation to John is the war that had broken out in Jerusalem in 66 CE when Jewish groups attempted to expel the Romans from occupying Judea. The Romans not only quelled the rebellion but also committed tremendous violence against the Jews and destroyed the Temple.

John's text then is a text that contains vivid imagery of war, the "Four Horsemen of the Apocalypse," but it also eroticizes this divine war through the physical violence done to the "great whore." The "great whore" sitting on a "scarlet colored beast." She is garbed in purple and scarlet and covered in jewels. She is covered in royal colors but holds in her hand "a golden cup full of abominations and filthiness of her fornication." She is labeled, named on her forehead, "Babylon the Great, The Mother of Harlots and Abominations of the Earth."

Yes, this is Rome—blood-spilling, rapacious, war-like, torturing Rome—and the divine judgment on Rome is coming brutally. But this ferocious penalty will be brutally completed on the body of a woman as the battlefield, this whore, who will be made "desolate and naked, and [the beast] shall eat her flesh and burn her with fire." This brutal sexual assault and murder is paired with other sexual imagery, a pregnant woman who is "clothed with the sun, with the moon under her feet and on her head a crown of twelve stars" (Rev. 12:1). This is certainly Israel, as the number twelve would indicate, and the desired reproductive life of the community that "good" women represent. This mirrors the dualism on gender in ancient Israel that divides women into the controlled reproductive vehicle or the threatening chaos that must be brutally subdued and/or destroyed, as has been noted.

The saints will be saved, however, and will be taken up into heaven as in Revelation 11:12, though the final taking up of the righteous into heaven will not take place, per Revelation, for more than 1,000 years. They will also experience the tribulations on earth such as war, disease, and starvation per the biblical text.

There is tremendous controversy among contemporary conservative Christians, however, about whether the saints will even have to experience these woes or whether a "pre-tribulation" Rapture will take place, as Barbara Rossing explains in her book *The Rapture Exposed*.[26]

Belief in the Rapture became popularized during the 1970s, especially due to the best-seller *The Late Great Planet Earth*. The advent of nuclear weapons and the threat of nuclear war figured prominently in Lindsey's prediction that the Rapture was nearly upon us. What is crucial to note, for the purposes of this argument, is how there is a lurking eroticism in Lindsey's descriptions of nuclear war in his bestseller. Lindsey's book uses fear, but it is exposed as erotic longing for a spasm of violence as in the references to "awful climax."[27] Keep in mind that a synonym for "rapture" is "ecstasy."

This book exhibits a kind of lust for the ultimate destruction of humanity, and it is clearly dangerous; it is the underlying desire for violence that gives tremendous energy to the erotic normalization of both war and the War on Women.

Augustine: Projecting Desire

When Augustine probes not only how, in God's providence, barbarians could have sacked Rome but also how God could have allowed them to rape consecrated virgins, his projection of desire in the violence of war is exposed.

Augustine sees history not as linear but as a struggle between the City of God and the Earthly City, moving on toward a final resolution in the eschaton in a far more complex, but ultimately similar, to war in Hal Lindsey. In Augustine's schema, Rome is Babylon, the earthly city, even the City of the Devil, in contrast to Jerusalem, the City of God and now the Holy Church. According to Augustine, Rome is the second Babylon, and Babylon is the first Rome. "One empire took the place of another." So Rome is not innocent. But what about the consecrated virgins who are raped?

Recall from Chapter 4 that, for Augustine, there is more than one war in human life. There is the war without, the war between nations. There is also the war within, the war with sexual drives and the struggle with lust as part of the condition in which human beings find themselves caught because of original sin.

In treating Augustine's views on sexuality and on war together, we come to understand how, in an Augustinian sense, conflict in the self, like conflict in the city, is a clear sign of sin, especially the sin of disobedience. This is clearly seen in how Augustine condemns both "passion" for injuring in war and having "lust" in war. By that, he does not mean sexual lust but rather the "lust for power." For Augustine, the chief moral risk in war is that you will enjoy it, even as in the sex act, the chief moral risk also seems to be that you will enjoy it.[28] This leads Augustine to the disreputable position that what is ultimately wrong about sexual assault in war is that the victim of rape will enjoy it.

The body/soul dualism that carries through Augustine's work, an inheritance of Platonism, directs Western Christian thought away from what happens to the body in war and away from what happens to the bodies of women when treated violently. Yes, these raped women may have experienced pain, but what was happening in their souls is what really matters. Thus when Augustine's conviction that God is provident over history with the body/soul dualism, there must have been something of God's will in it, and it is their bodies that betrayed the women. Those Christian women who were raped, Augustine argues, may yet have "had some lurking infirmity which might have betrayed them into a proud and contemptuous bearing" so that their "humiliation" in rape and in the taking of the city was to teach them "humility."[29]

Augustine starts off on the right track, that there is indeed a perverted passion in war and the War on Women. But his overriding conviction of God's plan for history, again, not unlike Lindsey's, leads to his frankly impossible notion that violence in war and violence against women in rape can serve God's purposes. Augustine, unlike Lindsey, briefly glimpses what is corrupt and cruel about war and even the War on Women, and he loses that insight when he tries to rescue absolute divine providence from the realities of injury and death.

Ironically, it is not the theological wrestling of Augustine on these issues that is the late twentieth-century legacy but the erotic normalization of war and desire.

Woman as Temptress

Joseph Campbell has a section titled "Woman as the Temptress" in his major work on mythology that is riddled with the key assumptions about the female, the body, sexuality, and the erotic that so fuel violence against women. In order to attain "total mastery over life" the "hero," according to Campbell, must attain mastery over women as they ultimately symbolize life. But life—that is, women—"is necessarily tainted with the order of the flesh" and the hero feels revulsion. "[L]ife, the acts of life, the organs of life, woman in particular as the great symbol of life, become intolerable to the pure, the pure, pure soul."[30]

The "acts of life" and the "organs of life" clearly refer to the sex act, and Campbell is saying that sex itself is disgusting for the pure, pure (male) soul. This revulsion and attraction are vividly expressed in Christian asceticism, and it is not a surprise that Campbell's examples of the struggles with the temptations of the flesh are of Christian asceticism, and the justifications for violence against women that are the result.[31]

An especially perverse form of eroticized violence in the medieval period appears in the persecution of those accused of "witchcraft," most of whom were women. This was an outpouring of torture and death that continued in Europe for centuries. While Augustine had argued that witchcraft was actually impossible because of his conviction of God's providence over history and that only God could suspend the laws of nature, Thomas Aquinas was persuaded of the reality of the demonic. In the *Summa Theologiae*, Aquinas argued that the world was full of evil and dangerous demons, and he associated demons with women and sex. Demons do not procreate, Aquinas states, rather what happens is that while there are those who are "occasionally begotten from demons," it is from "seed of men taken for the purpose; as when the demon assumes first the form of a woman, and afterwards of a man" and thus secures the semen.[32] Women, he argues in the same passage, are known by "many persons" to have had intercourse with "incubi"— that is, a male demon that has intercourse with sleeping women. Women's sexuality, in Aquinas's view, is a portal to the demonic and hence to the devil.

It did not take much, then, for this view that women are the "devil's gateway" to become murderously violent. Thousands on thousands of women and vulnerable men were killed.[33]

We are so accustomed to knowing that women in particular were persecuted as witches that it is hard to step back and ask, "Why women?" But an analysis that does not privilege gender alone can reveal the persecution of women as a "safe" outlet for state violence.[34] This violence helped consolidate hierarchical state power, supported by hierarchical understandings of gender. Eroticized violence against women is not random; it serves social, political, and economic purposes.

The persecution of witches was not confined to continental Europe and England, and it was justified in Catholic and Protestant theology alike. Cotton Mather, Harvard graduate and minister of the influential Old North Church in Boston, was profoundly influential in the tragic circumstances that led to the Salem Witch Trials in Salem, Massachusetts, in 1692. In 1689, Mather published a bestselling book on the subject, *Memorable Providences, Relating to Witchcrafts and*

Possessions, detailing an episode of supposed witchcraft a year earlier involving three children who had been "behaving strangely" and an Irish washerwoman named Goody Glover whom Mather concluded had bewitched them. Mather's account, describing the symptoms of witchcraft, was widely read and discussed throughout Puritan New England. The book was in the meager library of Samuel Parris, the Salem minister in whose house began the events of 1692 that resulted in 24 innocent people being killed as witches.

Analyses of the Salem Witch Trials often emphasize the economic disparities between the accusers and the accused, but the theologies of gender and society need to be emphasized far more than is often the case. Gender persecution, through the eroticized violence of witch hunts, provides a means of control for social and religious elites such as Mather.

Eroticizing violence against women as a means of social control is also a tremendous engine of the construction of the racist and sexist ideologies that justified the slave trade and made it not only profitable but also an object of desire.

Eroticizing African Women's Bodies in Slavery and Colonialism

In 1853, Solomon Northup, a New York man kidnapped and sold into slavery, published his personal memoir of being a slave. It sold out within a month of publication. Frederick Douglass, the great abolitionist and slave-narrative author himself, said of the book that "it chills the blood."[35]

The 2013 film *12 Years a Slave*, based on Northup's memoir, won best picture. The memoir and the film show the unrelenting, interlocking relationship of sexual obsession, possession of enslaved women's bodies, and brutality in American slavery. Some critics of the film sought to mitigate its portrayals of the extremities of violence, especially the sexual violence, but many slave narratives contain the same stories of totalizing sexual and physical violence that characterized the slave system.[36]

The memoir and the film capture the complete physicality of this slave system. Patsey, an enslaved African woman, is the object of obsessive control and sexual violence by Epps, the white master on a plantation in Louisiana. The totalizing effect of this eroticized violence is portrayed not only as Epps invades Patsey's quarters and forces her to have sex with him but also as his wife deprives her of soap with which to wash. When Patsy takes a day trip to another plantation to retrieve a bar of soap, Epps is jealous and forces Northup to whip her. When Northrup cannot whip Patsey sufficiently in Epps's view, he takes over and nearly whips her to death. As Epps makes no secret of his fixation with Patsey, Epps's wife throws heavy objects at Patsey's head in her warped victim blaming and tells Northrup to whip Patsey when her husband is not around.

The hatred that is at the root of the eroticized violence against slave women is visible in the film and vivid in the narrative. The repeated rapes, the denial of soap, and the whipping form a continuous loop that exposes the corrupt system of slavery that was based on the physical desire for total control of the bodies of enslaved Africans.

The erotic desire projected onto the bodies of African women was constructed as part of the colonial project, as should be clear from the analysis of the paintings of Rousseau. A historical example that is even more telling, however, is of Sarah "Saartjie" Baartman. Baartman was the best-known of at least two African women of the Khoikhoi people in southern Africa who were taken to Europe and exhibited as part of the freak show attractions popular in the nineteenth century.

Baartman was born in 1789 and was working as a slave in Cape Town, in what is now South Africa, when she was "discovered" by the ship's doctor and taken to London where she was put on display for what were considered her "unusually large buttocks and genitals," not actually a feature all that unusual for a Khoisan woman. She was called the "Hottentot Venus." "Hottentot" was a term used for the Khoikhoi people, now considered denigrating, and "Venus" to make clear the sexualized connotation of her body shape. She moved to Paris where she was known as "La Belle Hottentot," and she attracted the attention of French scientists, especially Georges Cuvier. She could not maintain herself financially and eventually became a prostitute. She died at the age of 25. Cuvier made a plaster cast of her body, then removed her skeleton and, after removing her brain and genitals, pickled them and displayed them in bottles at the Musee de l'Homme in Paris.

One hundred and sixty years later, they were still on display in Paris but were finally removed from public view in 1974. In 1994, President Nelson Mandela of South Africa requested that Sarah Baartman's remains be brought home, but it still took eight years for that to be accomplished due to French concerns about other countries claiming their "stolen treasures." Finally the French allowed this "scientific curiosity" to be returned to South Africa in 2002 and her grave is a national heritage site. A poem by Khoisan descendant Diana Ferrus in 1998 is considered to have played a major role in helping bring Baartman home. The poem places Sarah Baartman in a beautiful land, safe finally from the eroticized violence of "poking eyes" of both the political "imperialism" and the wretched theologies that made her "Satan" and thus suitable for dissection.[37]

Racism "dissects" African women's bodies and does so with seeming impunity with theologies that deny their sacred dignity and worth. Womanist theology has made constructing a theology of black women's bodies central to its task. This work is profound and difficult as the dissection and denigration is deeply rooted in Western culture. In a chapter called "The 'Loves' and 'Troubles' of African American Women's Bodies: The Womanist Challenge to Cultural Humiliation and Community Ambivalence," Cheryl Townsend Gilkes points to the "historically conditioned responses of white people to the differences among African American women and their bodies" that are sexist and racist pathologies. "We find that our history of racial oppression has always been sexualized," she stresses.[38] This has its origins in the "abuse and degradation of slavery" that are "so specialized and so deep that they even carry over into pornographic depictions." The slave auction drew "white prurient interests" and "[b]lack women's bodies were the objects of intense public curiosity," not unlike the display of Sarah Baartman. Postslavery, the stereotypes about the sexuality of black women as Jezebel were used to justify segregation and "supported the lynching of their men."[39]

As Rita Nakashima Brock and I have written in a section on "Racism and Colonialism" in our book, *Casting Stones: Prostitution and Liberation in Asia and the United States*, the American history of slavery and its aftermath are foundational to the understanding of power and sexuality in this country. This racism extends into US immigration laws that are also are shaped by the Western colonialist enterprise not only in Africa but also in Asia and Latin America. We write, "For a time, every Asian woman trying to enter the United States had to prove beyond all doubt that she was not a sex worker." The idea of the foreign "other" is a blend of threat and attraction, a dangerous mix of "exotic eroticism" that can be used to justify sexual violence.[40] Women and girls held in the vast network of American immigration detention centers, according to the American Civil Liberties Union, are subject to widespread sexual abuse as the vulnerable, alien others.[41]

This erotic normalization of violence against women has deep roots within slavery, as well as colonialism, and carries enormous cultural weight today. It is a perversion and a perversion of considerable power.

We have traced some of sources of the "European-American male tradition," per Audre Lorde, that corrupts the erotic as creative power and harmony and employs it in objectifying, disempowering, and even injuring and killing women through theological and philosophical sources. The humanist traditions of the Enlightenment, developed around and through colonialism and the slave trade, are part of this tradition. That period of the Enlightenment was also the time in Western culture when the modern idea of the "erotic" was invented.

Enlightenment: Monstrous Reason

What is called the "Enlightenment" is a complex European intellectual movement of the late seventeenth and eighteenth centuries. Enlightenment thinkers emphasized reason and individualism rather than tradition. The Enlightenment was a revolutionary period, and it gave rise to political, social, scientific, artistic, and even gender and sexual experimentation. The Enlightenment also gave rise to experimentation in the nature of war. Remember that it was Leonardo da Vinci, artist and weapons maker, who encouraged realism in the depiction of war. The Spanish, for example, invented guerrilla warfare in resisting the incursions of Napoleon, starting the process of making the bodies of all citizens into the battlefield in war. The Enlightenment also contained a theological revolution, building on the Protestant Reformation and its political as well as religious rebellion against the Papacy and Catholicism and emphasizing the spirit in the life of the individual believer.

Huge changes swept over European and then the American colonies, with ideas of personal liberty giving rise to several political revolutions that could find an abundance of philosophers and political theorists to support their cause. What is less well-known about the Enlightenment, however, is that it was a period where the production of what is called "Erotica," or sexually explicit literature, simply exploded, as Peter Wagner argues in *Eros Revived: Erotica of the Enlightenment in England and America*. "No single person can possibly read the thousands of erotic books, pamphlets and broadsides" published in "the Age of Enlightenment." Wagner seems not to be a critic of this production, as he refers to the Enlightenment as "this macho century."[42]

Macho or not, there is a connection here between the rational and the erotic, especially in its normalization of violence and violence against women, that needs to be explored. It can best be seen in the artistic outpouring of the period as the contradictions are there to "see" if one will but look. There is a "Janus-face of Enlightenment," Thomas Crow, an art historian, writes, as "the very creation of art in an age of reason entailed a dangerous flirtation with madness. More than any other period in history, the Enlightenment was a time when artists questioned the received ideas of absolutist politics and hierarchized religion, embracing in their stead new subject matter painted in innovative styles."[43]

We have seen, in earlier chapters, how prominent eroticized violence against women became in the European painting of this period. According to Crow, whereas once the "violent or erotic narratives from ancient history and religion" may have served to channel "libidinal desire toward a socially sanctioned outlet," in the Enlightenment, they are promoted as violent and erotic for their capacity to create "psychic release." Thus, he says, "violence and eroticism . . . were now liable to pour forth in a flood." The use of the Rape of Tamar in European painting, following this script of using "violent and erotic narratives from ancient history and religion," is discussed in Chapter 2. But this interpretation by Crow has its own dangers for the potential to cause pain and injury to women's bodies, since he regards this "violence and eroticism" as a "psychic release" for some—one assumes males of privilege who viewed and even paid for this art. The reproduction of "violence and eroticism" would not have been a "release" but rather another trap for women for whom such representations simply normalized the violence against them in a new cultural and intellectual climate.

The Enlightenment is not all about reason, in other words. Crow uses the work of painter Francisco Goya to make his point about the "dangerous" flirtation of reason with madness in Enlightenment in his print #43 from the *Los Caprichos* (or *Follies*) from 1799, titled *The Sleep of Reason Produces Monsters*.[44] The print depicts the sleeping artist beset by monsters that represent evil in Spanish folktales. These monsters, especially when reinterpreted through critical physicality, pose a deep critique of the much-vaunted reason of the Enlightenment. The Enlightenment is a period where "freedom" and "liberty" did not extend to women, lower economic classes, and racial minorities, especially enslaved minorities, who were in fact often subject to eroticized violence. In fact, it should be argued that the outpouring of the erotic normalization of violence against women in this sexist, racist, classist context is precisely how the Western understanding of "freedom" gets constructed, so much so that the US Constitution could be written by male slaveholders about equal rights and freedom secured by the Creator and explicitly legalize the disenfranchisement of women and legalize slavery.

The life and work of the Marquis de Sade (1740–1814) makes much more sense in this analytical framework of critical physicality, where far from being an aberration, de Sade's philosophical discourses on pornography and violent sexual expression as eroticism are the "madness" that is the very close companion of reason, its "shadow," to use the term of Carl Jung. De Sade's life, and his sexual exploitation of very young girls as well as his servants of both sexes, has been seen as a radical expression of "liberty," but in fact, this "liberty" just flows right along the established lines of sexual, racial, and economic hierarchies of European culture. The married lover of the author of *The Story of O*, Jean Paulhan, was an admirer of the work of de Sade.

The erotic normalization of violence against women, and violence itself, is a structural part of Western understandings of freedom and democracy. This becomes clearer and clearer as the women's rights struggles of the nineteenth and twentieth centuries are met not only with derision but with the modern construction of the "War on Women."

Twentieth Century: Women's Rights and Women's Objectification

The War on Women in the twentieth century is, some respects, a "Dirty War" like the one waged by the Argentine military junta from 1975 to 1978 during which so many men and women were "disappeared." The difference is that women and girls in Euro-Atlantic culture both appear and disappear, though some quite literally are "disappeared," like immigrant women and girls killed along the US–Mexican border or the thousands of women and girls who are lured, trapped, or kidnapped into prostitution and domestic slavery.[45]

Elite white women, on the other hand, are thrust into an eroticized public presentation in the increasing cultural production of consumerism that dismembers them, establishes impossible white standards of "beauty" as a cultural norm, and cements the erotic desire for products by using this media-mediated form of violence. Their body "type" is so thin that many die of anorexia, fulfilling the ideal of *The Story of O* that the only way to be "perfectly feminine" is to be dead.

One narrative frame of the twentieth century in the West is that this is the century when "democracy" starts to work for women as they succeed in getting "equal rights" through the passage of the 1920 suffrage amendment. Yet it should also be recalled that the citizens of the United States were unable to get an Equal Rights Amendment passed in the 1970s. How can we best explain this?

One way to explain this seeming contradiction is to examine the underside of freedom and democracy. Yes, it is true that in the twentieth century, women not only get the vote but get increasing access to the workplace, first through the rising industrialization and factory work and then, during World War II, into many trades and fields. But women's bodies are eroticized in this period, making a mockery of their supposed gains as citizens and workers.

One important lesson we should take from *The Story of O* is that the erotic normalization of violence against women is constructed as dominance and submission. Certainly this was true in slavery and in the class context of industrialization. Sexual violence in the workplace was included in an 1887 report on *Women Wage Workers*. But despite strong efforts, especially in the last quarter of the twentieth century, a history of the struggle against sexual harassment in the workplace, up through the legal definition and the passage of laws, shows just how little change has actually taken place. Judges routinely refused, and refuse today, to connect gender, unwanted sexual advances, and employment, breaking them apart and sabotaging efforts to change workplace culture.[46] The assumption is still an eroticized version of "she must have been asking for it" logic.

A rising capitalist consumer culture adds substantially to eroticized violence against women. There is a construction of desire that takes place, indeed a violent construction of desire that has one end: selling products. Young white women (and women of color who resemble white women) are sliced and diced in cropped and now digitally altered photos that brutally (but softly) cut off their heads, shrink their bodies almost out of existence, enlarge their breasts, show them in submissive, childlike poses, and increasingly portray them caught in violently eroticized scenarios of bondage and sexual threat. They are so cropped, diced, and hideously thin that they disappear in plain sight. African American women, when shown at all, are often in "jungle" settings with animals, animal skins, and poses suggesting animalism. This is a strong echo of the Henri Rousseau theme of colonial eroticization of African women in jungle settings.[47]

Predatory capitalism is intimately, inextricably related to war as was noted earlier in the monstrous war in the Congo that is really about minerals needed to produce cell phones and other technology. That war too is conducted on the bodies of women and girls. What is called "disaster capitalism" has a close, even intimate relationship, with war. This is capitalism run amok around the world.[48]

Predatory capitalism constructs desire to sell its products, drawing on a well-spring of images and concepts from Western culture of the erotic as the degradation and submission of women. This construct is dangerously accelerating in the age of new media.

Videogames, Cyberstalking, and Videotaped Rapes

Anita Sarkeesian, a Canadian-American feminist, media critic, and blogger, reported death threats a day after she released a new episode of her series, *Feminist Frequency*. The blog deals with games that feature sexualized female victims or female characters introduced solely to highlight either a villain's aggression or provide motivation for players to complete their missions. This is where the "heroic" and the "erotic" in fact merge.

The effect of introducing these "mature themes," she argues in that posted episode, is the trivialization of painful experiences that are all too common. Sarkeesian alludes to a 2011 study by the Centers for Disease Control that found nearly one in five US women reported having suffered either a rape or an attempted rape, while one in four reported having been beaten by a domestic partner.

"When games casually use sexualized violence as a ham-fisted form of character development for the bad guys, it reinforces a popular misconception about gendered violence by framing it as something abnormal, as a cruelty committed only by the most transparently evil strangers," she says in the video. "In reality, however, violence against women—and sexual violence, in particular—is a common everyday occurrence, often perpetrated by 'normal men,' known and trusted by those targeted."[49] Sarkeesian has been relentlessly cyberstalked—that is, harassed electronically—and has received death threats, as noted earlier.[50]

A profoundly disturbing new trend that is certainly related to the contemporary construction of eroticized violence is videotaping the raping of women and girls and then posting the videos to the Internet. In May of 2013, three teenaged boys were caught after they allegedly raped a 12-year-old girl and posted the video of the attack on Facebook. In 2012, an 11-year-old Texas girl was raped and the rape was recorded on a cell phone and then circulated around the girl's school. In the same year in Halifax, a 17-year-old girl committed suicide after having allegedly been raped at 15 and a photo of the event circulated around her school. One of the best known of these kinds of attacks took place in Steubenville, Ohio, where in March 2013, two boys were convicted of raping a classmate and then sharing images from the night and "hundreds of text messages from more than a dozen cell phones." It was a collection of gleeful, callous boasting that the judge later declared "profane and ugly."[51]

This is an electronic version of the Enlightenment paintings of the rapes of women that became so prevalent in Western culture but magnified exponentially by the reach of social media. The power and dominance exercised by a rapist is visited upon the survivor of the rape again and again, but it is also power and dominance over other girls and women, as the images and the commentary weave a cybernet for rape culture.

The Porn of Class: Fifty Shades of Grey

Fifty Shades of Grey, an "erotic romance novel" by British author E. L. James, became a publishing phenomenon in 2011. It began as an ebook and a print-on-demand book and subsequently set the record as the fastest-selling paperback of all time.[52] The plot of the novel and its sequels revolves around a relationship between a recent college graduate, Anastasia Steele, and a young business executive and billionaire, Christian Grey. The novels are characterized by sexual practices of sadomasochistic bondage and the familiar dominance/submission erotic renderings of violence against women's bodies. The writing is remarkably poor, but that has hardly hurt its sales.

British tabloids have dubbed this book "mummy porn" as the buyers of these books are apparently "frustrated middle-aged mothers."[53] The feminist blogosphere quickly pointed out the "erotization of male dominance," of *Fifty Shades of Grey* and its similarities to *The Story of O* in terms of dominance/submission themes in the sexual violence.[54]

Yes, but why this and why now? When there is a huge surge in buying badly written books (*The Late Great Planet Earth* is another example), large cultural issues are in play, as Eva Illouz points out in her 2014 book, *Hard-Core Romance: "Fifty Shades of Grey," Bestsellers and Society*. Illouz analyzes what bestsellers reveal about the culture from which they come. The ideas in a bestseller are not, she argues, radical ideas but ideas and experiences that people already have and the bestseller articulates them.

Illouz postulates that *Fifty Shades of Grey* is part of women's self-help culture, where individual women are supposed to work on themselves (in this case on their sexual "freedom"). Illouz's academic treatment of *Fifty Shades of Grey*, however, ends up as an apology for the erotic fiction of violence against women. She argues the sadomasochistic relationship at its heart is "both a symbolic solution for and a practical technique to overcome" the deep-seated social contradictions of the relationship between men and women. Read as self-help books, the book advertising states, these "hard-core romance" novels are "a cultural fantasy as a sexual one, serving as a guide to a happier romantic life."[55]

This is quite similar to the "self-transcendence" interpretation of the erotic normalization of violence used to describe *The Story of O*, and it is just as much an apologetics for the accumulation of justifications of violence against women as the earlier commentaries on the 1954 novel.

The cultural analysis offered by Illouz actually bogs down in the self-help-culture swamp and fails to address the larger cultural shifts of our age. What is required is informed race or class analysis. Self-help culture for women in Western culture is an economic production that is class and race situated, and as was noted in the previous section, it functions to facilitate overconsumption. The more inadequate women feel, the more they will "work on themselves" with self-help and will buy products.

The cover of *Fifty Shades of Grey* is the key to a different analysis of why this form of eroticized bondage and submission took off right now. The cover shows a slightly loose, expensive, silver patterned, male tie. What is being eroticized, in my view, is dominance by male billionaires. The erotic rendering of vulture capitalism is the point. This novel makes greed erotic and that is the real fantasy. We fantasize that we like male CEOs dominating us, even though in real life they may look like the Koch brothers, the billionaire industrialists and funders of conservative politics. But it is not really these men who are eroticized, it is their money and power.

When eroticism is recruited in the service of normalizing violence against women, we have to ask over and over, "Who benefits?" The violence that is being normalized here, once again using women's bodies not as the end but as the means, is economic violence.

It is very easy to do this, as the author of *Fifty Shades of Grey* has demonstrated, because of the enormous amount of religious, philosophical, artistic, and historical productions of Western culture and their accumulated weight. These accumulations are there, always available to structure cultural control mechanisms. People today are anxious, and they are anxious about the economic polarization of our times into the increasingly large class of the poor and the "about-to-be-poor" middle class versus the obscenely wealthy upper class. When people are extremely anxious, they regress. Then these regressions can easily be focused as sexual fantasies of dominance and submission, and dominating women in order to subdue chaos (i.e., anxiety) is such a strong, strong theme over millennia.

The default structure of Western culture is the eroticized normalization of violence against women, and our anxious times are helping facilitate a resurgence of these deep themes.

The War on Women

The so-called War on Women that erupted in the 2012 presidential campaign was a slogan used to describe policies that penalize women's equal pay and reproductive rights and to point out the justifications for the continued assault on their bodies in rape and domestic violence.

As has been shown to this point, these policies and practices are the tip of the iceberg in terms of the actual War on Women that is the continued product of a deep-seated, multifaceted, and resilient set of ideas in Western culture. These ideas are critical for the persistence of the violence against women and the violence of war that so stubbornly resist efforts to end them.

Just War theory developed as an attempt to rein in unbridled war making, but it has been less than effective in totally restraining war and not been used at all to put a stop to the constant War on Women. The reason for this may very well be that Just War theory is highly dependent on these very same ideas, the ideas that drive both the heroic and the erotic misconceptions of violence in war and in the War on Women.

7

Just War and the War on Women

[R]ape victims searching for help at Bob Jones University in Greenville, S.C., were told to repent and seek out their own 'root sin' that caused them to be raped.

Tom Boggioni[1]

By a vote of 7 to 3, the City Council repealed the local law that makes domestic violence a crime.

The New York Times, October 11, 2011[2]

The phrase "War on Women" is not a metaphor. The War on Women is an actual war where women's bodies are the battlefield in a violent conflict where injury and death routinely occur.

The phrase the "War on Women," as has been noted, burst into political prominence in the American presidential contest of 2012 as tone-deaf statements by certain politicians on violence against women, as well as about women's equal rights, received intense scrutiny.[3] But the War on Women is not just a rhetorical problem. The War on Women is an actual war that is the product of strong forces in Western culture that drive the assumptions that normalize this violence, especially by shifting the blame for violence done to women onto the women victims themselves.

Women's bodies have been battlefields in the War on Women for millennia. Women have been dismembered to create a cosmos and elevate a warrior class as in the *Enuma Elish*, they have been battered and raped to justify the triumph of order over chaos in the formation of civilization as parts of the Hebrew bible demonstrate, and their bodies are philosophically "disappeared" in Greek philosophy. Over and over, the cosmic female body is splayed open for dismemberment, made into religiously justified "spoils of war," and physically and/or philosophically disappeared. These philosophical and religious sources are used to justify injury and death to women.

The War on Women shares many sources and norms with war itself, and it should be clear that it is not just women who have been injured and killed on battlefields in human history. Human beings have used the organized lethal force of war against each other and have justified the use of that force over the same millennia.

The difference, however, is that human beings have also tried to avoid or limit war over this same period and forms of moral reasoning on preventing or eliminating the use of lethal force have been developed. Historically, these have been Pacifism and Just War. A newer paradigm called Just Peace is a later addition to the list and will be considered in following chapters.[4]

Concepts in Western philosophy and Christian theology have provided and shaped all these theories on war and peace. Augustine and Aquinas are often cited as key architects in the development of Just War theory, though the classical tradition, through Plato and Aristotle as well as Cicero, played an important role. It can be argued that Just War theory was developed and then refined in the Christian tradition to create a space between divinely authorized war, or Crusade, with its nearly unlimited sense of moral justification for the use of force, and Pacifism, the dominant tradition of the first three centuries of Christian history and its various arguments against Christians participating in war as combatants.

Yet it is demonstrable that while Just War theory and Pacifism have been used to attempt to avoid or limit the use of force in injuring and death in war, Just War theory, and surprisingly to some, Pacifism, have been absent or ineffective in preventing or even limiting the War on Women. Sometimes, in fact, they can be shown to be complicit. Why would this be so?

Just War theory has not been used to limit or prevent the use of force on women in the War on Women precisely because its sources, in the classical and religious origins of the theory, are the very same ones that serve to normalize the War on Women and justify making women's bodies into battlefields. Pacifism has been slightly more useful in creating a rhetorical climate to challenge the War on Women, but Pacifism, as it developed in Western culture, shares many of the same attitudes toward women's bodies that facilitate violence against them leading to pacifist silence or complicity in violence against women.

The War on Women can also illuminate just why Just War theory has been largely ineffective in preventing or drastically limiting war itself. For example, Just War theory does not account for the erotic desire for violence that is part of how Western culture normalizes both the War on Women and war. As Chris Hedges argues in *War Is a Force That Gives Us Meaning*, "War is an enticing elixir," and he quotes General George S. Patton who once famously said, "Compared to war all other forms of human endeavor shrink to insignificance. God, I do love it so!" The general was not exaggerating about his love of war; some of the construction of love as desire is part of the drive to exercise power through physical force.

Critical Theory and the War on Women

Theoretical and practical struggle against violence against women has also been developed. In the last third of the twentieth century, many feminists and Womanists began to elucidate the way in which the violence against women is justified and how both Western philosophy and Christian theology have been complicit in excusing, hiding, or even requiring violence against women. While women in

Western culture had protested their treatment in church and society for centuries, these fields of critical work began to treat this issue in a sustained fashion.

Rosemary Radford Ruether, well-known feminist historian and liberation theologian, broke new ground from the late 1960s in her work connecting the history of the exploitation of women to major Christian texts, theologians, and doctrines. Ruether identified that the Christian theological contribution to violence against women was specifically to charge women as "disproportionately responsible for sin." While Genesis origin stories imply this, it is the New Testament narratives where this particular theological connection is made as in "First Timothy 2:12–14" that reads, "I do not allow women to teach or to have authority over men. They must keep quiet. For Adam was created first and then Eve. And it was not Adam who was deceived. It was the woman who was deceived and broke God's law."[5]

From these and other texts, Ruether argues, Christian theologians such as Aquinas, Luther, or Calvin spun "theories of women's inferiority."[6] She goes on to point out that not only was the work of these theologians crucial in "depriving them [women] of legal rights and excluding them from higher education and professional and leadership roles in church and society, it also took the form of certain legal justification of physical violence."[7]

The medieval Christian church gave some refuge to women who took holy orders, Ruether continues, but in ecclesiastical eyes, "[t]he married woman was the epitome of the carnal Eve," and she effectively deserved her subordinate status and physical punishment because of her sin. Canon lawyers argued the niceties of how a husband might beat his wife—that is, striking her but not whipping her like a slave. He could also confine her or starve her, though "not unto death." It is no wonder that medieval towns passed laws like that of the city of Villefranche that reads, "All the inhabitants of Villefranche have the right to beat their wives, so long as death does not ensue."[8] It cannot be overemphasized how much medieval Villefranche is a distant mirror for what is happening in the United States in the twenty-first century, as for example, when the City Council of Topeka, Kansas, repealed the law making domestic violence a crime, as was noted earlier.

Ruether, like many other liberation theologians, turns to the Hebrew prophets and Jesus of Nazareth, as well as other sources, to draw attention to the foundations of religious resistance to violence against women.

Important advances were also made in critical theory and violence against women beginning in the 1980s. Womanist Christian theology and ethics emerged in that decade, especially with the work of Katie Geneva Cannon and Dolores Williams.[9] "Womanist" is a term originally coined by Alice Walker in her book *In Search of Our Mothers' Gardens* and means "A black feminist or feminist of color."[10] Womanist theology and ethics put the bodies, minds, and spirits of African American women at the center of the theological task, as well as the violence done to them and their communities through racism and the institutions of patriarchy. All these factors interlock and reinforce each other in the violence done to African American women. Williams writes, "I remember hearing the bloodcurdling screams of the woman in the house next to ours when her husband beat her for acting uppity—showing off her education, he said. She had been a schoolteacher."[11]

Womanist theologians and ethicists identify the physical, sexual, and existential violence of slavery and its aftermath as a crucial factor in their work. Shawn Copeland's scholarship is particularly instructive in bringing critical race theory to bear in a critique of white Enlightenment thinkers and their ideologies of racial superiority over any and all other races. Copeland juxtaposes this European construct with the narratives of emancipated black slave women and their realization of their own personhood. Copeland uses this realization to examine the often antagonistic relationship Christianity has had with the body, and she posits the need to reclaim the centrality of the incarnation for a changed praxis.[12]

Traci West, in *Wounds of the Spirit*, identifies specific social mechanisms that contribute to the reproduction of intimate violence. West insists that cultural beliefs as well as institutional practices must be altered if we are to combat the reproduction of violence and suggests methods of resistance which can be utilized by victim-survivors, those in the helping professions, and the church.

Violence against African American women's bodies, minds, and spirits is a constant theme in Womanist writing. Location matters, and it matters tremendously for what kind of change either becomes possible or is strangled at birth. Womanist critical theory causes us to ask, "Which woman's body, in which context, and under which social, political, intellectual, and religious regime?"

These critical perspectives are crucial to examine the legacy of Just War theory in regard to the War on Women.

The Just War on Women

Mary Potter Engel, liberation theologian and historian, has spelled out exactly how the rationales for violence against women have been justified, and she parallels them with the criteria of Just War theory.

Just War theory, as it has developed, has a number of specific criteria, traditionally six, that cover the justification for the use of violence (*jus ad bello*) and some regarding how the violence may or may not be administered (*jus in bello*).

Engel puts popular French literature of 1150 through 1565 and its astonishing amount of tales of justifying wife beating side-by-side with several of the criteria of Just War theory. This literature includes rhymed tales of the "follies of family life" that were first repeated by traveling storytellers over and over and then which passed into written tales of the same stories. Added to this cultural formation of attitudes on violence against wives were the "exempla, brief concrete illustrations of vice and virtue used by uneducated priests to teach their illiterate congregations religious or moral doctrines."[13]

All the tales, both oral and written down, combined with the sermon manuals, Engel argues, provide a wealth of material that is generated in European culture that can be used to understand how Western culture normalizes violence against women as part of its social fabric. What she found was the "normalization and control of gender relations" that reveal the relationship among "the ideology of subordination and the practice of violence" that was supported in both secular and ecclesiastical laws.[14] In other words, for the citizens of medieval Villefranche to decide that it is perfectly legal for men to beat their wives, though not to death, and for the citizens of twenty-first-century Topeka, Kansas, to effectively decide the same thing, there has to be a wealth of cultural and religious supports for the idea that this violence is actually justified.

The same rationales for deciding that war is justified—that is, Just War theory— are apparent in the French popular literature of the Middle Ages.

Violence, whether in war or wife beating, is not simply granted carte blanche. There has to have been provocation so that, the first tenet of Just War theory— that is, "just cause"—can be fulfilled. A nation, or a husband, has just cause when there are "acts of aggression" that are "unjust" and that "gives a group a just cause to defend itself." Wives, per this ideological inversion, are the aggressors and this gives husbands just cause.

As she read these medieval sermons and tales, Engel reveals, the outline of this justification became shockingly clear. The ideology of gender inequality mandated that violence be used by husbands to control wives. This is the pattern: "All women are created to be subordinate to men. All wives, therefore, are subordinate to their husbands. Because the health of society depends on this ordered relationship, if a wife is insubordinate in any way, not only domestic peace but the entire social fabric is threatened. The husband, then, has not only a right but a duty to discipline her. This social responsibility may be called 'the office of chastisement.'"[15] Thus it is the *wife* who is the aggressor because she has dared step out of her subordinate role (or she is accused of having done so). This provocation then justifies, actually demands, that the husband reassert his authority.

The husbands portrayed in the French folks tales and sermons, per the idea of a "just battering" tradition when it comes to domestic violence, had just cause because they were provoked by the misbehavior of wives who would not be submissive. But this is not the extent of the conditions of Just War theory that appear to be used in a Just Battering tradition in the Christian West.

In fact, Engel argues, all six of the criteria commonly found in Just War theory are present in these sources. The first is

> the *condition of just cause*, based on the assumption of female subordination. Second and third, the discipline must be administered after other corrections have failed and in moderation, that is, so as to correct effectively (i.e., not maim or kill). These are the conditions of *last resort and just means*. Fourth and fifth, the wife must be disciplined not out of rage or revenge but out of love, with an aim to preserve the peace of the household and the right order of society. These are the conditions of *right intention and just end*, which is based on the distinction between punishment and correction. Sixth, it must be the husband as head of the family who administers the blows. This is the *condition of right authority*, based on the assumption of male dominance. Violence against wives is acceptable moral and social behavior when some or all of these conditions are met.[16]

A fundamental theme that runs through all these conditions of Just Battering of women, as represented in Just War theory, is power and subordination. In the Western philosophical and Christian theological traditions, this understanding of a hierarchy of human authority is crucial to any notion of justified violence in the home, in society, and in war, as is argued in Shawn Copeland's work cited earlier.

Power and subordination are cornerstones of the battered-wife syndrome in evangelical and fundamentalist Christianity to the point where God becomes the author of the battering of wives by husbands. There are more blatant examples of excusing abusive male authority among stricter proponents of complementarianism and submission theology. In June 2007, professor of Christian theology at Southern Baptist Theological Seminary, Bruce Ware, told a Texas church that women often bring abuse on themselves by refusing to submit. And Debi Pearl, half of a husband-and-wife fundamentalist child-training ministry team, as well as author of the bestselling submission manual *Created to Be His Help Meet*, writes that submission is so essential to God's plan that it must be followed even to the point of allowing abuse. "When God puts you in subjection to a man whom he knows is going to cause you to suffer," she writes, "it is with the understanding that you are obeying God by enduring the wrongful suffering."[17]

Ideologies of power and subordination do not begin with Christianity; in the Greek classical tradition, power and submission were also related concepts. Ideologies of dominance and subordination as "natural" root themselves in Aristotle. As has been noted in Chapter 3, Aristotle posits a natural superiority of maleness and form, and inferiority of femaleness and matter. This whole power structure is fixed and immutable, as "it is clear that the rule of soul over the body, and of the mind and the rational element is natural and expedient . . . the male is by nature superior, and the female inferior; the one rules, and the other is ruled; this principle of necessity extends to all mankind."[18] This provides what we might call a biologically based defense of the use of force, when extrapolated, to justify violence in the home and in the capture of slaves in war.

Aristotle's justification for the use of force is developed in the same section as the "natural and expedient" rule of the male over the female. The use of force is justified due to a hierarchical notion of biology in regard to women. This effectively undermines his claim that the violence in war, in this section in regard to the capture of slaves, must subject to some notions of "justice." This reveals a major flaw in Just War thinking, in fact, because the use of force will always be qualified first by a natural hierarchy, and as will be discussed later, this means the use of force on peoples and nations deemed "inferior" will first be rationalized by a presumption of natural domination and subordination and only then subject to Just War criteria.

In regard to just cause, then, biologically fixed notions of power hierarchies will bias the use of force toward the self-justification of the dominant over the subordinate and undermine the concept of justice. In fact, according to Aristotle, when force is used by the virtuous (i.e., a dominant member of society) for the good, it is not monstrous because "in a certain manner *virtue when it obtains resources has in fact very great power to use force, and the stronger party always possesses superiority in something that is good*, so that it is thought that force cannot be devoid of goodness, but that the dispute is merely about the justice of the matter."

This notion of the goodness of the use of force on women and slaves and in conquering in war as separable from the "justice of the matter" is the predominant reason those in power feel justified in their use of violence despite theories designed to prevent or limit the use of force.

The Christian theological heritage of this claim of the "virtuous" use of force can be seen, as again was noted earlier, in Augustine. Augustine believed Christians could wage war in peaceful ways to attain the end of peace even as the father in the family can physically chastise women, children, and slaves to maintain order and obedience.[19] This is the major flaw in his thinking and thus in Just War thinking as it is a physical absurdity that a husband "peacefully" beats his wife and children. The lens of women's bodies as battlefield reveals that there is no such thing as engaging in violence and justifying it as peace. The use of violence causes pain and harm to human bodies and can even cause the death of human bodies. Whatever "order" is established or reestablished by this pain and injury is not peace. It is not peace because this is an order created and maintained by the threat of physical destruction.

Any subjugated person or people are viewed as an implicit threat to a hierarchy of power and authority, and force is justified then to remove this threat in advance of any actual threat. In my view, this is actually a seventh justification for battering of wives implicit in Engel's analysis of these French folktales that she does not make explicit but that has become highly contested in the twenty-first century. This is the doctrine of preemption, today what has been called the "Bush Doctrine."[20] In this perspective, violence is justified to prevent what is presumed or feared to be an aggression that has not occurred and that may not even be imminent. According to Engel, in the French folktales, all women are portrayed as having evil natures as the "Gateway to Ruin, Temptress, Adulteress, Deceiver, or Shrew." All women have these evil tendencies by nature because they are all Eve who caused the Fall, the temptress who led Adam into sin and got them both kicked out of the Garden of Eden. Thus women, as descendants of the sinner Eve, are always deserving of punishment even when they are not, in fact, transgressing male rule in any way. "The *fabliaux* contain several examples of husbands beating their wives because they 'feared their wives would commit adultery or squander their resources in other ways.'"[21] This is exactly the Bush Doctrine, especially as a justification for the broad use of force against wives without specific provocation.

It should be emphasized that Aristotle, Augustine, and their religious and cultural heirs as represented in the medieval folktales and sermons are one aspect of how a Just Battering as well as a Just Rape tradition comes to be established in religion, law, and culture in the modern West, especially in the United States. But without the addition of critical race theory, and especially from a Womanist perspective, any particular modern example can be incompletely or even incorrectly analyzed.

As an example, one might think that idea that women "provoke" violence against themselves as seen in the medieval French folktales and sermons was part of a more recent controversy, that of football player Ray Rice and his then-fiancé, Janay Palmer. After a first video was released of Rice dragging what appeared to be the unconscious Palmer out of an elevator, Rice was suspended for two games.

ESPN sportscaster Stephen Smith made rambling comments on a sports debate show that included several remarks that seemed to blame women who "provoke wrong actions," as well about "elements of provocation" by women as a factor in battering of women. This produced a storm of criticism of Smith, including Smith's ESPN colleague Michelle Beadle, who called him out on Twitter, emphasizing that "violence isn't the victim's issue, it's the abuser's."[22] A second videotape was then released showing more of the violence that knocked Janay Palmer unconscious, and Rice was cut from the Ravens and suspended indefinitely by the NFL.[23] But men's-rights advocates on the social media thread r/MensRights continued to blame Janay Palmer for "poking the bear" and increased their defense of Ray Rice.[24] The NFL's attempts to protect its image and profit, not to address issues of domestic violence, can be seen in its incoherent responses.

Domestic violence by players in the NFL does, however, have some overlap with a Just War/Just Battering tradition. In an article on how the NFL and the police look the other way when wives try to report battering by their husbands, a wife of a Saints player who chose not to be named said she was severely beaten by her husband and neighbors called the police. Instead of arresting him, the cops came and chatted with him about the game. The next day, a players representative called her. "[The rep] said she called to 'check on me.' . . . I knew what the call meant. I think every wife knows innately what that call means: 'Your husband needs this job, and you don't want to take his dream away now do you?' I lost more than my dignity. I lost my voice, my self-confidence, my identity. I was just a football player's wife, collateral damage."[25]

Collateral damage is most often used as a military term where noncombatants are accidentally or unintentionally killed or wounded and/or noncombatant property damaged as result of the attack on legitimate enemy targets. In Just War theory, a war can still be considered "just" if noncombatants are killed, it is just not moral to target them. A battered NFL wife considered herself "collateral damage" in the War on Women, as she is not the primary concern of her husband, of the NFL, or of law enforcement. The laws about justice do not apply to her, as her injuries are accidental to the main target, protecting the corporate profits.

Which bodies are battered in which ways and how these actions are considered justified or unjustified forms a large part of how critical physicality both grounds and complicates traditions that serve to justify violence against women.

In addition, the existence of such traditions in Western culture of justifying violence against women exposes the flaws in Just War theory. Just War theory has not, in fact, been very successful in either preventing war or even limiting it despite the existence of a strong set of criteria designed to do just that. The fact that violence against women is so often justified by *using these same criteria*, the very criteria that are supposed to limit or prevent war, reveals that the philosophical and theological sources of Just War theory are themselves skewed toward the very conditions that are conducive to violence.

A Just Rape Tradition

Is there a parallel Just Rape tradition in Western culture to that of Just Battering? To some extent, yes, but the Just Rape tradition does not line up with Just War theory in the same way that domestic battering has been shown to do.

Rape has occupied a different category in Western legal history than domestic violence because it has more often been illegal. But laws prohibiting rape have frequently defined rape as a property crime by one man (the rapist) against another man (the one whose property the woman raped is established to be). In fact, there has never been a commonly accepted legal definition of rape in the West, as the term "legitimate rape" used in the 2012 elections shows. It was only in 2012, in fact, that the Federal Bureau of Investigation revised its definition of rape from "the carnal knowledge of a female, forcibly and against her will," to include any form of forced sexual penetration of a man or a woman and to include "nonforcible rape."[26]

When rape passed out of the legal definition of property crime of one male against another, the redefinition of rape in the United States became part of race, gender, and economic struggles beginning in the nineteenth century. For rape to even occur, some seemed to argue, a woman had to physically fight back, "proving" that she did not consent. A verbal "no" was not sufficient and is not, in some quarters, even sufficient today. There is a strong bias in Western culture to deny that rape has occurred and to limit the focus of what can be considered rape. There has been a continuing effort by dominant males to define rape out of existence and redefine it as consent on the part of the victim of sexual assault. If any sexual penetration occurred, in other words, the woman must have consented. In 1913, a doctor wrote that rape wasn't really easy, because "the mere crossing of the knees absolutely prevents penetration . . . a man must struggle desperately to penetrate the vagina of a vigorous, virtue-protecting girl." Rape has been successfully prosecuted in American history, but these charges and convictions have been highly politically, racially, and economically dependent, as Estelle B. Freedman argues in her book *Redefining Rape: Sexual Violence in the Era of Suffrage and Segregation* demonstrates. Freedman argues that the effort to define and thus prosecute rape is struggle for who gets to be a citizen in the United States and thus who gets to write law.[27]

Varied definitions of rape have thus been part of a political, social, and racial struggle, Freedman argues, and undertaken by "generations of women's rights and racial justice advocates" who "have contested the narrow understanding of rape as a brutal attack on a chaste, unmarried white woman by a stranger, typically portrayed as an African American male." The history of slavery and Jim (and Jane) Crow laws have contributed to the history of rape as legal on the bodies of slave women, a pretext for lynching in the anti-emancipation backlash, and a "private matter" in more recent times. "On a rhetorical level," Freedman contends, "the constructions of black women as always consenting, white women as duplicitous, and black men as constant sexual threats all justified the very limitations on citizens that reinforced white men's sexual privileges."[28] The goal, as is often the goal, is the unfettered access to the territory of women's bodies without legal, moral, or social constraint.

A Just Rape tradition depends heavily on the idea that some bodies, in this case those of African people, can be owned by others. The body and the will are separated, as the enslaved woman or girl has no will other than that of the slave-holder. In this case, Brownmiller's groundbreaking volume is partly incorrect in its title, *Against Our Will*. Slavery in Western culture broke apart the body and the will. This is similar to the way patriarchal understandings of marriage subjugated the will of the wife, but it is not identical. Since it was legal, under various laws in slaveholding US states, to kill a slave, it can be argued that the breaking of body and will in slavery was more fundamental.[29]

African American women, therefore, have been considered nearly "unrapeable" as their very being was defined, and continues to be defined, as sexually available. Prostitute bodies are "unrapeable" as Rita Brock and I contend in our *Casting Stones* book.[30]

Even sexual violence and abuse against LGBT and particularly transgender bodies was basically unrecognized legally until March 2013. Leading up to its reauthorization, lawmakers worked to include LGBT individuals in the Violence against Women Act (VAWA). Specifically, the act states that social-service organizations receiving funds from the VAWA cannot discriminate against battered and abused individuals based on "sexual orientation" or "gender identity" and may not "ask questions about the beneficiary's anatomy or medical history or make burdensome demands for identity documents." The inclusion of LGBT individuals in VAWA will aid them in receiving social services such as transitional housing and victim and legal assistance.[31]

But sometimes, the legal is not even the most difficult issue in analyzing rape in this critical physicality framework. It is the struggle over whether any violence actually occurred in regard to rape.

As part of the contemporary struggle against rape, colleges and universities are being pushed into better policies and education on rape. In September 2014, discussing Ohio State University's new policy (discussed more at length later in this chapter) that mandates students get explicit consent before engaging in sexual activity with another person, conservative commentator Rush Limbaugh precipitated a storm of controversy. Limbaugh argued that a woman saying "no" to sex can mean "yes." "How many guys, in your own experience with women, have learned that no means yes if you know how to spot it? . . ."[32] Limbaugh is a kind of cultural bellwether that taps into white, male, hetero-patriarchal views and fosters a politics of resentment. Limbaugh articulates the entitlement argument regarding women's bodies. His view, well established in Western culture, is that rape actually rarely occurs because, if sexual activity takes place, women are consenting to some extent, even when they refuse. The undercurrent of this attitude is that men are entitled to sexual activity with women, and women actually do not have the right to say "no." Hence rape does not actually exist in almost all cases.

Limbaugh's comments are symbolic of the "define rape out of existence" perspective. But they incompletely represent how the Just Rape tradition in the United States functions, whether on a college campus or anywhere else. The female body is never a body without a social, political, economic, racial, and gender context. This does not limit but rather expands the idea of a Just Rape tradition, since it shows how women's bodies are not generic battlefields but rather specific battlefields in specific struggles over specific territories. The race, socioeconomic status, sexual orientation, national origin, previous sexual history, and even dress, as well as a host of other factors will all enter in to the struggle over defining rape, and these provide a host of barriers to successfully ending it.

Another location of the struggle to define rape, both historically and in contemporary terms, is colonial conquest. Wars of colonial conquest were (and are) wars to acquire territory to occupy and dominate.

Colonization in the War on Women

The war of colonial conquest of Native American peoples is crucial in the effort to understand the depth of the Just Rape tradition. Rape is not well understood when it is seen only as a tool of patriarchy; it is also a primary "tool of racism and colonialism," as attorney, professor, and Native American activist, Andrea Smith, argues.[33] In fact, Smith, quoting Ann Stoler, explains how "racialized colonization" functions as a way to make it acceptable "to put [certain people] to death in a society of normalization."[34]

The physicality of this death-dealing normalization thorough rape, mutilation, and murder must be witnessed in its specific physical horror. Massacres of Indians by settlers and armies routinely included rape and sometimes mutilation and the creation of "trophies" of body parts. "I heard one man say that he had cut a woman's private parts out, and had them for exhibition on a stick . . . I also heard of numerous instances in which men had cut out the private parts of females, and stretched them over their saddle-bows and some of them over their hats."[35]

Far from a restraint on such brutality, specific accounts grossly implicate Christianity in these genocidal wars and in the atrocities.[36] The Sand Creek Massacre, which truly lives in infamy for mutilations and "trophy" taking of massacred Indian bodies was led by Colonel Chivington, a former Methodist minister. An estimated 70–163 peaceful Cheyenne and Arapaho, most of whom were women, children, and infants, were killed and mutilated by Chivington's troops. These soldiers took scalps and other body parts as trophies, including human fetuses and male and female genitalia. There was an investigation of the massacre by the Joint Committee on the Conduct of the War. The conduct of Chivington and his men was condemned, but there were no criminal charges.

In the perspective of critical physicality, the racist colonizing of Native Americans requires not only their deaths but also the actual remaking of their bodies. Their futures are also targeted, as can be seen in the massacre and mutilation of women, including pregnant women as well as children and infants. These bodies of a specific people and culture are made into a kind of consumer product of a different culture, a conquering culture. The actual trade in objects made of the skin of Native Americans places this in the context of profit-generation. In colonial domination as a tactic of war and the War on Women, it is not enough to take the land; the physicality of the conquered must be absorbed and transformed into something else, a profit center.

The taking of physical trophies from the mutilated corpses of massacred Indians and turning them into profit centers casts the controversy over the name "Redskins" for the football team that plays in Washington, DC, into sharp relief. Native American activists against this team name are clear: "'Redskins' is part of that mentality from colonial times when our people were hunted by soldiers and mercenaries who were paid for the scalps of our men, women and children. How can anyone claim this is a proud tradition to come from? The labels, racism and hatred that Indian people continue to experience are directly tied to those racial slurs. Let me be clear: The racial slur 'redskins' is not okay with me. It's never going to be okay with me. It's inappropriate, damaging and racist."[37] And it is very, very profitable, as racist and colonial conquest continues to be.

The commodification of Native American bodies in sports images, especially in regard to the reference to bodily dismemberment per the logo and name of the Washington football team, is a colonial context for the War on Women.

Video-game culture is another example. In 1982, a video game made for the Atari 2600 by Mystique, a producer of "adult" video games for that system, released *Custer's Revenge*. The game also came to be known as "Westward Ho" and "The White Man's Game." The player of the game takes on the character of Custer, the American General at Little Big Horn. In this version, however, Custer as the player character is wearing nothing but a cavalry hat, boots, and a bandana and has a visible erection. The goal of the game is for the Custer player to reach and rape a naked Native American woman tied to a pole on the opposite side of the screen. The Custer character has to dodge arrow attacks to reach the woman.[38] When Mystique went out of business, they sold the rights to the game to a company called Playaround. In a vivid example of the reversals of which the Western colonial mentality is capable, Playaround changed the game, calling it *General Retreat/ Westward Ho*.[39] They reversed the male and female roles, and it is the woman who has to overcome cannonballs launched at her in order to have sex with Custer. It was released only in Europe.

The revised title of *Westward Ho* is enormously instructive as it speaks to the sexualizing of violently colonized women and girls, equating them with prostitutes and, by extension, desirous of even violent forms of sex. This is a common projection of dominant, racist, patriarchal cultures onto the bodies of women and girls in prostitution.[40]

Gendered analyses of justifications of rape are partial, especially when they are taken out of racial, political, social, and economic contexts. The colonial mentality extends to globalization today and informs how the construction of desire relates to the justification of war, as well as the justifications for the War on Women.

"You Know You Want It": The Virtuous Use of Force

The projection of desire onto people and nations that are the objects for conquest is a completely overlooked aspect of Just War theory, and it is a crucial reason the

War on Women, in the violence of both battering and sexual assault, has been considered just in so many ways. The failure to recognize the role of desire in the longing to exercise force as dominance and control undermines the effectiveness of Just War theory in actually preventing and restraining war, as the real motivations for conquest remain hidden.

One example from the wars of conquest of Native Americans by the United States of this unarticulated and yet very real reversal of desire can be found in the first State of the Union Address by President Martin Van Buren in 1837. Van Buren argues that Indians benefit from being conquered by the Americans. Rather than a violent assault in conquest, it is a form of rescue. Van Buren refers to these brutal wars as a "system of removing the Indians west of the Mississippi, commenced by Mr. Jefferson in 1804, has been steadily persevered in by every succeeding President, and may be considered the settled policy of the country." That this removal was in large part genocidal is hidden and recast as benefit and, in fact, as protection from "evil practices." The clear implication of the terms used is that the genocide was actually a divinely inspired (blessing) of Native American people who need to be saved from themselves and their evil ways.

Native American women in particular were told that the conquest of their people, their sexual violation, and their eventual imprisonment on "tribal lands" at the hands of the conquerors was for their own good. Native American women needed to be saved from their own culture. Andrea Smith notes that "Thomas Jefferson argued that Native women 'are submitted to unjust drudgery. This I believe is the case with every barbarous people. It is civilization alone which replaces women in the enjoyment of their equality.'"[41]

This amazing rationale by Jefferson for raping, slaughtering, robbing, and eventually confining Native Americans as a form of civilization that is of benefit to Indian women is strikingly similar to what was said to justify the US war in Afghanistan, the so-called Operation Enduring Freedom. There was a rhetoric of "saving Afghan women" that produced flights of rhetoric about civilizational "clashes" and theologies of "good versus evil" cast as the freedom-loving West versus the fundamentalist tyranny of the Afghan government demonstrated by the ill-treatment of Afghan women.

Yet as Ainab Rahman notes in her article, "The War for Afghan Women," "[d]espite the rhetoric of the US moral crusade for the liberation of Afghan women, women's actual security and empowerment have yet to be prioritized in the decision-making and peacekeeping processes on both the policy and grassroots level in the war in Afghanistan." Afghan women's lives, health, education, and full citizenship were never a "key policy objective" for the US government, the women were merely a handy symbol. From ignoring Afghan women before 9/11 to trading away women's rights and even safety in making deals with the Taliban under the guise of "reconciliation," Afghan women's situations have become less and less secure.[42]

The distorted view that a war of conquest is about rescuing women when it is really about geopolitical and, especially, global economic issues that have nothing to do with women is most often disastrous for women themselves. One such example is the US coalition with the Northern Alliance, a group that is "'notoriously misogynistic' and 'comprised of soldiers who lead campaigns of rape, torture, and slaughter in Afghanistan before the Taliban takeover.' They were also known for their frequent participation in the abduction of young girls and women, gang rapes and lust-based murders."[43]

In fact, engaging in poorly conceived, and mostly rhetorical, exercises in the "liberation of Afghan women" created an Afghan backlash against the foreign invader that was then refought on the bodies of Afghan women. Sexualized violence against women was justified as repelling an external attacker and preserving traditional Afghan culture from alien Western practices. Thus the Taliban attacking women physically and sexually to "control" them and reestablish "traditional Afghan culture" was framed as self-defense from the incursions of Western invaders.

What the colonialist either does not see or, in my view, willingly ignores, is that wars of conquest routinely make women's situations worse when thin rationales for "women's liberation" are used as part of the justification for the attack. That translates directly into physical and even sexual attacks. Rahman underlines this crucial aspect of war and its connection to the global War on Women. "Conditions of war tend to exacerbate pre-existing patriarchal behaviors and attitudes, which may intensify as a responsive mechanism to undergoing oppression, being involved in conflict and/or as a 'backlash against occupying forces,' and often lead to a reinforcement of neocolonial paradigms."

Wars of colonial conquest make women's situations more vulnerable in both the violence against them perpetrated by the invaders and the violence against them justified by some in the culture under attack as repelling foreign values. If ever there were an instance where it is crystal clear that women's bodies are battlefields, this is it. Women's bodies are trampled, bruised, raped, mutilated, and killed as the very site of struggle *by both sides*. The fiction of the virtuous use of force, especially when it is wrapped in a rhetoric of "protecting native women," is dangerously delusional as witnessing what actually happens to women's bodies in these conflicts testifies.

It is crucial to understand what actually happens to women, children, and to whole populations in wars that are presented to the public as "Just Wars" and also to understand why violence against women is so often justified. These two issues are rarely considered together, but when they are, the whole Just War framework is revealed as deeply flawed, and ways to improve theories to prevent or limit violence, both violence against women and the violence of war, can be found.

The Flaws in Just War Theory

"Would an Invasion of Iraq Be a Just War?" was a question considered by a panel of experts at the United States Institute of Peace just prior to the invasion.[44] Four experts on Just War theory, myself included, debated the issues.

The various positions on the panel illustrate some of the parameters of an appraisal of the Just War tradition, though working on this book has persuaded me that the critique needs to be taken much further. It is the case that the traditional

Just War position can yield some useful insights, especially in regard to when war should not be undertaken, as both Gerald Powers, director of the Office of International Justice and Peace of the US Conference of Catholic Bishops, and George Hunsinger, professor at Princeton Theological Seminary, effectively argued. There was no extreme, imminent danger, and the risk in causing civilian suffering in particular was great from a "long drawn-out bloody war."

Robert Royal, president of the Faith and Reason Institute, however, brushed all the civilian suffering aside and the concerns about the shedding of blood in a protracted conflict and said confidently, "I take as axiomatic that the classic conditions of *jus in bello* [the rules for conducting war in a just fashion] can be reasonably achieved by American military planners. And the traditional *jus ad bellum* [the rules for whether a nation can get into a war] principles—just cause, right intention, right authority, reasonable hope of success, and proportionality of good achieved over harm—can be met as well."

Not one thing Royal argued ended up to be true, especially the "proportionality of good achieved over harm," not only in light of a half a million deaths and the policies of torture and rendition, but also in light of the massive suffering of the population as illustrated in the deformation of children's bodies and the blighted lives of Iraqis suffering from cancer in Fallujah.

My argument was fundamentally different from those of my colleagues at the panel on Just War and the Iraq War in 2002, however; I did not stay within Just War theory but contended it was an "old narrative" that will not help us deal with these times. I said, "[T]his is not the time of Aquinas or Augustine; there is no orderly universe just waiting to be upheld again." I argued that the easy assumption by someone like Royal that, 'oh, yes, we can conduct war justly' is the worst of this unwarranted confidence that there is a rational way to conduct war. There isn't. This is a convenient fiction that allows us to ignore and excuse "the lust for power that underlies both globalization and worldwide militarism." Any assumption that the Iraq War could be waged "justly" then became completely morally bankrupt in the face of "shock and awe" that rained down fire and death on Iraqi civilians—the bloody, bruised, and injured bodies of the tortured and in light of women's wombs made toxic by our bombs. It follows then that Christian theologies that aid and abet us in turning away from deformed children, tortured bodies, and those who bled and died as fire rained down from the sky in March 2002 are also revealed to be bankrupt.

There are three areas where the deep flaws in Just War need to be further examined in light of the fact that the War on Women has been so consistently defended as just in Western philosophy, religion, law, culture, and practice. This wholesale justification of violence against women in turn sheds light on how manifestly unjust wars, and the Iraq War is only one of many examples, have routinely been declared "just" despite violating all the criteria of Just War.

These three areas are the lust for power, the presumption of race and gender hierarchies, and the "nonexistence" of the body.

The Lust after Power

There are clearly flaws in Augustine's body/soul dualism, but one thing Augustine got right is his conviction that the chief moral flaw in war is the lust for power.

Augustine argues that war is horrible when waged out of the "lust for power" and the "passion for inflicting harm"; under those conditions, it is sin. He even laments the pain and suffering caused by wars, as one "thinks with pain on all these great evils, so horrible, so ruthless" and has to "acknowledge that this is misery." But this is where Augustine's body/soul dualism trips him up, because it is not the physical injury and death per se that renders a war unjust but actually the inflaming of the passions in desire to injure and lust after power.[45]

But the "lust after power"—the eroticized normalization of the desire for violence—is always present in the decision to go to war and in the making of war. Always present. But the lustful desire for power is hidden, wrapped in the "it's for your own good" fantasies as described earlier in relationship to the war against American Indians. This came to dominate the interventionist perspectives on the wars in Afghanistan and Iraq. Former Vice-President Dick Cheney is perhaps the poster child of this point of view. According to former British Prime Minister Tony Blair, Cheney "thought the world had to be made anew, and that after 11 September, it had to be done by force and with urgency. So he was for hard, hard power. No ifs, no buts, no maybes."[46]

Surely the term "hard power" is easily understood as a phallic metaphor. It does not take feminist or Womanist critical theory to understand how sexualized such a term is and is meant to be. It is an aggressive representation of power in foreign policy as a male erection. The rape connotations are not difficult to see either, especially when contrasted with the other, "companion" term, "soft power," meaning cultural power, a "feminized" alternative.[47]

Hard power as a phallic metaphor is key to understanding the culture of war and the culture of violence against women in Western society. There is an entitlement ideology that a particular gender, race, or nation is entitled to exercise power over others and their very autonomy is literally insulting and provoking. Per Augustine's insight that what is unjust about war is a "passion for inflicting harm," what stimulates that passion is the rebellious autonomy of others.

Economic autonomy of others as provocation for the desire for power is a crucial aspect of what is missing from Just War theory. The missing dimension of desire for control contributes to understanding the question of whether the attack on Iraq was about oil.

Yes, signs abounded at rallies that read "No Blood for Oil," but what kind of economic calculation about oil went into the actual attack? Even more conservative economic theorists finally acknowledged, "Of course it's about oil, it's very much about oil, and we can't really deny that."[48]

But even a "Western-orientated Iraq" or the prospect of access to oil and the fears of oil dependency are insufficient explanations. The fundamental issue is the desire for power over others, a desire to remake other countries in our image: not control of their oil, control of them. And like the Western justification for battering of wives as "provoked" by them daring to be even mildly autonomous or the responsibility of women for their own rape because of what they wear, do, or say, the violence against Iraq is justified because it is provoked. In a Just War sense, countries that have the audacity to act on their own interests rather than those of the United States or even more broadly of the West are just asking to be invaded.

It is incorrect, therefore, to see this critique of Just War as merely a critique of how this theory neglects economic calculations. As Jason Stearns so well argues in *Dancing in the Glory of Monsters* about the Congo War, it is important to avoid "Congo reductionism" and reduce the conflict to "Western greed for raw minerals"; "Rwandan meddling"; or just "globalization," "sexual violence," or "conflict minerals." In fact, argues Stearns, analyzing the Congo War is the opposite of Occam's famous razor—that is, the simplest solution is the best one. "Get into the grime and grit of the story, rub up against its intricacy," he advises.[49]

Violence against women or economic globalization or any other factor is distorting when used as a single lens to illuminate the multiple engines of conflict. What connects them, however, is the hidden nature of the lust for power as control. When the lust for power is hidden rather than revealed, as it is by Just War criteria such as just cause, the deep longing for power over others is never examined. Simple equations ranging from "opening markets" to "fighting terrorism" to "women's rights" can be used in an uncontested way to justify violence.

Presumption of Race and Gender Hierarchies

Hierarchy is central to the Western philosophical and Christian traditions that inform Just War theory. To posit a hierarchy in being itself is to predetermine what is just or unjust in war and what will be justified in the War on Women. This point bears repeating. To posit a hierarchy in being itself is to totally determine the outcome of any consideration of what will be considered the justified use of force. Those at the top of the chain are literally justified in whatever they do to those further down the chain. In Western philosophy and theology, the top of the chain of being is virtually synonymous with white-male superiority.

Thomas Aquinas, perhaps the most important architect of Just War as well as an influential Western theologian, believed hierarchy was natural and was even a part of God's plan before the Fall (*Summa Theologiae*, 38). This rigid, hierarchical chain is also causal and leads from God as first cause through all secondary causes, linking existence in a reasonable, orderly fashion to the creator. While Aquinas frequently quotes the works of Augustine, the tension at the center of Augustine's theology, the stress and strain of a City of God in vivid contest with an earthly city as both move toward Armageddon, is absent. Instead in Aquinas, there is this inexorable march of reason that governs all, from top to bottom.

This is political through and through. The great chain of being is really a "great chain of ruling" and a justification of "natural rulers" (*Summa Contra Gentiles* book III, chapter 81) who possess superior intellect and hence are best able to rule. It is ruthlessly efficient and drives attention up the chain and away from what is happening to the body, especially the bodies of women.

Aquinas takes over some of the biologically based misogyny of Aristotle and uses it to shore up the hierarchy of gender in the great chain of being. Women are "defective and misbegotten," and this sets up the hierarchy in being and in rule because women's defective nature means they are unfit for rule in either the home or the society.

Now it can look like, in the chain of being, that women are not misbegotten because they have a crucial role, that of procreation, in nature. But this is a step backward in terms of violence against women, since rape as not nearly as sinful as, for example, masturbation or homosexuality, because rape of a female by a male is "unlawful" but it is not against nature; masturbation or homosexuality, on the other hand, are considered to be against nature (question 154, article 12). Thus the violence done to women's bodies and, by extrapolation, violence done to bodies in war, are not the worst offenses in a fairly lengthy list of offenses. Instead, violence done to the ordering of nature, which is from "God himself," is the worst.

Slavery fit into the great chain of being because there is a natural structure to the whole universe that gives some men authority over others, including women, children, and slaves. Aquinas justified this by pointing out the hierarchical nature of heaven itself, where some angels were superior to other angels.

Challenging this hierarchy in heaven and on earth was an achievement of the Enlightenment and of the Protestant Reformation to some extent, but this was an incomplete challenge. The struggle for human rights, part of the democratic experiment, has been shown to be complicit in valuing the humanity of some over others—that is, a US Constitution that, at the time of its writing, included legal slavery and the disenfranchisement of women and unpropertied males.

The legacies of hierarchies of gender, race, and class influenced ideas of what constituted justified and unjustified violence. Rebellions by slaves were ruthlessly suppressed, and militias were armed and supported to put down slave revolts. Women's efforts not only to get the vote but also to actually use it, with male allies, to support laws to protect women from battering and rape have been met with obstruction at every step of the way.

A hierarchy in human worth gets carried along from Greek philosophers through Christian theologians up to the present. The "reasonableness" of this very idea is foundational to which violence gets justified and which does not.

Hiding the Bodies

The body in pain is the indispensable location from which to examine issues of violence, both in war and in the War on Women. But in Just War theory, the body never seems to show up, or when it does make an appearance, it is brushed aside as "collateral damage" in an otherwise perfectly justifiable exercise in the bloody mess that is the reality of war. This was seen earlier in the comments of Robert Royal, who pushed aside civilian suffering and the concerns about a "long drawn-out bloody war" and instead offered reasonable planning by the American military as a rationale for this dismissal.

Just War must be indicted for the very way it hides the injury and death inflicted on bodies in a reasonable set of categories that bear little relationship to the struggle to injure and kill bodies that is the reality of war. War and the War on Women are much more difficult to wage unless you hide the bodies. One way to hide the bodies is for them not to actually exist or not to exist in a way that really matters.

Plato's discourses on materiality, and the feminine and female bodies in particular, play a key role in directing our attention away from actual bodies. Plato was, of course, unable to completely do away with physical existence, but our attention is directed toward eternal forms. The "she"—that is, the "nurse"—of matter is not real, only the forms that "enter into and go out of her" are real. The body is submerged under abstractions.

This is precisely what Plato's metaphysics sets up for Western culture, the absolute negation of embodiment, especially female embodiment, as subject or agent. "She" has no agency but is merely astonishingly formless and passive, not even what we might think of materiality at all. "She" has no power and, as Judith Butler reminds us, "'Materiality' designates a certain effect of power or, rather is power in its formative or constituting effects."[50]

It is not just female bodies that are rendered so formless and passive but also the bodies of those with less social status, the bodies of those maimed and killed in war. Per Butler, "How can we legitimate claims of bodily injury if we put into question the materiality of the body?"[51] Per Just War theorists, how can we put war into question if we do not have a way to account for the body? If the body does not matter, then the battlefield itself will not matter. And women's bodies as battlefields will not matter at all.

Turning from the Just War paradigm to those that emphasize peace and justice, the question remains, do bodies matter and why? Is power examined or ignored? Are race, gender, and other hierarchies repudiated, or do they get carried along in as yet unexamined ways?

Such investigations are a crucial next step in getting to a framework that will help prevent and limit both war and the War on Women.

8

Peace and the War on Women

During the interview, Father Mizuno [Japanese Catholic priest who helped develop a shelter for women and girls trying to escape forced prostitution] told Rita the story of a major peace conference in 1987 protesting the U.S. military base in Okinawa. Because of the presence of so many international protestors, the American soldiers were confined to the base for the duration of the conference. When he called a friend who worked for a sex worker shelter in Okinawa and asked how the women had fared without a source of income for five days, Father Mizuno was told that they had the best business they had ever had for a single five-day period.

Casting Stones: Prostitution and Liberation in Asia and the United States[1]

I have spent years as a peace activist, as a domestic violence counselor, and as a professor teaching about these issues and also helping students deal with violence done to them (or done by them). Based on these experiences, I am not overly optimistic about human nature or about the human capacity for completely eschewing violence. I do not believe, actually, that "peace," especially when understood as the absence of conflict, is even possible. Yet it has also been my experience that human beings can form movements that sustain and promote nonviolent conflict resolution and reduce intimate as well as communal and international violence.

Peace is the product of a culture and requires religious, legal, economic, and political support for resolving problems without violence and for providing a just and equitable means to live for all. Gender justice must be part of that culture in a central way.

Human beings are social in their nature, and peace work is able to be more effective when it is understood as a social enterprise. This is, for me, a deeply spiritual work and as Beverly Harrison so well said, "God is in the connections" to one another.[2] Those connections are especially powerful when we work together for peace and justice. These movements are not perfect, and the human beings who compose them are not perfect.

When even those committed to peace, like those men attending the peace conference in Okinawa, Japan, in the late 1980s referenced at the beginning of the chapter, are able to use women as sexual objects in prostitution and apparently see no conflict with their peace activism, we learn something profound not only about human nature but also about peace and justice work itself. There is no possibility of a return to innocence, even through committed activism to eradicate violence. Yet this does not mean that human beings are only sinners and only capable of cruel violence. Human beings are complex in their individual and in their social natures.

Peacemaking Is Not Innocent

It is important to continuously recognize that there is a Western culture of misogyny so pervasive that it structures even the best efforts at resisting violence, including movements for "peace." This misogyny has elements of the heroic, the erotic, and the identification of femaleness with weakness and subordination. But these structural legacies of both Western philosophy and Christian theology are well disguised in peace traditions.

One of the great weaknesses of the peace movement, in fact, is that there is a deeply held, and yet often not examined, conviction that resisting war, especially as a faith commitment, makes one a peaceful person and more "innocent" than those who support war. This very self-understanding of innocence makes the systemic oppression of women within pacifist communities almost impermeable to critique. Few in the peace movement itself, whether in classical or more contemporary Pacifism or in the more recent paradigm of Just Peace, have dared to examine the fact that men who support war and men who oppose war share almost exactly the same attitudes toward women. And we cannot forget that since the culture of misogyny is pervasive, women themselves are subject to its formative character. Women can, and often will, internalize these demeaning and submissive cultural messages.

Many whom I have met in the peace movement seem blind to the fact that both peacemaking and war making in the West are products of the same male-dominant culture. As Rita and I write, "Male dominance is common in U.S. peace movements, as we both discovered to our dismay when we were active in several peace movements."[3] While one might expect men who are strongly committed to peace to recognize the correlates between militarism and male attitudes of dominance over women, this does not in fact often happen. Or, if it is perceived, it is not owned as a problem shared by men in a male-dominant society. Women have critiqued their treatment in peace movements, however, and it could be argued that the patriarchal attitudes toward women in the Vietnam antiwar movement helped fuel women's movements that emerged in the 1960s and 1970s.

The impact of the opposition of Dr. King to the Vietnam War was substantial, especially with his 1967 speech called "Beyond Vietnam—A Time to Break Silence" to 3,000 people at Riverside Church in New York City.[4] But in the seven powerful ways Dr. King chose to "break the silence" on Vietnam and on the destructive domestic as well as foreign effects of American militarism, he does not mention the way it perpetuates gender injustice. This is surprising, because for years prior to this address, Dr. King would have been hearing about the negative effects of sexism. African American women leaders had been very clear about their objection to a lack of attention to the recognition of women's leadership in the movement. They raised that concern repeatedly. Dorothy Height, a prominent member of the National Council of Negro Women, recalls, regarding the March on Washington, "there was a low tolerance level for . . . questions about women's participation" in terms of visibility. Height recalls being accused of making "a lot of fuss about an insignificant issue, that we did not recognize that the March was about racism, not sexism."[5] Height was equally clear that it was the women who were doing the majority of the grassroots work in the Civil Rights movement, a structural legacy of patriarchy.[6]

Sexism is not, in fact, insignificant when it comes to transforming social structures away from the deforming effects of a militarization of society through nonviolence. It is at its heart.

There are powerful and yet infrequently examined legacies from Western patriarchal culture that are present even in movements dedicated to ending racism, war, and economic inequality. One of these inheritances is the strong association of nonviolence with weakness and thus a despised femaleness. Movements that advocate nonviolence can exhibit this legacy, as can movements that advocate armed resistance, whether in opposing war or racism or economic inequality and even, truth be told, in movements dedicated to gender justice.

The deep roots of this ideology and its philosophical and religious supports can be seen in the identification of (heterosexual, white, elite) maleness with strength, the "warrior" who defeats Ti'amat and establishes order and political rule. A male peace activist, for example, will refer to himself and others in the movement as "warriors" for peace, tapping into the heroic paradigm that is so prevalent in the West as a virtue and ignoring how the warrior is so deeply rooted in an ideology of aggression toward women. Thus to return to the beginning of the chapter, peace activists using prostituted women becomes more intelligible.

Yet, and this is a challenge, these sexist ideologies (as well as the racist and elitist) do not make peace and justice movements worthless. It makes them more imperfect than they need to be. This can change. Or, put more positively, a movement for peace and justice must include gender and sexual equality, racial equality, and a decent standard of living for all people in its very structure, not just in its mission statement.

The problem is that "peace" has been defined very narrowly in Western culture, and this has been an ultimately dangerous shortcoming.

Peace in Western History

Ideals of peace certainly existed in Western antiquity, in fact, argues historian Roland Bainton, "[a]ll the peoples of antiquity with the exception of the Assyrians had the myth of a one-time warless world in a lost age of gold, whose recovery was the object of desire and endeavor."[7] This age of gold was a mythological time when the earth freely gave of its bounty and without human beings having to work to reap its benefits. There was no private property, no slavery, and no war. In the poem of Hesiod, this myth is described along with a chronicle of its deterioration through the stages of silver, bronze, and finally the current age of iron, in which familial and political enmity rule.

In the Hebrew bible, the lost age of gold is the Garden of Eden, and there are clear parallels to Hesiod, especially in the second creation story in Genesis. God plants a garden in Eden and "[a]river flows out of Eden to water the garden, and from there it divides and becomes four branches. The name of the first is Pishon; it is the one that flows around the whole land of Havilah, where there is gold; and the gold of that land is good, bdellium and onyx stone are there" (Genesis 2:10–14). The other three rivers are also described, including the Tigris and the Euphrates.

But like the devolution of the age of gold in Hesiod, in Genesis, human beings also mess up the golden age. This is the disobedience of Adam and Eve to God's command that they not eat of the tree of the knowledge of good and evil. Adam and Eve do eat of that forbidden fruit, and they are cast out of the garden.

The return to the "age of gold" is also a common theme. In Hebraic thought, as extensively described in Isaiah but also in others of the biblical prophets, the return of peace would be a gift of God, anticipated certainly in the Sabbath but finally restored in a messianic age where a "Prince of Peace" would come and institute a "government and peace there shall be no end" (Isaiah 9:6–7). Swords would be beaten into plowshares (2:4), and abundance would again return. "He will make her wilderness like Eden, and her desert like the garden of the Lord" (51:3). There will be no more enmity, as even human beings and animals would live in peace (11:6).

In the New Testament, the book of Revelation comes closest to this idea of the return to a golden age, but in the view of John of Patmos, this would only occur as the completion of a process of intensifying Christian witness, persecution, violence, and then punishment by God that would eventually come to completion with the end of the current order and a "new heaven and a new earth." A "New Jerusalem" would occur, ruled over with peace and justice by the risen Christ.

This New Jerusalem is clearly a restored Eden, as an angel shows John a vision of "the river of the water of life, bright as crystal" flowing through the city. John sees a tree that bears fruit each month, and "nothing accursed will be found there any more" (Revelation 22). The return to this Eden is through a violent cataclysm, but it is a vision of peace nevertheless.

But until that return, it is also clear that early Christians did not fight in Rome's wars. While it is commonly held that the early Christian church was "pacifist," there is debate about what that meant. But one thing is clear, "From the end of the New Testament period to the decade A.D. 170–80 there is no evidence whatever of Christians in the army."[8] After that, there is more (but sporadic) evidence of Christians participating in military service, more on the frontiers of the Roman empire than in the interior. The eastern frontier has the most service, but also an articulated rejection of military service, coming mostly from groups holding ascetic or monastic ideals.[9] This anticipates the sectarian pacifism that continues after the "Peace of Constantine," when Christianity is adopted by the Emperor and military service became acceptable, even sacralized, over succeeding centuries.

There are some intriguing arguments against military service both in the East and in the West in these centuries. Clement of Alexandria issued a plea for an equal code of conduct for women and for men. When this met the objection that women, unlike men, were not trained for war, Clement countered by arguing against military service for men. "In peace, not in war, we are trained. War needs great preparation but peace and love, quiet sisters, require nor arms nor extensive outlay." The positive feminine metaphor of "sisters" for the training needed for Christian service is nearly unique. The Word of God is all Christians need, Clement argued, and it is an "instrument of peace." Christ calls all to a "bloodless army he has assembled by blood and by the word, to give to them the Kingdom of Heaven." Christ calls, and Christians should respond and "put on the armor of peace."[10]

Other theologians and church leaders in this period such as Irenaeus or Tertullian quote texts on "beating swords into plowshares," and call Christ the "son of peace." Clement seems unique among these early Church Fathers in making a gender equality argument along with a dictum to refrain from military exercises. The gender injustice that accompanies militarism is not examined in his work, however, but it is in contrast to the general thrust of the other theologians who weighed heavily the risk of idolatry in the cult of the deified Emperor as a crucial reason not to serve.

It is often commonly held that the idea of the imminent return of Christ in the eschaton is the reason serving in an earthly military was avoided by early Christians. But the hope for an immediate return of Christ was fading by the third century and even in the second.

A much more evident response is the adherence to the law of love in combination with being guided by heavenly, not earthly, things. As Clement put it, "If you enroll as one of God's people, heaven is your country and God your lawgiver. And what are his laws? . . . Thou shalt not kill . . . Thou shalt love they neighbor as thyself . . . To him that strikes thee on the one check, turn also the other." Other theologians in the period echo this view. Tertullian emphasized the love of enemies as the "principal precept."[11]

There are many interpretations within Tertullian's "principal precept," but it seems that the law of love in the early Church was regarded as incompatible with killing.

Thus it is not only the risk of idolatry issue that shifts in Christianity post-Constantine but there is also an ethos shift that is related to a Church in an increasingly close relationship with a state and the introduction of that political hierarchy into the ecclesial structure itself. The advent of Just War thinking after Constantine was more than a way to justify the move from the pacifism of the early church to the demands of being a state and defending that state. Inevitably, that justification of the use of state force affects the Christian ethos profoundly, moving it inexorably toward greater support for power inequality, hierarchy, and a further contempt for the body (though there are antiphysical sentiments in groups like the Montanists in the earlier centuries that are also pacifist).

Peace theologies do not disappear after Just War thinking, but they were highly sectarian enterprises as anticipated in the ascetic and monastic objections to military service in the first three centuries. In the main, Just War thinking was dominant, and this had a hugely deleterious effect as the Holy Roman Empire crumbled under increasing barbarian invasions. The Church labored in vain to be what Constantine had hoped, the "cement of the state," but failed in the main. There was so much private war in feudal society that gradually the idea of the "Peace of God" and the "Truce of God" was put forward. The goal was to greatly limit those against whom war could be fought, not only clerics and the unarmed civilians, but also the stealing or killing of livestock, the burning of homes and crops, and a complete ban on knightly combat from the beginning of Lent until the end of Easter. This "peace" or "truce" was violated so much that "peace bands" were formed to enforce it, and then those bands got out of hand!

This set the stage for sending war elsewhere and calling it peace. In other words, the Crusades. Pope Urban II, in inaugurating the Crusades at the Council of Clermont in 1095, connected these dots. Urban goes from the infighting and banditry that was plaguing Europe and urging the "peace" or "truce" that had actually so far failed, to going as the "Christ's heralds" to invade another country and kill other people as a holy war to impose a Christian "peace" conducted under the auspices of the church.[12]

Even monastic Pacifism collapsed under this thrust, and groups of warrior monks such as the Templars, the Hospitalers, and the Knights of St. John were formed. The only critique of the Crusades that verged on pacifism was by the Franciscans, but that was a critique that the Crusades should confined to a missionizing effort.

The power of Crusade as a Christian paradigm of war for a holy cause is still plaguing the world today and is especially resented in the Middle East and among the Muslims who were painted by Pope Urban as "a despised and base race, which worships demons." This anticipates the racist wars of colonial conquest by the West and lays the groundwork for invasion as "bringing peace."

Europe itself returned to a form of Just War thinking in the post-Crusades era, as nation states fought with one another, each claiming just cause. But the Renaissance and the Enlightenment saw another form of peace thinking emerge, that of humanism.

One of the most outspoken humanist pacifists was Erasmus of Rotterdam. His best known tract, *The Complaint of Peace,* is a first-person litany of complaints by Peace—a female person, the "nurse," and the "patroness" of earthly blessing.

The tract is a kind of romance, where Peace as the trusting, caring woman wants nothing more than to love and be loved of "Man," but it does not seem to be going well. Still, she lures her "Man" and ultimately appeals to reason. "You'd be so much better off with me," she says.

"Why aren't things going well?," Peace wonders as she begins her complaint. She gives everything to her "Man."

"Now, if I, whose name is Peace, am a personage glorified by the united praise of God and man, as the fountain, the parent, the nurse, the patroness, the guardian of every blessing which either heaven or earth can bestow; if without me nothing is flourishing, nothing safe, nothing pure or holy, nothing pleasant to mortals, or grateful to the Supreme Being," then why isn't it working?

Why does "Man" love war and not me? Peace wails. War is horrible.

War is a vast ocean of "plagues and pestilences" that turns everything to "bitterness." War is not holy but "unhallowed" and a deadly threat to piety and religion. It is a threat to reason, where those whom war has turned "stark mad" spend their treasure to "purchase endless misery and mischief."

It turns out, Peace has been betrayed by her "Man." So many of "Man" disappoint, Peace laments, even Kings, Scholars, and Priests. But then, she thinks she has found one "Man" who will love her, and she will be loved in turn. It is not to be. "At length I felt a wish that I might find a snug and secure dwelling-place in the bosom, at least, of some one man. But here also I failed. One and the same man is at war with himself. Reason wages war with the passions; one passion with another passion. Duty calls one way, and inclination another. Lust, anger, avarice, ambition, are all up in arms, each pursuing its own purposes, and warmly engaged in the battle."

Peace is an intrepid heroine, and she does not give up in her indictment of all in scripture and religion, as well as in politics, that should rightly make the world safe for peace, and yet does not. She labors on, indicting one after another and finally makes a clarion call based on reason. "Let the public good overcome all private and selfish regards of every kind and degree; though in truth, even private and selfish regards, and every man's own interest, will be best promoted by the preservation of peace."[13]

I have called this a romance, and it is, very much in the genre of Renaissance romance literature. Epics are about war, but romances are about love. Erasmus wrote a romance about peace seducing (very gently) the part of "Man" tempted by war. Romance literature is vast, of course, but there is some overlap with this fascinating tract by Erasmus. It is interesting to note the contrast in the romance slant of this tract by Erasmus, where it is not the "hero" as love-sick warrior who is the protagonist, but a feminized "Peace" who is, in fact, the hero of the piece. It is also important to recall that the less elite forms of this genre, the earlier French fabliau, was where a Just War on women was so evident as Mary Potter Engel has shown.

Erasmus exhibits a strong influence from classical themes as well, especially in showing Peace as personified and the emphasis on peace being a reasonable way to achieve social well-being. The Christian side is the theme of the "beating swords into plowshares" and the ideal of the Christian community not being disrupted by the new nationalism. These latter will be critical themes in the emergence of the pacifist traditions in the so-called left-wing of the Reformation.

But it is crucial, for the purposes of this chapter, to underline the romantic tone of the tract that is personified as the caring female, trying every way she can think of to convince her "Man" to love her and not nasty old war. Peace is feminized in this work by Erasmus and, given the association of peace with weakness that is so much a legacy of Western culture, it perversely undermines his argument even as he makes it very persuasively.

Pacifist Sects

The sixteenth century in Europe was turbulent; wars broke out that took on a distinctly religious cast, and there was widespread violence and religious intolerance as evidenced by the Inquisition. This is also the period in which not only Erasmus had Peace make a complaint but also when the Protestant Reformation began.

Martin Luther rejected Crusade as practiced by the Roman Catholic Church, largely because it was part and parcel of the exercise of what he viewed as the Church's abusive power. Luther, and Lutherans, like all the Protestant state churches that emerged in the Reformation, favored Just War. Luther's rationale for this was deeply rooted in his theology of the two kingdoms. Drawing on Augustine, but with his own drive to indict the "The Mighty in the Church," Luther developed the theology of the two kingdoms: the Kingdom of God or Christ and the Kingdom of the world (civil affairs). The fall of Adam and Eve from the innocence of the Garden of Eden due to their sin of disobedience made the coercive power of the state necessary.

The very clear line that Luther drew between the spheres of church and state led Luther to two moralities: the spiritual that governs the church and the coercive power that governs the state. This prefigures the work of Reinhold Niebuhr in his *Moral Man and Immoral Society* and Niebuhr's support for World War II and the Cold War (but not for the Vietnam War). Luther plainly accepted the Augustinian position that the goal of war is peace, and this fit smoothly with the civil administration of the home and a Just War on Women who dared to disobey.

It might seem that women's situation would have improved in the Reformation as marriage was advocated for all, and clerical celibacy was not the definition of holiness. Women, having long been associated with sexual temptation, could perhaps escape that spiritual stereotype. But in fact, women's situation did not improve in the Reformation. It may have gotten worse, since there were no longer all-women conclaves in nunneries in which women could remain unmarried. Instead, women had one choice: to be a wife. The male head of the household became a model of the civil rule in an accepted hierarchy of dominance and submission. The wife was to obey the husband "as her head," and women had no other role than wife (motherhood is rarely mentioned). As Luther said, "The word and works of God is quite clear, that women were made either to be wives or prostitutes."[14]

Women, like the peasants who dared to rebel, had no authority to challenge their subordination. When the Peasants' War in Saxony threatened, Luther informed Prince John Fredrick that he had an obligation to use the sword to "smite, stab, slay and kill" because a rebellion cannot be just. It is disorder, not order, in Luther's view, and just like the ancient theory of establishing order over chaos, often represented by women's disobedience, Luther was explicit. No challenge to the state hierarchy can be just.[15] This is a vigorous application of Just War thinking and the civil (and domestic!) part of Luther's two kingdoms theology.

Some churches used aspects of this same theology of two kingdoms, and also humanity's fallen nature, to craft a very different approach to war and peace. The period of the horrific religious wars of the sixteenth and seventeenth centuries also gave rise to sectarian pacifists such as the Anabaptists (now the Mennonites and the Hutterites), the Quakers, and the Brethren. There is a theological continuum represented in these groups, from Anabaptists to Brethren to Quakers. The Anabaptists are the most sectarian, separating themselves from the kingdom of "this world" and all its fallenness, and the "kingdom of Christ" and Christ's followers. According to these Anabaptists, there was no state or sword in Paradise, and it is to the Paradise to come to which believers must turn. Quakers were (and are) at the other end of the continuum on this issue, not separating themselves from the world per se, even being willing to serve in government but refraining from war. The Brethren have taken a middle position, preferring not to engage the world very much.

These sectarian pacifists are organized by the doctrine of human nature, in effect, with the Quakers being most optimistic about human nature (think of all the "Friends" schools built by Quakers) and the Mennonites (the Anabaptists) being the least optimistic. The Quakers, therefore, were closest in their views to Erasmus and often appealed to rulers not to engage in war. George Fox, the founder of the Society of Friends (Quakers), proclaimed that his mission was "to stand a witness against all violence and against all the works of darkness, and to turn people from the darkness to the light and from the occasion of the magistrate's sword."[16] It is to Quakers and their principled allegiance to their right of conscience in regard to nonviolence that we owe the idea of conscientious objection to fighting in war.[17] Their struggle for religious liberty, combined with their sense of inward conviction, helped frame this concept in the West.

Quakers played a major role in the abolitionist movement against slavery in England, then lobbied the colonies, and subsequently were active in United States to end slavery. The strong Quaker belief that all people are created equal in the eyes of God led them to oppose one person owning another. In 1657, George Fox wrote, "To Friends beyond sea, that have Blacks and Indian slaves" to remind them of Quaker belief in equality. He later visited Barbados and his preaching, which urged for better treatment of enslaved people, was published in London in 1676 as "Gospel Family Order." Fox urged compassion in his preaching, asking his hearers, *"now I say, if this should be the condition of you and yours, you would think it hard measure, yea, and very great Bondage and Cruelty. And therefore consider seriously of this, and do you for and to them, as you would willingly have them or any other to do unto you . . . were you in the like slavish condition."*[18]

In the eighteenth century, Quakers in the American colonies began to oppose slavery and lobbied against it. By 1761, Quakers were barred from owning slaves, and any member who did own slaves was disowned from the fellowship. Quakers also tried to pursue and urge just and friendly relations with Indians. For nearly a century, they advocated this policy in Pennsylvania but were ultimately drawn into controversy in the legislature in 1756 when they objected to a bill that would authorize war against the Delaware Indians. Despite their conscientious objection to fighting in the war, they ultimately voted for it, but then their leadership could not abide it, and thus Quakers in the legislature subsequently either resigned or declined to run for office, effectively removing Quakers from that political body.

The sectarian ideal of peace could not compete with a King and their other legislative member, Benjamin Franklin, who wanted war.

The Quaker conviction of the equality of all people extended to women as well. Quaker women were early preachers in the movement. Quaker women were sometimes the majority of traveling preachers, and they were accorded time to travel alone and to publish. This was not a gender paradise, as Quaker business meetings were dominated by men, but George Fox eventually established separate women's meetings. Fox was criticized that the women's meetings for "discipline" were actually the first needed to pass on a couple's intention to marry. This gave women effective authority over men when it came to who could marry. These women's meetings gave women experience of leadership and organization, and though they declined in the nineteenth century, it is no surprise that Quaker women were in the forefront of abolitionism, women's suffrage, and peace activism.

Quakers, and especially Quaker women, were heavily involved in the struggle for women's equal rights in the United States, and the landmark 1848 Seneca Falls Declaration was in large part due to the work of Quaker women.[19] Quaker women were not of the same mind on the issues of women's proper place, the meaning of "public," and especially the relationship between church and society, however. As a subculture, Quaker women reflect the development of American gender roles in relationship to peacemaking. Quakers, as sectarians, illustrate how the dominant narrative of "women's place" was subverted by a theology of the equality of all persons. Their "public character" in "holding most of the offices in their church" and running their own business meetings, as well as being "among the first women to begin to limit their fertility in the nineteenth century, and as philanthropists, humanitarians and reformers" shows the impact such a theology can have on issues of peace and war, as well as human rights and women's rights in particular.[20]

The Anabaptists, however, were deeply pessimistic about human nature and its possibility for redemption in this world. Part of this pessimism might certainly have come from how grievously they were persecuted and killed by both the Catholics and the Protestants. Anabaptists based their sectarianism and their pacifism on a rejection of the Old Testament in favor of the law of Christ and especially the Sermon on the Mount.

The Anabaptists have not been especially "creedal" but are more a faith that is founded on obedience, discipleship, and imitation of Christ, especially the Christ that is to come. An example of the extremes of separation from the world can be found in the *Schleitheim Confession* of the Swiss Brethren (Anabaptists). In the section called "On separation of the saved," the *Confession* exhorts, "A separation shall be made from the evil and from the wickedness which the devil planted in the world; in this manner, simply that we shall not have fellowship with them [the wicked] and not run with them in the multitude of their abominations . . . For truly all creatures are in but two classes, good and bad, believing and unbelieving, darkness and light, the world and those who [have come] out of the world, God's temple and idols, Christ and Belial; and none can have part with the other." As a consequence, the *Confession* concludes, "Therefore there will also unquestionably fall from us the unchristian, devilish weapons of force—such as sword, armor and the like, and all their use [either] for friends or against one's enemies I would like the records—by virtue of the word of Christ, Resist not [him that is] evil."[21]

The work of peace as separation from a world effectively given over to the Devil means the shunning of military service and nonresistance to violence (evil). The community, by contrast, becomes the bearer of the "Light" and is, perforce, the "good." Yet Mennonite and Brethren churches have a fairly high incidence of violence against women and a tremendous difficulty in confronting this issue. Sectarian Pacifism needs to be confronted directly on their theology of obedience (and especially the submission of women), following the example of the sacrificial love of Christ (especially imposed on women to model Christ's suffering), as well as the pressures to be the self-righteous, "good" community against the evil world.

The infamous case of the sexual misconduct charges against John Howard Yoder (1927–97), one of the most prominent contemporary Mennonite theologians, is a prime example of how these theological perspectives can coconspire to facilitate violence against women and prevent an appropriate institutional response. It is also a very clear testimony to the theme that women are eroticized in Western theology and that this legacy can be carried through peace theologies, as well as through other perspectives on war and peace.

It is crucial, for the purposes of the argument of this book, to recognize that Yoder's sexual misconduct toward so many women is not something that should be treated as just a personal flaw and be separated from his pacifist views. Pacifism needs to examine its own deep inheritance in misogyny and to change not only by including women more in its authority structures but in its theological and biblical approaches as well.

Allegations that Yoder had sexually abused, harassed, and assaulted women had circulated in Mennonite circles for decades, but there were repeated institutional failures to actually address the abuses. This was in part due to the fact that Yoder's widely read works gave new prominence to pacifist theology. His best-known work, *The Politics of Jesus,* argued that a radical Christian Pacifism was the most faithful approach to following Christ and that this position was, in fact, a political stance as well. He contrasted his views with those of Reinhold Niebuhr and Niebuhr's "Christian realism" that posited a difference between the morality of individuals and that of nations.

But when it came to the abuse of women, Yoder himself engaged in a profoundly dualistic view of morality, denying abuse allegations until nearly the end of his life. When it came to a coherent response to women reporting sexual abuse and assault, the Mennonite church itself was singularly unable to deal with charges of violence against women. Finally, a group of victims threatened a public protest at Bethel College before a conference at which Yoder was to be a speaker. The college president rescinded the invitation to Yoder to speak. According to one of the victims, Bethel was "the first institution in the church that has taken this seriously" (*Mennonite Weekly Review,* March 12, 1992). A series of articles in *The Elkhart Truth,* a digital media outlet in northern Indiana, chronicle this case.[22] After this, Yoder was subject to the discipline of the Indiana–Michigan Conference of the Mennonite Church for allegations of sexual misconduct. His credentials were pulled, he was ordered to undergo rehabilitation, and he was urged to use his gifts for "teaching and writing," though many of the allegations were of his actions against women students.[23] His obituary in *The New York Times* did not mention his sexual misconduct.

Sixteen years after Yoder's death, *The New York Times* finally ran an article discussing Yoder's misconduct and quoted one complainant, Carolyn Heggen, who said more than 50 women had "said that Mr. Yoder had touched them or made advances." The article also discussed the recent formation of a support group for victims.[24]

Hand-wringing or exhortations to "reconciliation" have been some reactions to Yoder's sexual misconduct toward women but far from all of the responses have ducked the issues. One of the better efforts, called "Scandalizing John Howard Yoder," was by a team of writers—David Cramer, Jenny Howell, Jonathan Tran and Paul Martins—and was published in 2014. They attempt to make theological sense of what Yoder did from within Yoder's own writings on Pacifism. "Those looking to salvage something of Yoder's theology will find themselves confronted by the blatant inconsistencies between his sexual violence and his longstanding commitments to nonviolence. Christian nonviolence is what Yoder is best known for, as *the* twentieth-century Christian advocate for pacifism." But what seemed to keep Mennonites from making an institutional response was, in fact, internal to the kind of "person-to-person" method of reproving that proved, ultimately, completely ineffectual as Yoder was able to deflect and obstruct, wanting his accusers to "come forward" and ignoring (or relying on) the power differential between him and these women. But most damningly, the question of whether this behavior was in fact consistent with Yoder's separationist Pacifism is raised. "After all, Yoder described the 'original revolution' as 'the creation of a distinct community with its own deviant set of values and its coherent way of incarnating them.'" So, this article asked, is Yoder's theology thus proven wrong? No, because "[s]tymied by hushed and impotent institutions, Yoder's victims banded together and became the church Yoder could, apparently, only write about."[25]

As thoughtful as this piece is about Yoder and the pacifist theology he represented, it is contradicted by other writings by primarily Mennonite women about violence against women and pacifist theologies, as well as writings by women who were direct victims of Yoder. One effort that immediately preceded the formal discipline of Yoder was a 1991 conference on violence against women held at the Associated Mennonite Biblical Seminaries. The papers and responses were published as a volume called *Peace Theology and Violence against Women*. The ten contributors examine in depth the fact that while violence against women has, "on the surface" been "assumed to be wrong (therefore ethical debate was not needed) . . . actual practice has frequently been cloaked in silence and self-deception."[26]

A great strength of this volume is its willingness to see that the "situation in which we find ourselves as a church community—a state of professing peace while harboring violence—is intolerable."[27] Part of the problem, the authors argue, is the willingness to "sacrifice the sanctity of the individual for the good of the community," as well as the idea that marriage must be preserved at all costs. Certain "sins" are counted as sins while others are excused.

A crucial analysis, woven throughout the book, regards the pacifist neglect of the theological issue of power and the need to find a "liberation pacifism" that will not look the other way when both social and individual transformation are required in regard to violence and violation against women. Active resistance, not just passive nonresistance, needs to be theologically developed and brought into church practice. Central to this change is the need to reject the subjection of women as a biblically warranted abuse of power. And finally, the authors argue that Christologies of following the suffering Christ are misapplied to abused women and also must be challenged and changed.[28] The volume concludes with a very strong "Listeners' Report" that directly addresses the issue that "[t]he experience of women suggests that peace theology may subtly undergird patriarchy. Since most peace theology has been articulated by men, women's experience of violence has not been adequately addressed."[29]

Today the ripples of the abuse done by John Howard Yoder and the extensive failures of the Mennonite church to address issues of violence against women are continuing to be recounted, as in a blog called *Our Stories Untold*, a "website created as a safe and open space to discuss sexualized violence within spiritual communities (more specifically, the Mennonite Church)."[30]

Yes, "peace theology" does undergird patriarchy in many ways. A longing for the innocence of paradise in sectarian peace communities is an invitation both to perpetrating abuse and to covering it up. The nature of power is not systemically addressed and is assumed to be amenable to "person-to-person" resolution even when there are gross violations and power inequalities. A hierarchy of men and women, couched as biblically based subordination and domination, facilitates this abusive context. These all coconspire with an eroticized legacy of attitudes toward women and their sexuality.

Such peace theologies are clearly both the product of patriarchy and its facilitators, but what about the work of women as peacemakers? Are there similar structural flaws?

Women Peacemakers

A total of 46 women have won the Nobel Prize (Marie Curie won it twice, once in Physics in 1903 and once in Chemistry in 1911) since it was begun in 1901. Sixteen of those have been for the Nobel Peace Prize, more than twice as many as any of the other prize categories. Six women have won the Nobel Peace Prize in the twenty-first century alone.[31]

This is a complex statistic, as it can seem like evidence that peace is, indeed, "feminized" and that women gravitate to peacemaking as they are socialized to do. But, on the other hand, there are significant clues within the work of women peacemakers on how, in fact, to confront the nature of war and to work in organizing against it and to prevent its recurrence. But the toll on women peacemakers (and indeed, on all peacemakers) is very high.

Jane Addams was the second woman to win the Nobel Peace prize, in 1931. She had founded the Women's International League for Peace and Freedom in

1919 and the Nobel Prize website says, in her biography, that "[d]uring World War I, she chaired a women's conference for peace held in the Hague in the Netherlands, and tried in vain to get President Woodrow Wilson of the USA to mediate peace between the warring countries. When the USA entered the war instead, Jane Addams spoke out loudly against this. She was consequently stamped a dangerous radical and a danger to US security."[32]

Addams faced huge persecution not just as a peacemaker but especially for her courage in actually describing war.

Addams was a prolific writer on all these subjects and, in her book *Peace and Bread in a Time of War*, she chronicles her radicalization on peace and how it nearly crushed her. Addams admits that in terms of social change, she had always been "middle of the road," but when she returned from the Hague, she notes, "I was pushed far to the left on the subject of war" in order to give Pacifism itself a hearing. She spoke at a "large public meeting" in Carnegie Hall and tried to make clear that when she had spoken directly to soldiers in Europe, "War was to them much more anachronistic than to the elderly statesmen who were primarily responsible for the soldiers' presence in the trenches." This was, she notes, "my undoing."

After the Carnegie speech, Addams was vilified in *The New York Times* as a "choice specimen of a woman's sentimental nonsense" by a Mr. Davis who "himself had recently returned from Europe and at once became the defender of the heroic soldiers who were being traduced and belittled." Addams says she knew all too well that she had crossed a "popular and long-cherished conception of the nobility and heroism of the soldier as such." Instead, Addams saw the idealistic youth on both sides as war's true victims and quotes, "'we admire the soldier not because he goes forth to slay, but to be slain.'" Their countries demand a blood sacrifice, in other words.

Addams wrote that she endured a "bitter and abusive" response when she returned to Chicago that she labels "mass consciousness" that takes over a citizenry at war. She fell ill and was nearly an invalid for three years. Addams's introspection in this book is profound. She wrote about the lonely pacifist in wartime who found it strangely "possible to travel from the mire of self pity straight to the barren hills of self-righteousness and to hate himself equally in both places." But she was equally scathing about the "contradiction" of achieving peace by a "war to end all wars." In the end, Addams wrote, she persevered despite crippling doubts induced by "mass suggestion" because she fundamentally believed "that a man's primary allegiance is to his vision of the truth and that he is under obligation to affirm it."[33]

This was entirely consistent with Addams's upbringing as a Quaker. She remembered going to her Quaker father and sharing her struggle over the doctrine of predestination. Her father's response was to affirm to young Jane that she should always "be honest with yourself inside." Thus the lesson was that moral integrity was the most important religious value. As she matured, she wanted to "reconcile her 'childish acceptance of the teachings of the gospels' with an 'almost passionate commitment to the ideals of democracy.'" Her direction was not toward organized religion but ultimately toward founding Hull House and her work in peacemaking.

Addams's religious views were remarkably like the "spiritual but not religious" trend in the United States today, where a passion for actually doing something positive in the world is considered far more important than doctrinal niceties. She wanted to return Christianity to its roots, to a "deep enthusiasm for humanity." Addams evidenced a "desire to make social service . . . express the spirit of Christ."[34]

Critics have dismissed Addams and other women reformers who worked outside established religion, claiming that the social settlement movement "provided these young women a way out of their theological confusion by offering a 'secular outlet . . . for energies essentially religious.'"[35] Addams continues to be dismissed for her theological innovations, as Jean Bethke Elshtain does in her biography *Jane Addams and the Dream of American Democracy: A Life*. Elshtain pigeonholes her subject as belonging to "the generic liberal Protestantism of her day," though at least Elshtain takes Addams seriously as a religious figure rather than one of a group of young women who could not understand theology and who were therefore to be grouped as secularists.[36]

It is common for women religious peacemakers to work outside of religious institutions, and to be theologically innovative as well as effective not only in calling for peace but also in actually making peace.

In 2011, the Nobel Peace Prize was awarded to three women from Africa and the Arab world in acknowledgment of their nonviolent role in promoting peace, democracy, and gender equality: President Ellen John Sirleaf of Liberia, the first woman to be elected president in modern Africa; Leymah Gbowee, her partner in the extraordinary Liberian peacemaking efforts; and Tawakkol Karman of Yemen, a prodemocracy campaigner. The work of the Liberian women peacemakers begins the chapter on "Nonviolent Direct Action" in the volume *Interfaith Just Peacemaking: Jewish, Christian and Muslim Perspectives on the New Paradigm of Peace and War* that I edited, highlighting their work as "Just Peace," the new peace paradigm that will be discussed further in this book.

For more than 15 years, Liberia had suffered from the ravages of intense warfare. In 1990, two factions of the National Patriotic Front of Liberia, one led by Prince Johnson and the other by Charles Taylor, invaded the capital city of Monrovia. A bloody civil war resulted. Thousands of Liberian citizens had to flee their homes, and access to food, clean water, and adequate health care was nearly eliminated. Although a peace treaty was signed in 1995, violence continued. Murder, rape, and the use of child soldiers became commonplace, making living conditions unbearably dangerous, particularly for women and their children.

The 2008 award-winning documentary *Pray the Devil Back to Hell* tells the story—through interviews, archival footage, and compelling images—of contemporary Liberia. When rebels were once again closing in on the capital of Monrovia and peace talks were collapsing, the women of Liberia—Christian and Muslim—made a powerful series of demonstrations, putting their own bodies on the line to make a powerful statement that they would no longer put up with all the war. They organized a sex strike, which drew a lot of attention to their efforts. They decided to take public action and chose a field right where President Charles Taylor would have to travel twice daily, to and from Capitol Hill. They dressed in white with no jewelry or ornament, a kind of "sackcloth and ashes" statement and called themselves "Mass Action." Thousands of women came and they sat in the field and sang; they sang and chanted prayers and religious songs, and they often sang the slogan of their action:

> We want peace, no more war.
> Our children are dying—we want peace.
> We are tired suffering—we want peace.
> We are tired running—we want peace.

The women of Mass Action sat from dawn to dusk in the heat, suffering from rashes and pain. They sat in the pouring rain while their field flooded. "It was a kind of torture," Leymah Gbowee writes in her memoir, *Mighty Be Our Powers: How Sisterhood, Prayer, and Sex Changed a Nation at War*. It seemed a unified, spontaneous action, she notes, but it took tremendous work to mount such a grassroots effort and keep it going. "Every day we were on that field. *Every day*. We refused to go away. Refused to let our suffering remain invisible. If people didn't take us seriously at first, it was our persistence that wore them down." Bus drivers refused to take money from the women going to the field. Churches and individuals gave money. But not all were so supportive. One woman's husband beat her and threw her out for her actions.[37]

Peace talks were finally scheduled to take place in Ghana, and women from a well-established women's movement in Liberia, the Mano River Women's Peace Network (MARWOPNET), who were mostly women from educated, elite backgrounds, were invited to observe and then to participate. No one invited the women from Mass Action who had been demonstrating in the field, but they determined to go anyway and raised money for seven to go to Ghana. While in Ghana, their numbers grew to 500, including refugees and members of their group. But the talks stalled, and the women kept demonstrating outside the peace talks.

One of the negotiators invited women from Mass Action to sit at the table with the MARWOPNET delegates, but they refused. Gbowee said, "If we had stepped in to share their role, it would have suggested that we didn't trust them and that we were competing, which would have widened the divide between us." The MARWOPNET women thanked her.

But still the talks dragged on with no progress; the women sat in their field back in Liberia, and people were still suffering and being killed. Finally, the Mass Action women had had enough. They gathered as many women as they could right outside the door to the negotiating chamber and, just at lunchtime, sat down on the floor and looped arms. They determined to block the door until progress on peace was made.

They passed a note to the chief negotiator: "WE are holding these delegates, especially the Liberians, hostage. They will feel the pain of what our people are feeling at home."

Security guards rushed in to arrest Gbowee and the other women for "obstructing justice." She became so angry she said, "I will make it very easy for you to arrest me. I'm going to strip naked."

She explains, "In Africa, it's a terrible curse to see a married or elderly woman deliberately bare herself. If a mother is really, really upset with a child, she might take out her breast and slap it, and he's cursed. For this group of men to see a woman naked would be almost like a death sentence. Men are born through women's vaginas, and it's as if by exposing ourselves, we say, 'We now take back the life we gave you.' Fear passed through the hall."

Though peace was not finalized that day, the women stopped the casual, "circuslike" approach and the delegates began to get serious. "It marked the beginning of the end."[38]

There are enormous lessons to be taken from these women peacemakers. It is women who are doing the grassroots work, as Dorothy Height noted in the Civil Rights movement, and their work is critical to effecting the actual changes that build peace and reduce conflict. The Liberian Mass Action group did not happen overnight. They had done work for years in trauma healing projects, teaching about conflict and conflict transformation and in a program called "Shedding the Weight," where women came together to tell their stories of all the violence that had been done to them. This work all came together not only in the women dressed in white, refusing to leave the field in Liberia, but also in their creative engagement of their own bodies in the sex strike and the threat to remove their clothes, threatening to bring a female curse on male delegates who were failing to make peace.

The Liberian Mass Action illustrates one of what are called the "practice norms" of the new paradigm of peacemaking called Just Peace, moving from "pacifism" to what is called "peacebuilding."

Just Peace

Leymah Gbowee recalls that as she educated herself on not only the fact that her country, Liberia, "was a disaster" but how that had happened, and why, and what could be done about it. Ironically enough, she mentions she read John Howard Yoder's book *The Politics of Jesus*, "which talked of Christ as a revolutionary, fighting injustice and giving a voice to the powerless." But she added to Yoder. She also read "Martin Luther King Jr. and Gandhi and the Kenyan author and conflict and reconciliation expert Hizkias Assefa, who believed that reconciliation between victim and perpetrator was the only way to really resolve conflict, especially civil conflict, in the modern world." Without such processes, Assefa warns, the parties in conflict "both remained bound together forever, one waiting for apology or revenge, the other fearing retribution."[39]

Many of the influences that Gbowee named came together to influence the eventual creation of what is now called the Just Peace or Just Peacemaking paradigm. The work of Gandhi and King were definitive for changing the approach of peace in the twentieth century from sectarian commitment to nonresistance and nonviolence to a proactive approach of using techniques of nonviolence to make injustice visible, and to confront it truthfully but without retaliation.

The work of both Gandhi and King were highly influential on US Christian groups. The 1980s has been called a "peacemaking decade" because so many denominations produced peace statements not only condemning war but also urging nuclear disarmament. Many of the people who had worked on those statements knew each other, and during the mid-1990s, 23 of them—scholars, ethicists, biblical and moral theologians, international relations scholars, peace activists, and conflict resolution specialists—began to meet to discuss the possibility of a joint Christian statement on peace.

The group members' affiliations ranged from the historic peace churches, to mainline and Evangelical Protestant, to historic African American, to Catholic. The approaches to peace were equally broad, with all points along a continuum from classical Pacifism to human rights perspectives to political theory to traditional Just War represented. These perspectives are all, in some ways, represented in what came to be called Just Peace or Just Peacemaking as a paradigm. Women were consistently underrepresented in the two groups, never more than 5 percent, and racial/ethnic minorities were similarly underrepresented.

The group worked together for years and ultimately produced a volume called *Just Peacemaking: Transforming Initiatives for Justice and Peace*, edited by Glen Stassen.[40] The work was substantially revised and updated, with the addition of new collaborators, bringing the number to 30, to relate Just Peace to the challenges of terrorism in the new millennium.

The group faced many challenges posed by the wide range of perspectives represented, and indeed, without a professional conflict mediator hired for facilitation, it is likely the group would not have been able to come together sufficiently to produce a paradigm, let alone a volume. But it took more than mediation to bring off the new paradigm.

In the Introduction to the 2008 edition, Glen Stassen writes about the "fact-value" split that was driving the group apart: "The question was raised whether we should emphasize moral principles or political strategies. That led us toward abstract, historically disembodied principles or ideals rather than historically situated practices . . . We found reintegration by explicitly turning to the ethics of normative practices. A practice is neither an ideal nor a rule, but a human activity that regular takes place and that a sociologist could observe."[41]

There are great advantages in the "practice-norms" perspective, not the least of which is "demystifying" peacemaking—that is, not taking from a wish list of things that would be nice to have but are not practical in the "real world"—an unfortunate legacy of the influence of Christian realism on thinking about peace and war.

Just War, as has been previously noted, has a series of criteria that have been refined over centuries to provide some degree of clarity about not only when it is or is not justified for a nation to go to war but also what is and is not justified in the conduct of war. These criteria are not only necessary but they are also indispensable, argues Michael Waltzer. The nature of war is such that "[war] is distinguishable from murder and massacre only when restrictions are established on the reach of battle."[42]

Just Peace also contains a list of (ten) criteria but not ones that are framed as limits on the use of force. In Just Peace, the criteria are actions that historically have proven to reduce or eliminate the use of force. These are called "practice norms." Practice norms are a method that describes the normative nature of practices that have a proven track record in helping reduce violence and increase the presence of peace.

Yet Just Peace as a paradigm based on practice norms is far from perfect and is certainly a product of the different and often competing influences on those who designed and have promoted it. It is a sometimes unstable combination of Western human rights traditions and Western philosophical assumptions about the nature of war, elements of Protestant evangelicalism, pacifist ideas, liberation feminism, African American liberation theology, and Catholic moral reasoning. At no time has Just Peace seriously and directly confronted its legacies from these perspectives in regard to power, the body (and particularly women's bodies and racialized bodies), or a hierarchy in being, and I say that as one of the architects of the original paradigm and an editor and contributor to three volumes on Just Peace. That does not mean there are not latent critiques of these views, and these will be elaborated in the next chapter as a proposal for a Just Peace paradigm that takes power, being, and bodies into account in a far more fundamental way.

The deeply Christian and Western philosophical roots of the Just Peace paradigm were quite evident in the process that produced the first interfaith Just Peace document and then book. Over six years, Jews, Christians, and Muslims worked together and first produced *Abrahamic Alternatives to War: Jewish, Christian and Muslim Perspectives on Just Peacemaking*, edited by me and Glen Stassen. Subsequently, all ten Just Peace practice norms were examined in a book edited by me, *Interfaith Just Peacemaking: Jewish, Christian, and Muslim Perspectives on the New Paradigm of Peace and War.*[43] Fully a third of the participants in this process were women, and there was much greater racial diversity. But there was even less unanimity despite our shared commitments to peacemaking.

Muslim attendees at the many conferences it took to produce the full book, in particular, constantly raised the point that the very approach and structure of the Just Peace paradigm was a Christian and a Western human rights approach, not a Muslim approach, though it had useful practices. Jewish attendees also commented that the Just Peace paradigm, while admirable, was also not specifically Jewish, though it was congruent with many Jewish perspectives.

Not only is the Just Peace paradigm deeply Christian and deeply Western, but it is also rooted in the same traditions that have facilitated the War on Women for so long in Western culture.

Peace and the War on Women

It is crucial for peace work to be effective today, both in addressing the War on Women and the shape of modern war as a "Dirty War," to identify the ways in which patriarchy has affected even the most creative of peace paradigms.

The "practice norms" approach of Just Peace provides a way past some of the difficulties in recasting peace theologies so that they can be even more effective in the work of peacemaking, but much work remains to be done on the nature of power, hierarchy in being, and the legacy of contempt for women's bodies and sexuality.

9

Toward an Embodied Theology of Just Peace

A friend asked me, as I was writing this book, if I really thought the War on Women and war itself could be "ended." I replied in the negative, though it hurt to say so. There are so many deeply embedded forces in Western religion and culture that ensure that the War on Women, and war itself, will rage on. This does not mean these forces cannot be identified and impacted at the root. They can, but it is naïve in the extreme to think they can be eliminated. The practical goals are the prevention and reduction of violence. But this acknowledgement itself is rightly a cause of pain and grief and should always be judged against the ethical urgency that "this should not be."

To witness to violence and refuse to turn away and also accept that it can be prevented or reduced but not ever really eliminated is an aspect of the tragic. We are up against forces that seem to range beyond human control, the work of the "gods," in the Greek perspective of the *Iliad*, that are about ends we cannot really know. In a Christian sense, we could say it is "trans-tragic," as Christian theology has held that humanity is subject to an ultimate justice that judges the world.

The War on Women and war itself, however, are very much conducted in this world and serve this world's interests. Here and now, we have to deal with the constant realities of suffering, injury, and death of bodies from violence and the deeply embedded cultural, economic, political, philosophical, and religious forces that make this whole outrage not only possible but also necessary and justified.

The "here and now" is a crucial starting place for recognizing how Christian theologies need to change in order to be less complicit in the War on Women and war in general and instead more deeply support a changed practice that will strengthen peace movements.

Christian theology is therefore the focus of this chapter on the Just Peace paradigm. Christianity is, of course, only one of the religions of the world, but it is a primary inheritor of the philosophical and religious themes that have shaped Western culture. Just Peacemaking today is very much an interfaith work, as the Jewish, Muslim, and Christian contributors to the volume *Interfaith Just Peacemaking* would agree. Yet, through our debates, the reminders from the Jewish and Muslim contributors that the Just Peace paradigm came from Western culture and largely Christian sources were persuasive. I ultimately have come to agree with these colleagues and, in teaching on interreligious engagement, have more and more come to see that clarity about one's own faith perspectives is an indispensable way to engage in interfaith work. Interfaith work is often misunderstood as finding the religious "lowest common denominator." It is not. It is bringing the best of one's own faith tradition to the table, while also accounting for one's own faith and its legacies in violence and conflict.

I believe we cannot understand the changes needed in a Just Peace paradigm to better address Western legacies in the War on Women and war, unless Christian theological premises, and reconstructions, are closely examined.

Just Peace and Christian Theology

Liberation theological method is a way to take embodied human experience seriously in theology. When I teach this method, I often say, "Theology begins where the pain is." What that means is that the actual condition of human beings—especially as they are subject to such a wide range of suffering, injury, and death—is crucial information we need to know as Christian theologians.

Witnessing to the vast amount of human pain in the world is just a beginning, however. Another crucial change is to deeply question why this would be the case. This is the work of critical consciousness and it genuinely provides a way forward. As my colleague and friend, Mary Potter Engel, once said, "The most liberating question you can ask is, 'Who the hell set things up this way?'" The liberating question for this book is "Why is violence against women and the violence of war so ubiquitous and yet so hidden?"

The answer is that the prevalence of violence in the world is not the work of shadowy "gods," nor is it the way God, as conceived in dominant Christian theologies, exercises providential control over a world locked in sin. The liberating move of critical consciousness, based in theories that expose the underbelly of our civilization, reveals the unholy dependence of Western religion and culture on violence. Violence against women and the violence of war are absolutely critical to the functioning of Western culture and central to Christian theology as it has developed in that culture. Violence is not aberrant, in other words, it is foundational.

Christian theology has within it the very roots of this foundational violence. Christianity cannot be considered an innocent bystander to violence, but is, in some crucial ways, a major perpetrator. Exposing the complicity of some forms of Christian theology in violence, both violence against women and the violence of war, allows us to also work toward different Christian theological perspectives that can be more helpful partners in preventing, reducing, and ending violence.

A critical physicality approach to Christian theology can help construct theologies of peacemaking that are more fully engaged with what actually drives violence. This is a method anchored in the reality of the pain inflicted on the body while this reality is constantly subject to the reflection of critical theory and an engaged practice to prevent or reduce violence. It is a circular movement that starts with the body and returns to the body but asks critical questions regarding the contexts of specific bodies in specific social arrangements and continuously digs down to make crucial connections and to work for change.

To do this well, we have to be willing to really dig down into the dirt of our religious heritage.

Bodies and Dirt

One connection that is often, metaphorically speaking, buried in the dirt is the idea, strongly supported in traditional Christian theology and its sources, that women's bodies and sexuality are "dirty," and that violence is a way to clean that up.

Violence against women in war is called "War's Dirty Secret" as Anne Barstow and her colleagues have shown, and war today is more and more called "Dirty War." From Argentina's Dirty War that raged from the late 1970s to the early 1980s to the current Dirty Wars making the world itself a battlefield, per Jeremy Scahill's work, war is increasingly dirty. But, beyond a similarity of description, it is important to investigate the structural similarities in the War on Women and war itself in the twenty-first century in Western culture and its exports, and why these both are considered "dirty."

Federico Finchelstein, in his exploration of Argentina under the military junta *The Ideological Origins of the Dirty War*, argues, "the Dirty War was not a real war . . . but an illegal militarization of state repression." As Finchelstein describes the Argentine Dirty War, it sounds almost exactly like what I have described as the War on Women. Finchelstein contends that "[f]rom a historical perspective, the Dirty War did not feature two combatants but rather victims and perpetrators."[1] Dirty War is conducted on the bodies of the citizens of the nation conducting the war. This is very like the pattern of the War on Women. The War on Women is a war on their bodies but not a war with them as another combatant.

Dirty, in the descriptions of both these wars, is thus profoundly instructive, especially when we consider how much dirty is a concept deeply rooted in the biblical traditions that inform Christian theology. Dirty is a principal term in sexual morality, and it is opposed relentlessly to *purity* in assessing the sexual conduct of women, especially when women are considered property. In William Countryman's book *Dirt, Greed, and Sex: Sexual Ethics in the New Testament and Their Implications for Today*, these three elements of dirt, sex, and greed are shown to be intimately related.[2] For Countryman, biblical conceptions regarding proper sexual behavior arise from concerns for *purity*, defined as approved sexual conduct, especially by women in cultures in which women and children were often conceived as property.

Control of the body through sexuality understood as property is central in this understanding of dirty. Countryman quotes cultural anthropologist Mary Douglas who describes dirt as "essential disorder," and she invokes "the old definition of dirt as matter out of place."[3] Dirty can be understood as "matter out of place" when we consider that soil in a field about to be plowed is not considered dirty, but a kitchen floor with earth tracked on it by the farmer coming into the house is considered dirty. The dirt is out of place. When women's bodies are deemed "out of place," however, the existential ante has been upped because women's bodies, as has been argued throughout this work, are considered dangerously chaotic. Violence on women's bodies when they get "out of place" is deemed justified, even mandated, to control them and remove the "dirt."

When women are considered "out of place," this often means simply that they are asserting their own autonomy, sexual identity, and economic, political, and religious independence. In a similar way, civilians in repressive societies who try to exercise autonomy from the demands of the state are terrorized and tortured to control them in Dirty War. They are ruthlessly put in their place by violence, even when that means destroying their bodies completely. Sexual violence against women in the War on Women and violence, including sexual violence, visited on vulnerable women, children, and men in Dirty War merges these two forms of control. Violence is justified as a way to "clean up the dirt" of unruly bodies of women in patriarchal culture and to clean up the dirt of unruly citizens in a repressive society.

Bodies in Argentina's Dirty War, like the bodies of women in the War on Women throughout Western history and culture, were "disappeared" as one definitive way to "clean it up." The literal and metaphorical disappearance of the body in the Western tradition, especially in Christian theology, must be confronted and the body reclaimed as central to peacemaking. We have to keep our eyes on what is happening to bodies and expose the efforts to hide bodies. But this can never be the body in general. Some bodies are "dirtier" than others.

It is thus not enough to "put the body" at the center of peacemaking approaches like Just Peace in an effort to make this paradigm more effective. Reclaiming the centrality of the physical is only one correction needed. The deeply embedded mechanisms of hierarchy—especially hierarchies of gender and race—facilitate power inequalities and subordination. These need to be constantly exposed through critical reflection and rejected through changed practice. In this way, a more complex notion of embodiment can emerge.

Critical Theological Analysis

Protesting Hierarchies of Gender and Race

To posit a hierarchy of being itself is to predetermine what will be justified or unjustified in the use of force. Some beings, in other words, are authorized to use force and others are not; indeed, the "others" who are not authorized to use force are then cast as the designated victims.

In Christian theological terms, this notion of predetermined order in the use of force is rooted in the "rule of the soul over the body" and the "mind and the rational element" construed as belonging almost exclusively to elite, dominant-race males. Aristotle lays this out in no uncertain terms: "[T]he male is by nature superior, and the female inferior; the one rules, and the other is ruled; this principle of necessity extends to all mankind."[4] This provides what we might call a biologically based defense of the use of force, when extrapolated, to justify violence in the home and in slavery.

It is not that far, culturally speaking, from Aristotle to the United States today. For example, when I did domestic violence counseling of women at a center where there was a court-mandated program for male abusers, the man who ran those sessions told me that the male abusers were wholly convinced that *they had done nothing wrong*. They deeply resented being required to go to counseling, as they saw themselves in the right and believed their wives were the ones who had brought the violence on themselves through disobedience. He told me that if he was not able to break through this mind-set with someone, the court-mandated counseling would fail.

This is the Just Battering tradition in practice in an American suburb. To return to Aristotle and his legacy for Christian theology, what a hierarchy of being provides for Western culture is a way to make the use of force a good, not an evil, when it is used by designated elites against those lower down the chain, whether women, nondominant races, or in colonialism, whole nations deemed "lesser" compared to Western culture. Rape is similarly justified because women do not "deserve" to exercise sexual autonomy. Their very being is defined as in sexual service to those above them in the hierarchy.

God, as conceived in hierarchical theologies, sits at the top of the chain, imaged as "King" or "Ruler" in a merging of religious and political imagery. God will then logically be the author of war, as a "Holy Warrior," or the divine abuser who uses violence against women to punish them for (even imagined) disobedience. This is the connection between divine providence and the rape of the consecrated virgins, in Augustine's view. Even their imagined disobedience deserved punishment. Yet Protestant peace theologies that emerged as protest against the merging of unjust political and religious rule did not provide a real alternative when it came to the use of force against women as they managed to incorporate some of this body/soul dualism that is used to justify gender and race hierarchies.

Theologies that would more deeply confront violence must jettison the hierarchies that coopt God into being the ultimate perpetrator of violence. This is very difficult to do, as these hierarchies cannot be willed away by the individual or even by whole groups without sustained movements to continually act out the alternatives.

Movements to continuously act out alternatives are what I have come to call a "theology of protest." Individuals and groups that have been subordinated cannot merely think their way into a new way of acting; they must act their way into a new way of thinking. Protest movements themselves provide the way to enact a different theological anthropology and different doctrine of God in relation to the human person.

This work is difficult, perhaps even impossible, to do as a sole individual. Violence works to induce a sense of helplessness in the one victimized. Judith Herman observes how difficult it was for those who began to understand the widespread trauma visited on women and girls, like Bertha Pappenheim, to act on this knowledge without wider movements. It was not until the consciousness-raising movement of the 1970s that women began to find each other, tell their stories, and realize that the violence against them was not their individual fault but part of a very large and widespread pattern that we are calling the War on Women. Vietnam veterans did similar work, and much of what we know today about post-traumatic stress disorder came from the unruly work of those veterans who would not just sit down and shut up about what they had experienced in war. The Civil Rights movement protested the racial hierarchies that produced so much racial injustice and confronted the force used to sustain them, a force deemed justified by inequality in being according to race.

Group support and action in solidarity provide ways to actually merge body and soul and live in a different vision of oneself not as someone acted upon but an actor in one's own life and in the life of the world. Women's movements, antiwar movements, civil rights movements, movements for LGBTQ rights, and protests against economic injustice are crucial theological work because people actually put themselves physically in direct opposition to the kinds of hierarchies that would define that act—the act of protest—as the consummate disobedience.

It is crucial to be disobedient; in other words, it is crucial to understand oneself in the image of the disobedient God, the God of Jesus, the unruly Nazarene who protested moneychangers in the Temple and who was ultimately killed for his refusal to submit to the reigning political and religious authorities.

For women to be disobedient takes great courage but can be humanly defining in powerful ways. I remember my Great Aunt Helen telling me what it felt like the first time she and my grandmother decided to go to a rally for women's suffrage. They were teenaged, Hungarian immigrant women with traditionally long hair. They decided to cut their long hair before they went, she said, and she remembered going out on the street and feeling the wind on her neck. My great aunt was not given to poetic description and yet she remembered vividly feeling different in her body.

Feeling the wind on your neck as you move out into the world to protest injustice has always seemed to me to be a powerful metaphor for overcoming body/soul dualism through direct action. Wind functions religiously in powerful ways. In Genesis, the wind or breath of God moves over the "darkness and deep." The darkness and the deep, along with the formless earth, have been understood as the three elements of chaos. In the *Enuma Elish*, these are personified as Ti'amat, who must be subdued for order to be established by a warrior/god—namely, Marduk. This story is told in this way to provide support for the chaos/nomos theory of creation and to set up a theo-political justification of hierarchy in creation.

Wind, breath, or spirit, however, can take on different meanings when what is blowing are the winds of change, the storm wind of resistance. Chaos need not be the enemy, and the work of God-with-us may not be to subdue chaos but, in fact, to blow strongly and maybe create a little chaos in the face of repression. At Pentecost, the sound like the "rush of a violent wind" (Acts 2:2) blew through the room where the disciples were, and all of a sudden, Peter predicts upheaval in the society by both women and men, as "your sons and your daughters shall prophecy." In Judaism as well as Christianity, the spirit can create a little chaos, of course, especially through the prophets.

Human beings engaged in protest are often acting out of a prophetic challenge to the status quo; they are not willing any longer to be repressed and subdued through an imposed order. Not all protest is in the spirit of God, of course, but those who pour out into the streets are often doing so precisely to create enough chaos that they will overwhelm repressive regimes.

While theologies of protest have emerged, especially since the beginning of the twentieth century, they are far from perfect manifestations of justice as race and gender hierarchies structure the very movements designed to challenge hierarchy.

More subversion of the prevailing power structures is needed.

Subverting Power and Subordination

In my view, a primary connection between Christianity and the War on Women is the religiously sanctioned subordination of women. Hand-in-hand with hierarchy of being, power and subordination are crucial to sustain this inequality. Submission itself is institutionalized violence—a structure of unequal power that puts women in a vulnerable position in the home. This theological presumption of power inequality justifies abuse in the name of Christian obedience by women.[5]

Understanding how power functions theologically is only part of the challenge. The second is to actually subvert that power.

One primary way power functions in Christian theology to sustain dominance and subordination is through the idea of sacrifice, especially an understanding that the death of Jesus of Nazareth on a Roman cross was a sacrifice, not an unjust execution. For Christian theology, the symbol of the cross has been problematic as it can be seen to valorize physical violence.

As seen so startlingly in "The Dream of the Rood," but also in a much more contemporary way in *The Passion of the Christ*, the cross itself can function in Christian theology to create heroic myth and to justify violent retribution in a presumed battle between good and evil. The person and work of Jesus Christ have been used to support, even demand, this interpretation and then have been recruited to facilitate women being forced to submit to violence as a "sacrifice." So many times, women whom I have counseled who have been battered have told me that they first tried to tell their pastors about the abuse, and they were advised by these Christian leaders to "go home and forgive him as Christ forgave you from the cross."

The suffering and death of Jesus of Nazareth on the cross are not a justification for violence, either violence against women or violence in war. The cross subverts power as dominance and subordination because, through this unjust suffering, the meaning of the incarnation—the becoming one with humanity by Jesus—is a full and complete identification even with the most horrific forms of suffering inflicted by some human beings on others.

In a class I teach on violence, one year a woman student told about having gone to the dump to drop off some trash. While there, she was grabbed from behind and raped. Her rapist warned her that if she got up from the garbage heap, he would kill her. She lay there, and as she did, she had a vision of Jesus on the cross who said to her, "You don't have to tell me what you feel. I know."

That is why the protest memorial in Bolivia, shown on the cover of this book, is a profound theological subversion of the power that has driven femicide in that country. The cross itself can be a judgment on unjust suffering and, in conjunction with a protest movement, can subvert power conceived as dominance and subordination. It is not the crosses themselves, in other words, that challenge the prevailing power that commits femicide; it is the use of the cross as symbol by the very women who are the targets of that violence and who are saying, "You will no longer be allowed to do this to us because we will not submit."

It is extraordinary to me that the actual power exercised by Jesus of Nazareth that led to his death and ultimately to the committed movement of his disciples is not more often seen as the power of subversion of the regime of power exercised by the Roman occupying power in Judea and their religious collaborators, the Jewish religious authorities. I write about this extensively in *#Occupy the Bible: What Jesus Really Said (and Did) about Money and Power*.[6]

The way to subvert unjust power in Christianity is through a theology of subversion, understood as a sustained and critically informed way to contradict or reverse dominance in a system. But power is poorly understood not only in theology but also in politics. Understanding power is absolutely crucial to ending the War on Women and war itself.

Gene Sharp, who has been called the "Machiavelli of nonviolence," offers a perspective on power that is absolutely crucial to the transformation of society away from dominance and subordination. Sharp's key insight is that power is not monolithic, it is not "held" by those in power. Rather, any power structure derives from the obedience of subjects to the orders of the ruler or rulers. If subjects refuse to obey, the regime collapses. But the way regimes consolidate their power is complex and actually diffuse. There are the institutions of police, courts, and the military that provide enforcement and the moral or ethical norms (most powerfully of religion) that generate citizen obedience and thus prop up the power of the state. Citizens who obey are rewarded, and those who do not are punished.

Sharp argues that this consolidated power is absolutely dependent on this obedience, and thus his theory of how to exercise power in a conflict is for citizens to withdraw cooperation. This is the role of nonviolent direct action; it is a way to exercise the real power citizens have in order to engage effectively in conflict with repressive regimes. Because Sharp deals so directly with how to exercise power, he is often subject to critiques by pacifists: "When I used to lecture, I would always get complaints from the pacifists . . . They would say I wasn't pure. They said that what I was proposing was 'still conflict.'"[7] That much is true. Sharp's view is not "pure"; another way to state that is that he does not see peacemaking as "innocent" but rather as willing to get down into the dirt of repressive power and engage it there.

Sharp has advised rebels around the world. More than 20 years ago, he was invited to Burma, and he wrote a pamphlet. "I didn't know Burma well," he recalls. "So I had to write generically: if a movement wanted to bring a dictatorship to an end, how would they do it?" That pamphlet, *From Dictatorship to Democracy* (1993), "contained the idea for which Sharp is now known all over the world—that power is held only by the consent of the people over whom it is exercised, and that consent can be withdrawn." In 2005, he published a comprehensive work *Waging Nonviolent Struggle: 20th Century Practice and 21st Century Potential* that adds case studies of how to wage nonviolent conflict effectively.

Christian theologies that are based on a primary violence—especially violence against women conceived of as submission—serve what are effectively religious dictatorships. The good news from Sharp is that there are many, many points of subversion of this dictatorial theology because the more unruly women become in moving together against the violence being done to them, the more the system weakens from the inside.

Yet the physical and psychological effects of power exercised as dominance, either through physical violence or the threat of violence, are real. Suppressive power quite literally writes itself on the body in physical and psychological injury and in extinguishing life.

That is why the peacemaker must always return to the touchstone of the body and why dealing with the body in a primary way is crucial to the work of peace.

Reclaiming Physicality

We must put the body at the center of peacemaking because it is at the level of the body where the injuries and death caused by violence occur and where these assaults are experienced by survivors and carried in their bodies, minds, and spirits.

Violence is traumatic. "Unlike commonplace misfortunes," Judith Herman writes, "traumatic events generally involve threats to life or bodily integrity, or a close personal encounter with violence and death."[8] Unhealed trauma is shattering for the human self and can result in disempowerment, disconnection, and alienation. Trauma produces an existential crisis, a threat to basic trust in the self, others, the world, and God. Healing from trauma is central to reclaiming physicality in Christian peacemaking.

Trauma fragments the person and body, mind, and spirit become disconnected. This response can be a survival mechanism during the trauma. A rape survivor describes the way the detachment of body and spirit can occur to protect the person from intolerable pain: "I left my body at that point. I was over next to the bed, watching this happen . . . I dissociated from the helplessness. I was standing next to me and there was just this shell on the bed . . . There was just a feeling of flatness. I was just there."[9] This dissociation from the body is what happens to women in prostitution. Women who have been prostituted "get through it" by denying what they are feeling in their bodies, as Rita Brock and I have written. This disconnection from the body is dangerous for them. Women who work the streets in Chicago, for example, do so even in extremely cold weather. They can get frostbite because they literally ignore pain in their bodies. At Genesis House, where I volunteered, massage therapists would also volunteer their time to help women reintegrate their physical sensations. These women would actually have to relearn how to feel in their bodies.

Just Peace needs to deal with trauma theory more directly, both in terms of peace practices, and also in terms of peace theology. Leymah Gbowee's work is instructive in this way, because she describes how trauma work helped build the framework for the women's peace movement in Liberia. She went to work as a volunteer at the Lutheran Church in Liberia/Lutheran World Federation's Trauma Healing and Reconciliation Program (RHRP). The Lutheran pastors, lay leaders, teachers, and health workers had joined with the Christian Health Association since the civil war started in 1991, attempting to repair the social and psychological damage caused by the war. Leaders in the program would go to villages and encourage residents who had experienced violence to tell their stories and then they would teach them conflict resolution strategies.[10]

This is peacebuilding, Gbowee says. It is much more complicated than brokering treaties. "Peace-building to me isn't ending a fight by standing between two opposing forces. It's healing those victimized by war, making them strong again, and bringing them back to the people they once were." But victimizers too need to be helped in order to "rediscover their humanity" and to repair the whole society.

But something happened to that theory when women were invited to tell their personal stories. Gbowee expected to "hear about war," and in a way, she did. She heard about the War on Women. Women told about husbands demanding sex and "burdening them with too many children." They told about feeling that they "had no value as a person," and they talked about experiencing domestic violence.

"Women are the sponges," she realized. Women take everything in and are expected to hold it. But holding it in is misery and "as crippling as holding on to rage." It has to come out for women to heal from the trauma of all their lives; this trauma in Liberia intersected with war, but in crucial ways it was more foundational than war. These women's whole lives were traumatized by the war they were subjected to merely for being women. "Women who have suffered for nearly as long as they can remember come to a point where they look down, not ahead. But as we kept working, women began to look up and listen." In doing trauma therapy, they then began to heal their nation.

Trauma therapy, to be effective, must include telling the story of the actual injuries and the bodily sensations that were felt; without remembering the very physicality of the trauma, the work of reintegrating body, mind, and spirit does not occur or occurs less well. Unhealed trauma, then, risks being relived over and over. This repetition phenomenon can be rooted in a drive to actually try to integrate the traumatic experiences, but because the emotions are so powerful, they can simply overwhelm the person and doom them to alienation from their own bodies, minds, and spirits.[11]

This is illuminating for the problematic relationship Christianity has had with the body. While physicality is central to Christianity, since Jesus is understood to be God incarnate in human flesh, the crucifixion of Jesus is a founding trauma in the Christian narrative. The "body in pain" is there, as a central part of the faith drama. We have discussed the way the violent images in the writing of John of Patmos could have been a way to deal dramatically with the unhealed trauma of the brutal killings, not only of Jesus, but also of many of the disciples and followers.

To be a peace partner in helping provide healing from trauma from the War on Women and war, Christian theology itself needs to forthrightly reject the reenactment of the trauma of the killing of Jesus of Nazareth as violence we are doomed to live over and over. The life and ministry of Jesus, along with his death at the hands of tyrannical power, need to be at the center of our communal commitment to telling all the stories of violence and violation among us in all their physical manifestations. The work of Christian theology, then, can become the work of reintegration of our bodies, minds, and spirits in a supportive environment, along with the commitment to work together to protest hierarchical control and subvert power as dominance among ourselves and in our society.

American society is still reenacting several primary traumas as perpetrators, victims, and survivors in our history. From genocide against Native Americans, to slavery, through racism, the widespread violence against women, and violence against LGBT Americans, we are scarcely the peaceful, freedom-loving people of the dominant American myths. These traumas intersect and mutually reinforce, being recreated over and over in each generation. A Christianity that is captive to repeating a primary trauma cannot help such a society understand the damage done by these traumas, let alone get to a place where survivors and perpetrators can each confront their role.

Anyone in the movement against the War on Women or against war (or both) does not escape having a role in this national rollout of traumas. This is why critical theories of race, gender, and sexual orientation are indispensable to reclaiming the body in peacebuilding. We can so easily reenact the traumas of victimization and/or so quickly fall into the role of perpetrator even as we are trying to help one another heal and build movements of solidarity and change.

This is a given. There is no "getting over" our national traumas and no getting past the traumas of other nations or our roles in global trauma. Concerted effort toward healing must be part of our peace work. And let us remember, we ourselves can be survivors or perpetrators, and we are certainly witnesses of many forms of trauma.

There is only dealing with it. But that does not mean we cannot be creative about how we do so. In fact, creativity is indispensable to making meaningful space for real change.

An Erotic Peacemaking

Erasmus was right to have his personified figure of Peace lament, "Why don't you love me?" But he was wrong to cast his lament as a romance. Loving peace is not a pretty Renaissance romance, and Peace is not sitting around waiting for the peacemaker to come rescue her from bad, old war. Peacemaking needs an entirely different script, one that reconstructs erotic desire in fundamental ways.

Peace theologies often fail to recognize the role that the social construction of desire plays in why violence is so ubiquitous. War exists because it is made to seem highly desirable. In regard to the War on Women, the social construction of desire for access to women's bodies is a primary reason women are subject to so many forms of violence. Racism and homophobia each have deep aspects of desire in their structures.

We have also seen how the projection of desire onto people and nations that are the object for conquest is a completely overlooked aspect of Just War theory. War is desirable because violence has been eroticized, both politically and in terms of the primary Just Battering and Just Rape traditions of Western culture. The failure to recognize the role of desire in the longing to exercise force as dominance and control undermines the effectiveness of Just War in actually preventing and restraining war, as the real motivations for conquest remain hidden. It also undermines traditional peace theories as they underestimate how powerful the lure of conquest can be.

The erotic normalization of violence is constructed from an alienation from the body, a valorizing of power as dominance, and a hierarchy of being that delivers appropriate objects of violence to perpetrators. This kind of construction of the erotic as suppressive seems hidden and is yet everywhere visible if we will only look. Try this experiment for yourself. Google the phrase "the erotic," and my guess is that the same top search result will appear on your screen as did on mine: TheEroticReview.com. It is a website that allows customers to rate their experience with prostitutes (called "providers" on the site). The phrase "the erotic" to Google, and to millions of others around the world, means, first of all, purchased sexual services. Erotic means prostitution and is often then a synonym for pornography.

This notion of the erotic is the common reductionism of Western attitudes toward the erotic. It is what Audre Lorde, the Womanist writer and activist, describes as a "plasticized" erotic. The plasticized version of the erotic is a way to suppress feelings. In her view, the erotic is actually the opposite. It is a "measure between the beginnings of our sense of self and the chaos of our strongest feelings." Lorde, as noted previously, understands the erotic as truly "born of Chaos," from the Greek derivation of eros—"the personification of love in all its aspects." Thus, for Lorde, the erotic is the "assertion of the lifeforce of women; of that creative energy empowered, the knowledge and sense of which we are now reclaiming in our language, our history, our dancing, our loving, our work, our lives."[12]

According to Lorde, in a "patriarchal, racist, and anti-erotic society" women's empowerment through doing their own work in their own way is a measure of the erotic. In the argument I am advancing here, it means embracing the chaos of disobedience, the full-body work of protest and the right to get and give support for healing from trauma.

Can a more effective Just Peace method be advanced out of these insights and become one that works from the erotic, not against it?

First of all, the lives of women need to be prioritized in a way that they have not been in either Pacifism or Just Peace. There are those who will wonder why it is the "lifeforce of women" that is named by Lorde as the nexus of erotic power. One can hear the question echo, "What about the lifeforce of men?" But to quote the famous twentieth-century theologian, Karl Barth, albeit from a totally different context, "If you are defending everything but what is under attack, what are you doing?" The lifeforce of women has been under attack in fundamental ways in Western culture for millennia and this attack has been structured along sexual, racial, and even economic hierarchies. Today, in fact, it is demonstrably a model for modern war. This fact alone should make any person serious about peacemaking pay attention to Lorde and what she is saying about the power of the erotic and women.

But anyone who thinks this sounds like an easy task and that we can just reframe eroticism as the lifeforce of women in order to better advance peacemaking should do a close reading of Sharon Patrician Holland in *The Erotic Life of Racism*. She uses critical race theory as well as Womanism, queer theory, and sexuality studies to examine how, while racism is so profoundly "ordinary," it manages to operate as a powerful system that yet remains largely hidden. The personal and political dimensions of desire are embedded in racism itself. Holland moves into the territory of the erotic, understanding racism as constitutive of the practice of racial being and erotic choice. But this is not linear. Holland shows that "although contemporary sexuality studies and queer theory have committed themselves to a thoroughgoing analysis of racist practice, rarely do they actually succeed in this endeavor." There is, in fact, a vast amount of work to do to expose how desire works to demean and distort human relationships and structure them on a continuum from microaggressions to murder. Shifting how we construct desire away from its powerful role in normalizing violence to empowering peacemaking will be, as Reverend Susan Russell titles her blog, *An Inch at a Time*.

An erotic peacemaking has to privilege such insights, both from Lorde and from Holland, and make a serious attempt to engage critical consciousness about the way gender, sex, and race privilege have not only fundamentally structured war making but will also inevitably be embedded in even the most creative attempts to reframe peacemaking in Western culture. A reconstruction of the erotic as a measure of our individual and societal capacity to actually desire justice and peace must be undertaken, however. It is a way to profoundly engage justice in the work of peacemaking and will qualify our efforts as actually "Just" Peace. Yes, this work is long and complex, but more and more, critical theory helps provide clues for how to proceed.

Witnessing to Women's Lives

The War on Women is an invisible war that is going on all the time, hidden by cultural, economic, political, and religious views that normalize this violence. This war is dismissed and has not been considered a primary goal of peacemaking. Instead, wars (as the violent conflict between nations) or civil wars (as violent conflict within nations), have been the primary focus of peace work.

Both war and peace are gendered; war is masculinized as strong and heroic, and peace is feminized as weak and dependent. Even when war is decried, it receives a lot of attention because it is masculinized. And of course, very often war is not decried but is considered an object of heroic efforts to triumph over threat. Peacemakers are feminized and made nearly as invisible as women in the War on Women because their work is not heroic strength but is cast as weakness.

One of the hardest things for those dedicated to peace to do is to break through the weak/strong dichotomy, where war, as masculinized, is considered strong and peace, as feminized, is considered weak. This view is everywhere in the foreign-policy establishment, and it is very difficult to impact meaningfully. "Soft power" and "hard power" are obviously gendered versions of this same dichotomy. When she was secretary of state, Hillary Clinton attempted to break this impasse with "smart power," but it received little attention and ultimately had no traction.

The irony today is, of course, contemporary war strongly resembles the War on Women, and strategies developed to prevent or reduce the War on Women could potentially be very much needed in dealing with today's wars, where the whole world is a battlefield. This is why we very much need an embodied Just Peace that prioritizes just gender relations and that prevents or reduces violence against women.

Care must be taken, however, not to "instrumentalize" this focus on violence against women as it reveals the deep mechanisms of modern Dirty War and the ways in which bodies, especially of women and other vulnerable citizens, are the battlefields. Then, ending modern Dirty War becomes the real end game, and the War on Women is secondary, a good "byproduct" of the primary goal of stopping war.

Because of the prevalence and virulence of rape and sexual violence against women and other vulnerable civilians in modern Dirty War, the fields of international security and international relations have begun to take this form of violence more seriously. As noted by Jacqui True in *The Political Economy of Violence against Women*, "Physical violence against women perpetrated by enemy states or groups fits well within the remit of security studies, which largely focuses on physical security and threats to it within interstate contexts." The author points out the problem, however, that this approach does not consider "everyday violence" against women, and it is thus "limited as an approach to understanding the structural causes and consequences of violence against women."[13]

The "everyday" violence against women is, however, a structural mechanism that runs in and through Western culture, priming it to accept as normative the physical, psychological, and spiritual pain visited upon women and others deemed legitimate victims. Thus witnessing women's lives in the Just Peace paradigm cannot be something "added" to the various practice norms such as democracy or economic justice. Addressing the structural causes of violence against women is the only way for a Just Peace paradigm to actually get at the deep sources of conflict among and within nations and within homes and on the streets of every city and town.

For Christian peacemakers, prioritizing violence against women needs to be a theological conversion, where the roots of violence against women in Christian faith are understood to be part of what normalizes violence in Western culture. This much-needed conversion actually addresses one issue that frequently arises in relationship to prioritizing women's physical, mental, and spiritual safety in society; the priority of this work is challenged because "violence against women is part of the culture" in a given context.

I agree. I work within my own context, and I can say for certain that, in that context, violence against women is deeply and profoundly cultural. That's what I am trying to change. Violence against women is also part of many other cultures around the globe. I am not willing to prescribe for other cultures and other religions that may be part of that culture what they need to do in terms of examining their own faiths and cultural norms to prevent and reduce the War on Women. That is for them to do. But I am saying that they need to do it.

The War on Women is a war, and it is not a Just War. It is a profound moral wrong and must be challenged with every resource a culture can provide, especially resources from its religious faiths.

Conclusion

"Can I Get a Witness?"

Witnessing to the vast global War on Women is challenging. There are so many forces that push us to look away and to not even see violence that is going on right in front of us. This witnessing, however, is the indispensable starting place to begin to perceive how women's bodies are made into battlefields. Seeing what happens to the body, and doing contextual analysis of what these bodies mean in Western culture, suggests paths for change in how we go about the work of peacemaking in a world where the War on Women and war itself is everywhere.

Peacemaking itself is a challenging task, and those of us who worked on the original Just Peace paradigm nearly quit several times because of how vast and daunting this work was. The breakthrough moment was the identification of what came to be called "practice norms." These are historically based, concrete examples of work that, when undertaken, have been shown to reduce violence and increase the likelihood of peace. This model has been described as breaking through the fact/value split in the peace movement, between realists and idealists.

Yet further work remains to be done, work that is likely unending. There is no completely escaping the legacies of denigration of the body, hierarchy of being, and power as dominance that are so deeply embedded in Western culture. Those practices that were selected as normative, in the Just Peace paradigm, have also come from the very histories and ideas that have been shown to be foundational for violence against women.

It is actually fortunate, therefore, that the Just Peace paradigm was generated from so many traditions and perspectives, some of which are genuinely in conflict with others. Religious perspectives from the historic peace churches, mainline and Evangelical Protestantism, historic African American churches, and the Catholic Church were combined, not always successfully, with human rights perspectives, political theory, and the philosophy of Just War. Women, sexual minorities, racial/ethnic minorities, and frankly, their voices and views, were consistently unrepresented or underrepresented, mirroring the legacies of Western culture.

I say this is fortunate because the paradigm of Just Peace actually benefits from this multiplicity. Making peace with justice is not a linear process, and it is often quite contradictory. It requires intensive contextual analysis, not only of conflict in a given culture, but also of the social locations, beliefs, attitudes, and practices of those who would engage as peacemakers. Just Peace, like the other dominant paradigms of peace and war, was not primarily generated out of the experiences of women, sexual minorities, and racial/ethnic minorities. But the diversity of the architects, and the paradigm they created, is less unitary and thus lends itself better to both internal and external critique in its application.

Critical physicality adds tremendous complexity to the contextual analysis required of Just Peacemaking. In this conclusion, I will make suggestions of what a critical physicality adds to the Just Peace paradigm both in terms of critical questions and needed changes.

What happens to the Just Peace paradigm when we desire the well-being of the body and make it central to the task of peacemaking? Just Peace, like the other paradigms of war and peace, has not made the well-being of bodies, and the well-being of specific bodies in specific contexts of suppressive power and domination, central. In order for Just Peace to be less complicit in the War on Women, beginning with the bodies of women and applying critical theory to the practice itself, illuminates further work that needs to be done. The following are just a few examples of this kind of work. It is suggestive rather than definitive, mirroring the circular process of critical physicality.

Support Nonviolent Direct Action

Many of the twentieth- and twenty-first-century practices of nonviolent direct action, not only marches but strikes, boycotts, and public disclosure, have been directed toward more visibly public injustices such as the suppression of political and economic rights. Suppression of women's rights is not only part of political and economic suppression but also includes the forms of intimate violence such as rape and domestic violence.

Engaging in nonviolent protest is absolutely foundational for an embodied Just Peace and especially for an embodied Just Peace that tackles the drivers of the War on Women. Women themselves are the primary actors in this work, as they need to put their bodies "out of place" in order to experience a new humanity, to be seen by the larger society as refusing submission, and very importantly, to directly exercise power. Women who have survived trauma are often very engaged in social movements and can find it healing to try to make right what is so deeply wrong with the world. "Public truth telling" is one of the practices of nonviolent direct action, and survivors realize better than most people the drive to shove the violence out of sight and to silence those who try to tell the truth.

Nonviolent direct action is frequently misunderstood, however. It is, as Sharp has shown, an exercise of power and coercive power at that. Those who engage in such actions are embodying their own power and forcing suppressive regimes to confront their own powerlessness. This is profoundly enraging to suppressive regimes, and they will respond with physical violence to what they perceive (rightly, it turns out) as a threat.

Women who engage in nonviolent direct action are seen as particularly threatening, and they are frequently subject to physical violence. A suffrage parade in 1913 in the United States was subject to violence, perhaps especially because it was racially diverse. Members of the Black sorority Delta Sigma Theta marched as a delegation, while Black journalist and antilynching activist Ida B. Wells participated as well. Women suffrage activists who silently picketed the White House were subject to mass arrest, and when they went on hunger strikes, they were force-fed. Delores Huerta, a domestic violence activist as well as cofounder of the United Farm Workers Union, was so badly beaten by the police that she was on disability for much of her life.[1]

But violence against women in mass action is not done exclusively by repressive political powers. Women in peace and justice demonstrations can also be attacked; when I was in Egypt after the January 25 revolution, Egyptian women told me about going to Tahrir Square to join the demonstrations and being subject to horrific sexual abuse and sexual violence by the Egyptian men demonstrating for democratic freedoms. Women were not safe from sexual violence in the Occupy encampments either.[2]

In our early work on defining Just Peace practices, I added "safe spaces" to the more traditionally understood work of nonviolent protest. Domestic violence shelters and rape crisis centers were created primarily by women who were survivors and who came together to provide physical safety for women who had been victimized in the War on Women. The War on Women attacks them in their bodies and securing the physical safety of bodies is thus illuminated as indispensable to the work of peacemaking. In both the War on Women and in war, the bodies of women are made into battlefields, and so the struggle must begin at the level of their physical and psychological safety.

Physical safety as a practice norm is not limited to women, of course, as peace activists are routinely subject to beatings, arrest, incarceration, torture, and murder for their work. The importance of the body in peacemaking, therefore, cannot ever be less than an absolute priority, and the dynamics of the War on Women reveal this.

Take Independent Initiatives to Reduce Threat

The strategy of "independent initiatives" was first proposed by Charles Osgood in 1962. Osgood's argument was that in a relationship of distrust and heightened threat perception, nations are blocked from initiating peacemaking steps themselves. A new strategy was needed to initiate concrete and verifiable changes that would reduce threats. Hopefully, the "other side" would follow suit.

This strategy is one that comes from the public-policy arena, though it was strongly supported by Glen Stassen, a Baptist member of our original Just Peace group, who argued it was highly congruent with his Evangelical interpretation of the teachings of Jesus. It has been useful as a tool of foreign policy, but it is one of the practices that is least helpful when applied to the War on Women unless it is rethought from a gendered-power analysis of the weak/strong dichotomy. It is also a Just Peace practice, I would argue, that is not all that helpful in Dirty War, as Dirty War so resembles the War on Women.

The War on Women is not a war on them but a war about them that is conducted on their bodies. The same is true for Dirty War. The bodies of women and/or vulnerable citizens are not safe, so any move to lower perceptions of threat will likely be a source of increased violence against them rather than a reduction of tension. The "lack of consent to vulnerability," as Mary Potter Engel argues is so characteristic of those who perpetrate violence against women or other vulnerable people, means the power dynamic between nations or even between armed groups is not the same as in the War on Women or in Dirty War.

If the issue is with the violence perpetrated on the bodies of women, but the conflict is not with them but about them, this suggests that "taking independent initiatives to reduce threat in the War on Women" requires the reconstruction of masculinity away from violence as a way to achieve power and status in a masculinized society. The very definition of "strong" must be remade, and this requires independent initiatives taken by men with men. There are many examples of this, the "White Ribbon Campaign" begun in Canada in 1991 being but one example. The group was formed after an antifeminist man murdered 14 female engineering students at the École Polytechnique in Montreal. Men in the group attempt to challenge the culture of silence about violence against women. The men wear a white ribbon, not to indicate that the wearer was a "great guy," nor "an act of contrition, nor a symbol of misplaced collective guilt," but rather, the wearing of the ribbon was "a personal pledge never to commit, condone or remain silent about violence against women."[3] This campaign has spread around the world and is now linked to the 16 Days campaign.

The difference in this campaign from the independent-initiatives model by Osgood is that the initiative does not presume a shared context of conflict but rather a one-sided effort to change the structure of violence itself. Dirty War cannot be ended through independent initiatives by citizens being persecuted, tortured, and disappeared as the power inequalities are so vast; the attempt to do so by citizens would leave them vulnerable to attack. Repressive regimes could potentially take independent initiatives, but this is unlikely in the extreme given the one-sided notion of power among those who conduct Dirty War. Pressure on repressive regimes by other world powers has had some effect; this is analogous to the White Ribbon as men ending the culture of silence on the War on Women puts pressure on other men.

Another example of the way independent initiatives need a different dynamic in the War on Women is how women have struggled to take independent initiatives to control their own bodies through contraception and abortion. The struggle for women's reproductive freedom is a titanic and ongoing struggle by women to actually take the independent initiative to claim their bodies as their own. Theologian and ethicist Beverly Harrison's book on this struggle, *Our Right to Choose: Toward a New Ethic of Abortion*, remains the standard as Harrison argues that a truly moral society must centrally include women's free choice to bear children.

It is highly instructive to remember that most of what has been called the War on Women in the public square has been about women's access to contraception and abortion, as has been argued. This will continue to be a primary site of the war on them, because the war against women's freedom and self-determination is literally waged on their bodies. In 2015, when Congress shifted to having a Republican majority in both houses, these legislators introduced five bills designed to restrict women's access to abortion in the first three days of the new legislative session. As the United States faces suppressed wages, the need for immigration reform, increased threats from climate change, and a host of other urgent concerns, regulating women's bodies was these politicians' first choice for concerted action.[4]

This is a direct and even lethal threat to women and girls. In the US context, as one Planned Parenthood clinic after another is forced to close, women and girls are hurt in their reproductive health, and they are being injured and dying from efforts to end unwanted pregnancy. Even so, women experiencing this threat to make their bodies the site of political domination are still trying to take independent initiatives to exercise their own bodily choices. In Texas, after repressive anti-abortion-clinic legislation went into effect, women "put things in their vagina," or went to Mexico to get "clandestine abortions" in dirty clinics, or they take "miso"—pills that are abortifacients. These actions can clearly be harmful or fatal for women, as they can get infections or even bleed to death. Even the pills can be dangerous, as women taking the pills without medical help can take the pills incorrectly and suffer physical harm. Women volunteers have set up hotlines to help women understand how to take the pills. This "DIY culture" on abortion has been around globally for a long time, and now it is coming to the United States because of an American repressive regime that makes power over women's bodies a cornerstone of its political agenda.[5]

In domestic and global contexts, an embodied Just Peace must reflect the gendered nature of the power inequalities operative in any context in this weak/strong/masculinized/feminized dynamic. In terms of taking independent initiative, exercise of this practice norm, without critical consciousness about this dualistic understanding of power, will otherwise risk increasing not decreasing conflict.

Use Cooperative Conflict Resolution

Cooperative conflict resolution (CCR) is a well-established method used to engage parties in dialogue to find creative solutions with which they can all live. Cooperative conflict resolution, when looked at from the perspective of critical physicality, has some serious flaws, however, at least for some contexts.

Take the example of the recent movement often called #BlackLivesMatter that emerged to protest police or vigilantes killing unarmed African Americans with impunity. This movement began with the shooting death of Trayvon Martin by George Zimmerman and Zimmerman's acquittal. The website #BlackLivesMatter .com, created by three African American women—Alicia Garza, Patrisse Cullors, and Opal Tometi—describes the needed complexities. Garza writes, "Black Lives Matter is an ideological and political intervention in a world where Black lives are systematically and intentionally targeted for demise." Their work has been subject to theft, coopted for universalizing emphases such as an art project called "Our Lives Matter," that, in fact, "completely erased the origins of their work—rooted in the labor and love of queer Black women."[6]

The drive for "unity without struggle" that is characteristic of "progressive movements" according to Garza is a live risk of CCR as well; CCR comes from progressivism, human rights work, and its tendencies toward universalizing.

A related example is how calls for "racial dialogue" were made immediately following the killing of Trayvon Martin and continued to be made as killings of unarmed African Americans continued with no one being held legally accountable. No dialogue can really ensue while the assaults on African American bodies are ongoing. Yes, CCR does invite all parties to a conflict to understand the needs and desires of the other side, but when the need and desire is, "I'd really like not to have my body constantly subject to intrusive 'search and frisk,' not be routinely threatened with arrest despite acting lawfully, not be incarcerated at extraordinarily high rates, and I'd like not to be shot dead," the dialogue cannot even begin until that violation of African American bodies stops. And whose perspective counts in assessing the "needs and desires" of the African American community? The media, as well as politicians and self-styled community leaders, tends to gravitate to charismatic Black men, not queer Black women, as spokespeople. Who dialogues with whom? It is more likely to be elites with elites without a lot of work to insure this is not the case.

CCR can actually be dangerous if it is applied to situations of domestic violence unless the party who is being beaten—normally the woman in a domestic violence context—is physically safe during the whole process and afterward. Even then, a pall of threat can hang over the process and the person who has been treated violently does not feel she can really engage fully without risk, based on her previous experiences. CCR calls for participants to "take risks" and "make themselves vulnerable," but women who have been battered are already at risk and already vulnerable.

CCR is also not applicable at all in the case of rape. In fact, this is one of the fundamental flaws in college and university policies on handling campus rape. Campus rape is regarded as a conflict between two or more students that needs to be mediated, not a criminal assault that needs to be investigated and reported to the police.

Title IX of the Education Amendments of 1972 required that all colleges provide a safe space for all students to learn. In 2012, the Office of Civil Rights sent a letter to schools reminding them that if a student reports a sexual assault to the school, they must investigate it. But what happened was that colleges and universities adapted their disciplinary procedures that were used for things like plagiarism to this issue and, as a result, "disciplinary panels originally designed to decide cases of plagiarism are acting like criminal courts in rape cases with students, administrators, and professors questioning victims, alleged assailants, and witnesses and doling out punishments."[7] But these panels treat what is essentially a criminal assault as a problem to be mediated and resolved.

The power inequalities of gender and violence are hidden in this approach, and the "process" can just feel like another assault, as women activists on campus rape issues are showing. These activists have changed tactics from earlier anti-campus rape work that emphasized women's self-care and protection and are using drama, social media, and a recognition of their own power as those who fork over thousands of dollars to campuses that failed to keep them safe. They are realizing their power to hold their universities accountable.

Emma Sulkowicz, a Japanese-Chinese-Jewish Columbia University student and anti-campus rape activist, has become famous for carrying around a twin mattress typical of those used in dorm rooms to protest not only that she was raped at a Columbia University-sponsored event but also that at the "Columbia-adjudicated hearing during which the university found her assailant not guilty." She wants Columbia to expel him. The women leading this movement are very diverse and very aware of the power dynamics at play when universities try mediation as a way to minimize or dismiss sexual assault. The public pushback has been extreme, and conservative women in particular are trotted out to make charges that the women are lying about campus rape. Danielle Dirks, a sociologist at Occidental College, rightly points to the fact that this is a power struggle: "There are people out there who want to say that survivors today are feminism gone wild, railroading men for power."[8]

No, instead they are women activists who understand gendered power dynamics, and the way uncontextualized "mediation" can work to perpetuate violence against women. Great care must be taken with this Just Peace practice norm to recognize the embodied character of conflict and deal with the physical threats that continue to advance violence that cannot be mediated unless and until the violence stops.

Acknowledge Responsibility for Conflict and Injustice and Seek Repentance and Forgiveness

I had originally opposed including the practices of forgiveness in the genesis of the Just Peace paradigm because battered women, in the Christian tradition, have been so often pressed to forgive their batterers to the point where it becomes part of the abuse. Through our process of deliberation in crafting the paradigm, however, I became persuaded that this was a crucial norm for reducing violence against women, as well as impacting the long-term consequences of war and conflict, when the real process of a change in power relations became part of the norm.

Along with a Jewish and a Muslim colleague, I wrote the chapter on this norm in *Interfaith Just Peacemaking*, arguing that the example of how forgiveness is used against ending violence against women must be accounted for in this aspect of peacemaking and made central rather than merely included: "The 'forgive, forgive' dynamic in domestic violence fails at the crucial step of recognizing that unequal power relations are at the root of violent relationships, whether personal, national, or international. The 'spiral of violence' will not be interrupted unless the power inequalities that helped give rise to the violence are changed."[9]

The long-term success or failure of Truth and Reconciliation commissions (TRCs) around the world, as extensive studies reveal, depends to a great extent in how deeply these commissions are able not only to identify abuses but also to identify needed structural changes in societies that can be implemented and sustained. It has been challenging for TRCs to move from efforts to deal with individual trauma to national reconciliation; yet, there are also challenges since societies can stress the need to reduce national conflict, and individual healing, especially of the most vulnerable such as women, is given less attention.[10] TRCs can be artificial and can appear to include women but actually be political processes that do little to effect reconciliation and restorative justice, as Gbowee notes of the TRC in Liberia.[11]

Advance Democracy, Human Rights, and Interdependence

Women struggling to get the vote in the nineteenth and early twentieth centuries certainly believed they could improve their situation and that of other women through suffrage. But representational democracy is not a cure-all for the host of issues that afflict women's lives, health, and safety. Photos of Afghan women holding up ink-stained fingers after they had voted in Afghan elections were popular in Western media, but their ability to vote (though sometimes in the face of severe threat) has not, by itself, revolutionized their lives. Electoral democracy, without fundamental change in the host of issues that fuel the suppression of women, gives the appearance of change but can actually precipitate blowback, as has been previously described.

One critical issue in applying this norm is the public/private split in human rights. Historically speaking, what happens in the home has not been considered a human rights violation, though this is changing. Amnesty International has been a leader in exposing and preventing human rights abuses and has, along with a host of other human rights organizations like Human Rights Watch, taken a far more comprehensive approach to the gender-based violence that is epidemic around the world. Amnesty's work targets a "global culture of discrimination" that "denies women equal rights with men and which legitimizes the appropriation of women's bodies for individual gratification or political ends."[12]

Yet there is more that a critical physicality approach that focuses on the body as a battlefield could contribute to this work. A 2009 Human Rights Watch report on the deterioration of women's rights in Afghanistan, *We Have the Promises of the World*, covers the extensive "rights violations" of women through attacks on women in public life, violence against women, child and forced marriage, lack of access to justice, and lack of access by girls to secondary education.[13] There is deterioration across the board, and the report acknowledges that the rights of women were not a priority in the invasion, but instead "armed conflict" was the concern and the goal. Yet the report calls for these same rights to be prioritized without in any way reinterpreting them in relationship to the primacy of conflict. This is a tragic flaw in this report, as these profound calls for women's rights will continue to be ignored because a deeper examination of the sources and norms of the larger conflict itself is not part of the recommendations for what needs to change. As has been previously argued, women's rights in Afghanistan were an excuse for invasion and now are an excuse for the Taliban to recapture power.[14] Women's rights were a rhetorical "promise" but not a reality.

In fact, in a study of six postconflict countries where foreign intervention was untaken supposedly to advance the transition to democracy, no improvement on women's rights—whether political, social, or economic—can be documented. Rather, the analysis shows democratization in this way does not "take into account women's unequal political, economic, or social status, nor do the address norms in the private and public spheres."[15] Such "liberal" goals of electoral democracy, market economy, and even establishing the rule of law do not actually achieve a sustainable peace when it comes to women's lives. Part of this can be due to the fact that improving women's lives is genuinely not seen as essential to rebuilding societies. Of the $21 billion committed to the reconstruction of Iraq in 2003 and 2004, only $500 million was allocated to support the social and political development of Iraqi women.[16]

But what is even more hidden within this Just Peace practice is that the transition to democracy, in postconflict zones, can actually facilitate an increase in violence against women. As societies transition out of war and the feelings of powerlessness that entails among people, men can desire to reassert their traditional masculinized power. Women actually voting can be seen as a threat to this, and women are more at risk of violence. Women coming out of their homes and engaging in public spaces are routinely more at risk for rape in these settings.

Human rights work and democratization processes must continually be attentive to the interlocking forces that drive the War on Women and strategize against them.

Foster Just and Sustainable Economic Development

Economic development work almost directly parallels the problems with democratization. An Oxfam study of violence against women in rural Bangladesh explored the relationship among "men's violence against women in the home, women's economic and social dependence on men, and microcredit programmes." This study suggests that microcredit can reduce women's economic dependence on men and thus their vulnerability, but when their economic roles are strengthened, this can provoke male violence against them. This paper suggests that microcredit programs have a varied effect on men's violence against women: "By putting resources into women's hands, credit programmes may indirectly exacerbate such violence."[17]

More work has been done since that Oxfam report to help structure microfinance to actually recognize and impact the multiple issues of power and subordination that, combined with economic dependence, are drivers of violence against women. A microcredit program implemented in South Africa is being replicated in South America that combines "education and participatory workshops in order to tackle gender norms and roles, enhance communication skills, improve women's influence in household decisions and create collective action mechanisms to combat violence against women."[18] This more comprehensive and supportive approach is much needed, and it illustrates the multisystemic nature of the role of economic deprivation in the War on Women.

Women's subordinate economic status to men is a worldwide driver of violence against them, and they can feel and actually be trapped in trying to escape violence.

Economic empowerment for women is clearly a Just Peace practice, but it must be undertaken with intensive critical analysis in order not to contribute to violence against women instead of being a way to prevent and end it.

Work with Emerging Cooperative Forces in the International System

There has been a huge increase in the number of international nongovernmental organizations since the beginning of the twentieth century, and groups working on issues of violence against women have proliferated.[19] For this practice norm to be effective for women in a global context, the emphasis on "work with" cannot be overstated. But sometimes, this is not the case, and thus a critical physicality approach to the work of these organizations is crucial and an emphasis on the "critical" is essential.

An example of how this might look is in regard to One Billion Rising, an international organization founded by Eve Ensler, the creator of *The Vagina Monologues*. Grassroots activists have been very critical of this high-profile effort, especially because of a "refusal to name the root cause of women's inequality; its outright refusal to point the finger at a patriarchal system which cultivates masculinity and which uses the control and subjugation of women's bodies as an outlet for that machoism," according to Natalie Gyte, head of communications at Women's Resource Centre, the national umbrella body for women's charities. Gyte acknowledges that Ensler's other charity, V-Day, has funded some good work at the grassroots level. But the high-profile, "dance your violence away" approach is more first-world gloss than a force for systemic change. Gyte quotes a Congolese woman who called One Billion Rising "insulting" and "neocolonial."[20]

Gyte is by no means the only woman raising such issues in regard to the kind of high-visibility, generalized approach to "ending violence against women" that One Billion Rising represents. In its uncritical assumption of the unity of gender oppression, such approaches are actually first-world, white supremacy packaged as global feminism. Policy and enforcement recommendations that emerge from such uncritical movements are blind to the ways in which the very structures being recommended for "ending violence against women," such as increased policing, are a huge part of the structures that facilitate violence against racial/ethnic minorities, indigenous peoples, and women in societies that are the object of this intended "help."[21]

A Just Peace practice that engages international cooperative forces in the work of peacemaking must be attentive to the embedded oppressions in any Western approach to global concerns. The fact that these efforts are "well-intentioned" in some ways makes them even more blind to these crucial contradictions. Those engaging this practice must be aware that power inequalities and hierarchies of race and culture are inevitable and must be constantly brought to consciousness and strategized against.

Strengthen the United Nations and International Efforts for Cooperation and Human Rights

The World Health Organization of the United Nations has done enormously important work in documenting the fact that global violence against women is a health epidemic. In addition, it has been very important that the United Nations adopted *The Declaration on the Elimination of Violence against Women* which defined violence against women as "any act of gender-based violence that results in, or is likely to result in, physical, sexual or psychological harm or suffering to women, including threats of such acts, coercion or arbitrary deprivation of liberty, whether occurring in public or in private life." Yet the state and legislative approach, especially when couched as "punishment," will inevitably be coopted into individual regimes of oppressive power and often used as a policed substitute for community-based forms of social change to actually improve the lives of women and their communities and reduce violence more organically.

Moreover, the United Nations and its workers are often critiqued for assuming the same kind of "we're here to help you," first-world mentality that characterizes the private, charitable organizations such as One Billion Rising. As Gbowee succinctly says, the "U.N. reps do not listen to the local people, and many disasters that could have been avoided."[22] This is a commonly heard critique.

Tragically, another commonly heard critique is that United Nations "peace-keepers" have been documented perpetrators of gender-based violence, and this has gone on for a long time. The important 1996 UNICEF study, *The Impact of Armed Conflict on Children* reported that "[i]n 6 out of 12 country studies, the arrival of peacekeeping troops has been associated with a rapid rise in child prostitution." A review eight years later concluded that prostitution and sexual abuse followed most UN interventions.[23]

Clearly, reform of the United Nations on these issues of power and abuse is crucial, even as the work of peacekeeping and world health and a host of other important work done by the United Nations continues.

Reduce Offensive Weapons and the Weapons Trade

Reducing offensive weapons is perhaps one of the most important Just Peace practices in regard to actually reducing femicide. The Justice Department documents that more than two-thirds of perpetrators who killed their spouses or ex-spouses between 1980 and 2008 used a firearm to carry out the act. In the United States, the power of the gun lobby is such that it has been difficult even to keep guns out of the hands of convicted domestic abusers, though states have begun to pass such legislation.[24]

Astonishing as it may seem, the first-ever international Arms Trade Treaty (ATT) regulating the international sale of conventional arms and ammunition that went into effect in December 2014, actually mandates for "arms exporting countries to assess the risk that their weapons will be used in the commission of GBV [Gender Based Violence] and deny authorization of any sales that present an 'overriding' risk." This is a crucial step in recognizing the disproportionate effect of gun violence on women, not just in killing, but also in threatening and intimidating. This aspect of the treaty was accomplished through the combined efforts of Amnesty International, the Women's International League for Peace and Freedom, the Women's Network of the International Action Network on Small Arms, and Oxfam. As Amnesty International notes, "Possession of firearms changes the balance of power in a relationship and emboldens both individuals and members of armed groups to use weapons to instill fear and exert control."[25]

Guns and other weapons are a power issue, and bringing a gender-based critical analysis to the arms trade is a significant step forward. More work clearly needs to be done, as the world, especially the United States, is awash in guns and other arms and weapons systems.

Encourage Grassroots Peacemaking Groups and Voluntary Associations

When I talk on the Just Peace paradigm, I often call this practice, "How to end war in your spare time." Grassroots peacemaking is the basis of all the other work of peace done around the world, and thus it is the most crucial to examine from the perspective of critical physicality.

Yet, grassroots peacemaking movements are not exempt from the structures that facilitate violence as power inequalities and hierarchies of race and gender. They reproduce these structures in leadership, advocacy strategies, funding, and a host of the practical issues that are part and parcel of this kind of work.

It is absolutely crucial to get at these structures within grassroots peacemaking efforts themselves, but this is a critical perspective that is nearly impossible to generate from within the group itself. We are all blind to our own captivity.

Grassroots movements that would be effective on the complex dynamics operative in the War on Women need to be deliberately collaborative with other groups that bring a different set of social locations. This precisely does not mean absorbing other groups but listening to them and being challenged to develop critical consciousness about race, class, gender and sexual orientation, religion, national origin, age, and disability. Rather than aiming at one giant movement to do peacemaking at the grassroots level, collaborative work that is open to listening (and acting!) on this challenge is a more effective way to disaggregate power.

Conclusion

Witnessing the reality of violence in women's lives and being open to recognizing the ways in which the very structures that give rise to that violence are so present, even within our best efforts to end such violence, can seem paralyzing. There is no way forward except through these contradictions, driving for greater collaboration, listening, and changing strategies.

This is not work any of us can do alone.

Notes

Introduction

1. Erich Maria Remarque, *All Quiet on the Western Front* (New York: Little, Brown, 1929), 64. Originally published as *Im Westen Nichts Neues* (Berlin: Ullstein A.G., 1928).
2. Sherry Kurtz, *The "M" Word: My Story of Being Gang Raped in the Military* (Charleston, SC: S. Kurtz, 2013). Kindle Edition.
3. World Health Organization, London School of Hygiene and Tropical Medicine, and South African Medical Research Council, "Global and Regional Estimates of Violence against Women: Prevalence and Health Effects of Intimate Partner Violence and Non-Partner Sexual Violence," World Health Organization, 2013, http://apps.who.int/iris/bitstream/10665/85239/1/9789241564625_eng.pdf.
4. Ibid., 4.
5. Susan Brooks Thistlethwaite, "Yes There Is a War on Women, and #YesAllWomen," *Huffington Post*, May 27, 2014, http://www.huffingtonpost.com/rev-dr-susan-brooks-thistlethwaite/yes-there-is-a-war-on-wom_b_5397167.html.
6. This book is about women's bodies as battlefields and the correlation between what happens to women's bodies in a "global War on Women" to what happens to the body in war. Men's bodies are also assaulted outside war, including sexually assaulted, and that is a crucial topic that some are beginning to address. It is not, however, the subject here.
7. Susan Brownmiller, *Against Our Will: Men, Women and Rape* (New York: Ballantine, 1975).
8. Elaine Scarry, *The Body in Pain: The Making and Unmaking of the World* (New York: Oxford University Press, 1985).
9. Susan Brooks Thistlethwaite, "#YesAllWomen and #YesAllWomen Differently," *OccupytheBible*, May 27, 2014, http://occupythebible.org/2014/05/27/yesallwomen-and-yesallwomendifferently/.
10. If critical physicality is to be at all useful in helping focus attention on the body and violence, it must not even temporarily essentialize the body. Gayatri Chakatri Spivak is an Indian literary theorist who is best known for her contemporary cultural and critical theories to challenge the legacy of colonialism; she created the concept of "strategic essentialism" as a way to temporarily essentialize the "subaltern,"(i.e. the colonized). She has expressed dissatisfaction, however, with how that term has subsequently been misused and even used to defend essentializing. In the same way, there is a very live risk that a constant focus on physicality in this book can overtly or covertly promote the idea that women's bodies are the same and subvert solidarity. Thus critical theory must be employed at every step of the way.
11. Works influential in this book include the following: Katie G. Cannon, *Black Womanist Ethics* (Atlanta: American Academy of Religion, 1988); Emilie Townes, ed., *A Troubling*

in My Soul: Womanist Perspectives on Evil and Suffering (Maryknoll, NY: Orbis, 1993); Kelly Brown Douglas, *What's Faith Got to Do with It? Black Souls/Christian Bodies* (Maryknoll, NY: Orbis, 2005); Susan Brooks Thistlethwaite and Mary Potter Engel, eds., *Lift Every Voice: Constructing Christian Theologies from the Underside* (Maryknoll, NY: Orbis, 2000); Rosemary Radford Ruether, *Sexism and Godtalk: Toward a Feminist Theology* (Boston: Beacon, 1983); Scarry, *The Body in Pain*; Susan Sontag, *Regarding the Pain of Others* (New York: Farrar, Straus and Giroux, 2004); Judith Butler, *Bodies That Matter* (New York: Routledge, 1993); Michel Foucault, *The History of Sexuality, Volume 1: An Introduction* (New York: Random House, 1978); W. E. B. Du Bois, *The Souls of Black Folk* (Chicago: A. C. McClurg, 1903); James Cone, *God of the Oppressed* (Maryknoll, NY: Orbis, 1997); Patricia Williams, *Alchemy of Race and Rights: Diary of a Law Professor* (Boston: Harvard University Press, 1992).

12. Scarry, *The Body in Pain*, 63.
13. The Michigan Women's Justice and Clemency Project, "Clemency Manual," http://www.umich.edu/~clemency/clemency_mnl/ch1.html.
14. "Fla. Mom Gets 20 Years for Firing Warning Shots," *CBS News*, May 12, 2012.
15. Douglas Kellner and Steven Best, eds., "Foucault and the Critique of Modernity," in *Postmodern Theory* (New York: Guilford, 1991): "I am just saying: as soon as there is a power relation, there is a possibility of resistance. We can never be ensnared by power: we can always modify its grip in determinate conditions and according to a precise strategy."
16. Jeremy Scahill, *Dirty Wars: The World is a Battlefield* (New York: Nation, 2013).
17. Anne Llewellyn Barstow, ed., *War's Dirty Secret: Rape, Prostitution, and Other Crimes against Women* (Cleveland, OH: Pilgrim, 2000).
18. Abraham Lincoln, *Address Delivered at the Dedication of the Cemetery at Gettysburg November 19, 1863*, http://www.d.umn.edu/~rmaclin/gettysburg-address.html.
19. Claire Laurent, "Femicide: The Killing of Woman and Girls around the World," *Academic Council on the United Nations System (ACUNS), Vienna Liaison Office*, http://acuns.org/wp-content/uploads/2013/05/Claire-Laurent.pdf.
20. "Bolivia Works to Reduce Violence against Women," *Femicide News*, June 15, 2013, http://femicidenews.com/2013/06/15/bolivia-works-to-reduce-violence-against-women/; "Critical State: Violence against Women and Impunity in Bolivia," *Pulitzer Center on Crisis Reporting*, October 14, 2014, http://pulitzercenter.org/projects/south-america-andes-bolivia-femicide-violence-against-women.

Chapter 1

1. The war in Afghanistan officially became the longest war, surpassing the Vietnam War, after President Obama announced its end in December 2014. Scott Neuman, "Ceremony in Afghanistan Officially Ends America's Longest War," *NPR*, December 28, 2014, http://www.npr.org/blogs/thetwo-way/2014/12/28/373597845/ceremony-in-afghanistan-officially-ends-americas-longest-war; Anna Mulrine, "War in Afghanistan Officially Over. Does That Mean End of Fighting for US?," *Christian Science Monitor*, December 29, 2014, http://csmonitor.com/USA/Military/2014/1229/War-in-Afghanistan-officially-over.-Does-that-mean-end-of-fighting-for-US.
2. "Infinite Justice, Out—Enduring Freedom, In," *BBC News*, September 25, 2001, http://news.bbc.co.uk/2/hi/americas/1563722.stm.
3. Witness for Peace, http://www.witnessforpeace.org/section.php?id=89.

4. See Introduction, Susan Thistlethwaite and Mary Potter Engel, *Lift Every Voice: Constructing Christian Theologies from the Underside* (Maryknoll, NY: Orbis, 1998).

5. Rachel Loxston, "July 21, 1861—Picnicking at Bull Run—A Dangerous Spectacle," http://www.7score10years.com/index.php/north/82-north/362-21-july-1861-picnicking-at-bull-run-a-very-dangerous-spectator-sport.

6. Susan Sontag, *Regarding the Pain of Others* (New York: Farrar, Straus and Giroux, 2003), 75.

7. Ibid., 52ff.

8. Ibid., 63.

9. Ibid., 8.

10. Ibid.

11. Alejandro Escalona, "75 Years of Picasso's Guernica: An Inconvenient Masterpiece," *Huffington Post*, May 23, 2012, http://www.huffingtonpost.com/alejandro-escalona/75-years-of-picassos-guernica-_b_1538776.html.

12. Michael Mandelbaum, "Vietnam: The Television War," *Daedalus*, Vol. 111, Issue 4, Print Culture and Video Culture (Fall 1982): 157–69, http://www.jstor.org/stable/20024822.

13. This is my own experience of resisting the war in Vietnam as a college student. In the spring of 1970, I helped to shut Smith College down and I volunteered in the strike school we set up. Patrick O'Neill, "A Just Peace Activist in the Age of Religion," *Divinity*, Vol. 7 (Fall 2007), http://divinity.duke.edu/publications/2007.09/features/feature4/print_feature4.htm.

14. "The Vietnam War: The Bitter End 1969–1975," *The History Place*, http://www.historyplace.com/unitedstates/vietnam/index-1969.html.

15. Ibid.

16. Elisabeth Bumiller, "U.S. Lifts Photo Ban on Military Coffins," *The New York Times*, December 7, 2009, http://www.nytimes.com/2009/02/27/world/americas/27iht-photos.1.20479953.html?_r=0.

17. Susan Brooks Thistlethwaite, *Dreaming of Eden: American Religion and Politics in a Wired World* (New York: Palgrave Macmillan, 2010), 212ff.

18. Seymour M. Hersh, "Torture at Abu Ghraib: American Soldiers Brutalized Iraqis. How Far up Does the Responsibility Go?," *The New Yorker*, May 10, 2004, http://www.newyorker.com/archive/2004/05/10/040510fa_fact.

19. "Disturbing New Photos from Abu Ghraib," *Wired*, http://archive.wired.com/science/discoveries/multimedia/2008/02/gallery_abu_ghraib.

20. Susan B. Thistlethwaite, "Can a Nation Lose Its Soul?," *Chicago Tribune*, May 4, 2004, http://articles.chicagotribune.com/2004-05-04/news/0405040065_1_torture-prisoners-reservist.

21. Jeremy Ashkenas, Hannah Fairfield, Josh Keller, and Paule Volpe, "7 Key Points from the C.I.A. Torture Report," *The New York Times*, December 9, 2014, http://www.nytimes.com/interactive/2014/12/09/world/cia-torture-report-key-points.html?_r=0; "The CIA Torture Details Are Appalling," *Business Insider*, December 9, 2014, http://www.businessinsider.com/the-senate-is-about-to-release-the-cia-torture-report-2014-12.

22. Kayvan Farzaneh, Andrew Swift, and Peter Williams, "Planet War," *Foreign Policy*, February 22, 2010, http://www.foreignpolicy.com/articles/2010/02/22/planet_war#33.

23. Ibid.

24. Ibid.

25. Ann Scott Tyson, "AP Photo of Dying Marine Criticized," *Washington Post*, September 5, 2009, http://articles.washingtonpost.com/2009-09-05/news/36926776_1 _santiago-lyon-casualties-service-members.

26. Ibid.

27. David W. Dunlap and James Estrin, "From the Archive: Not New, Never Easy," *The New York Times*, September 9, 2009, http://lens.blogs.nytimes.com/2009/09/23/archive-5.

28. Jason K. Stearns, *Dancing in the Glory of Monsters: The Collapse of the Congo and the Great War of Africa* (New York: Public Affairs, 2011), 33.

29. Ibid., 33–34.

30. Ibid., 33.

31. The UN estimates that about 69 percent of Palestinian casualties were civilian, but this is hotly contested. Of the 73 Israeli casualties, 6 were civilians and 67 Israeli soldiers. "Gaza-Israel Conflict: Is the Fighting Over?," *BBCNews*, August 26, 2014, http://www.bbc.com/news/world-middle-east-28252155; "The U.N. Says 7 in 10 Palestinians Killed in Gaza Were Civilians. Israel Disagrees," *Washington Post*, August 29, 2014, http://www.washingtonpost.com/world/middle_east/the-un-says-7-in-10 -palestinians-killed-in-gaza-were-civilians-israel-disagrees/2014/08/29/44edc598 -2faa-111e4-9b98-848790384093_story.html.

32. "Stealth Conflicts: Africa's World War in the DRC and International Consciousness," *Journal of Humanitarian Assistance*, January 1, 2004, http://sites.tufts.edu/jha/archives/ 71.

33. David Mayeda, "DRC Death Toll Exceeds 5 Million and Almost No News Coverage," November 26, 2012, http://www.sociologyinfocus.com/2012/11/26/aware-of-ongoing -violence-democratic-republic-of-the-congo/; See also "Stealth Conflicts," Ibid.

34. Mayeda, ibid.

35. Leslie Larson, "Mud, Blood and Terror: The Brutality of the Vietnam War Captured in Harrowing Images," *The Mail Online*, January 25, 2013, http://www.dailymail.co .uk/news/article-2268602/Mud-blood-horror-The-brutality-Vietnam-War-captured -selection-stunning-images.html.

36. David W. Dunlap and James Estrin, "From the Archive: Not New, Never Easy."

37. "Special Report: Congo," *International Rescue Committee*, http://www.rescue.org/ special-reports/special-report-congo-y.

38. "The DR Congo: The Facts," http://eng2bell7jennacox.blogspot.com/p/facts.html.

39. "Democratic Republic of the War Congo-Wounded Face Life of Penury," *Refworld*, February 11, 2011, http://www.refworld.org/category,COI,IWPR,,COD,4d6c93361e,0 .html.

40. "Baghdad ER: Documentary on US Military Hospital in Iraq Gets Cold Reception from Military," *Democracy Now*, May 17, 2006, http://www.democracynow.org/2006/ 5/17/baghdad_er_documentary_on_us_military.

41. Paul Farhi, "Strategic Retreat?," *Washington Post*, May 17, 2006, http://www .washingtonpost.com/wp-dyn/content/article/2006/05/16/AR2006051601879.html.

42. "Military Recruitment 2010," June 30, 2011, http://nationalpriorities.org/analysis/ 2011/military-recruitment-2010.

43. Sontag, *Regarding the Pain of Others*, 15.

44. David Wood, "Beyond the Battlefield: Back Home, Severely Wounded Veterans Wish More Would Ask, Not Just Stare," *Huffington Post*, October 18, 2011, http://www .huffingtonpost.com/2011/10/18/beyond-the-battlefield-7-reintegration_n_1011265 .html.

45. "Conference Overview," *Veterans in Society: Changing the Discourse*, http://www .veterans.vt.edu/Veterans_In_Society_Conference.

46. "Shell Shock," *BBC Inside Out*, March 3, 2004, http://www.bbc.co.uk/insideout/extra/series-1/shell_shocked.shtml.
47. Judith Lewis Herman, *Trauma and Recovery* (New York: Basic, 1992), 22.
48. Ibid.
49. Ibid., 26.
50. Robert J. Lifton, *Home from the War: Vietnam Veterans: Neither Victims nor Executioners* (New York: Simon and Schuster, 1973), 31, cited in Herman, ibid., 26.
51. Jeff Ousley, "Soldiers Continue to Struggle with Public Perception of PTSD," *VeteransUnitedNetwork*, April 12, 2012, http://www.veteransunited.com/network/soldiers-continue-to-struggle-with-public-perception-of-ptsd/.
52. Helena Carreiras, *Gender and the Military: Women in the Armed Forces in Western Democracies* (New York: Routledge, 2006), 1.
53. Jesse Ellison, "Gates, Rumsfeld Sued over U.S. Military's Rape Epidemic," *The Daily Beast*, February 15, 2011, http://www.thedailybeast.com/articles/2011/02/15/robert-gates-sued-over-us-militarys-rape-epidemic.html.
54. Hayes Brown, "Pentagon: Estimated 26,000 Sexual Assaults in Military Last Year," *ThinkProgress*, May 7, 2013, http://thinkprogress.org/security/2013/05/07/1972241/pentagon-sexual-assault-report/.
55. "Rape, Sexual Assault and Sexual Harassment in the Military," *Service Women's Action Network*, July 2012, http://servicewomen.org/wp-content/uploads/2012/10/Final-RSASH-10.8.2012.pdf.
56. Hillary Lake and staff, "W. Wash Woman Shares Story of Military Rape," *KOMONews*, May 24, 2013, http://www.komonews.com/news/local/W-Wash-woman-shares-story-of-military-rape-208822221.html.
57. Raphaelle Branche and Fabrice Virgili, *Rape in Wartime* (New York: Palgrave Macmillan, 2012), 4.
58. Jina Moore, "Confronting Rape as a War Crime," *CQ Global Researcher*, Vol. 4, Issue 5 (May 2010), http://www.nobelwomensinitiative.org/wp-content/archive/stories/women_new_security/CQ_Press_women_in_war.pdf.
59. "Committee Study of the Central Intelligence Agency's Detention and Interrogation Program," *Senate Select Committee on Intelligence*, December 3, 2014, http://www.intelligence.senate.gov/study2014/sscistudy1.pdf.
60. Kate Halper, "The Sexual Violence of the CIA Torture Program," *Feministing.org*, December 12, 2014, http://feministing.com/2014/12/12/the-sexual-violence-of-the-cia-torture-program/.

Chapter 2

1. Susan Thistlethwaite, *Sex, Race, and God: Christian Feminism in Black and White* (Eugene, OR: Wipf and Stock, 2009).
2. Gerard Loughlin, ed., *Queer Theology: Rethinking the Western Body* (Malden, MA: Blackwell, 2007), 9.
3. Susan Brownmiller, *Against Our Will* (New York: Fawcett, 1993), 229.
4. "Livy: The Rape of Lucretia from the History of Rome," *Fordham University Ancient History Sourcebook*, http://www.fordham.edu/halsall/ancient/livy-rape.asp.
5. Emily Detmer-Goebel, "The Need for Lavinia's Voice: Titus Andronicus and the Telling of Rape," *Shakespeare Studies*, 2001, http://www.questia.com/library/1G1-79826270/the-need-for-lavinia-s-voice-titus-andronicus-and.

6. Sara Kipfer, "Love Turns into Hate: The Rape of Tamar (2 Sam 13:1–22) in Baroque Art," *Society of Biblical Literature Publications*, http://www.sbl-site.org/publications/article.aspx?articleId=800.

7. Mary Wollstonecraft, *The Vindication of the Rights of Women* (Mineola, NY: Dover, 1996).

8. See Karen O'Brien, *Women and Enlightenment in Eighteenth-Century Britain* (Cambridge: Cambridge University Press, 2009).

9. Peter Erickson, "Images of White Identity in Othello," in Philip C. Kolin, ed., *Othello: New Critical Essays* (New York: Routledge, 2001), 134–35.

10. Justin Berrier, Melody Johnson, and Remington Shepard, "Republican 'War on Women' Is Not a Left-Wing Invention," *MediaMatters for America*, April 10, 2012, http://mediamatters.org/research/2012/04/10/republican-war-on-women-is-not-a-left-wing-inve/186151.

11. See columns by Susan Brooks Thistlethwaite at "On Faith." http://www.faithstreet.com/onfaith/author/susan-brooks-thistlethwaite.

12. E. J. Graff, "2012's War on Women," *The American Prospect*, December 31, 2012, http://prospect.org/article/2012s-war-women.

13. Juliet Macur and Nate Schweber, "Rape Case Unfolds Online and Divides Steubenville," *The New York Times*, December 16, 2012, http://www.nytimes.com/2012/12/17/sports/high-school-football-rape-case-unfolds-online-and-divides-steubenville-ohio.html?pagewanted=all&_r=0.

14. Adam Clark Estes, "CNN's Not the Only One Peddling Sympathy for Steubenville Rapists," *The Atlantic Wire*, March 17, 2013, http://www.theatlanticwire.com/national/2013/03/cnns-not-only-one-peddling-sympathy-steubenville-rapists/63204/.

15. Ruchira Gupta, "Victims Blamed in India's Rape Culture," *CNN*, August 28, 2013, http://www.cnn.com/2013/08/27/opinion/gupta-india-rape-culture/index.html.

16. Tricia Romano, "'Blurred Lines,' Robin Thicke's Summer Anthem, Is Kind of Rapey," *The Daily Beast*, June 17, 2013, http://www.thedailybeast.com/articles/2013/06/17/blurred-lines-robin-thicke-s-summer-anthem-is-kind-of-rapey.html; linked lyrics can be found at http://rapgenius.com/Robin-thicke-blurred-lines-lyrics#note-1644751.

17. Elizabeth Day, "Renault's Sexist Advert Drives Me Absolutely Mad: The Car Company's Efforts to Sell Its Products Demean All of Us," *The Observer*, July 20, 2013, http://www.theguardian.com/commentisfree/2013/jul/21/renault-weather-duchess-of-cambridge.

18. Francisco Goya, *The Disasters of War* (New York: Dover, 1967).

19. Beatrice Heuser, *The Strategy Makers: Thoughts on War and Society from Machiavelli to Clausewitz* (Santa Barbara, CA: ABC-CLIO, 2010), 24, 86.

20. The summary of the extent of rape, violence against women in war, and the frequent cover up is extensively documented in Anne Llewellyn Barstow, *War's Dirty Secret: Rape, Prostitution, and Other Crimes against Women* (Cleveland, OH: Pilgrim Press, 2000). For the preceding paragraphs, see 3–6.

21. Samantha Power, *"A Problem from Hell": America and the Age of Genocide* (New York: HarperCollins, 2002). There are nine references to rape in this book of more than six hundred pages.

22. Nancy Lemon, *Domestic Violence Law: A Comprehensive Overview of Cases and Sources* (San Francisco: Austin and Winfield, 1996).

23. Mary E. Hunt and Diane L. Neu, eds., *New Feminist Christianity: Many Voices, Many Views* (Woodstock, NY: SkyLight Paths, 2010), 109–13.

24. *Regimen sanitatis salernitanum: Conservandae bonae valetudinis praecepta longe saluberrima, regi Angliae quondam à Doctoribus Scholae Saliturnitanae versibus conscripta.*

Frankfurt: Christ. Egenol, 1582, cited in Elizabeth Fee, Theodore M. Brown, Jan Lazarus, and Paul Theerman, "Domestic Violence—Medieval and Modern," *American Journal of Public Health* (December 2002): http://www.ncbi.nlm.nih.gov/pmc/articles/PMC1447351/.

25. James A. Brundage, "Domestic Violence in Classical Canon Law," in Richard W. Kaeuper, ed., *Violence in Medieval Society* (Woodbridge, England: Boydell, 2000),183–97; Barbara Hanawalt, "Violence in the Domestic Milieu of Late Medieval England," in Richard W. Kaeuper, ed., *Violence in Medieval Society* (Woodbridge, England: Boydell, 2000), 197–214; Eve Salisbury, Georgiana Donavin, and Merrall L. Price, eds., *Domestic Violence in Medieval Texts* (Gainesville: University Press of Florida, 2002).

26. Del Martin, *Battered Wives* (New York: Pocket Books, 1976), 30.

27. Corinne Wieben, "'As Men Do with Their Wives': Domestic Violence in Fourteenth-Century Lucca," *California Italian Studies Journal*, Vol. 1, Issue 2 (2010): http://www.escholarship.org/uc/item/08p9b8gz#page-7.

28. Mary Potter Engel, "Historical Theology and Violence against Women: Unearthing a Popular Tradition of Just Battery," in Carol J. Adams and Marie M. Fortune, eds., *Violence against Women and Children: A Christian Theological Sourcebook* (New York: Continuum, 1995), 260n26.

29. Christa Grossinger, *Picturing Women in Late Medieval and Renaissance Art* (Manchester: Manchester University Press, 1997), 16.

30. Dorothee Kehler, "Echoes of the Induction in *The Taming of the Shrew*," *Renaissance Papers* (1986): 31, cited in Erin Furstnau, "Feminist Themes in and Critiques of Shakespeare's Taming of the Shrew." http://www2.cedarcrest.edu/academic/eng/lfletcher/shrew/efurstnau.htm.

31. Jessica L. Goldman, "Arresting Wife Batterers: A Good Beginning to Stopping a Pervasive Pattern," *Washington Law Review*, Vol. 69, Issue 3 (1991): n. 56.

32. See Ana Stevenson, "Project Title: The Woman-Slave Analogy: Rhetorical Foundations in Nineteenth-Century American Culture," University of Queensland, Australia, http://www.uq.edu.au/hprc/ana-stevenson.

33. J. W. Kaye, "Outrages on Women," *North British Review*, Vol. 25 (1856): 253.

34. Lisa Anne Surridge, *Bleak Houses: Marital Violence in Victorian Fiction* (Athens: Ohio University Press, 2005), 4–5.

35. Jo Chandler, "It's 2013, and They're Burning 'Witches,'" *The Globe Mail*, February 15, 2013, http://www.theglobalmail.org/feature/its-2013-and-theyre-burning-witches/558/.

36. *FotoEvidence: Documenting Social Injustice*, http://www.fotoevidence.com/BookAward-Detail/346.

37. See Douglas E. Beloof, *Victims' Rights: A Documentary and Reference Guide* (Santa Barbara: ABC-CLIO, 2012).

38. Ian Johnson, "Cuts Demanded in Keira Knightley's Anti-Domestic Violence Advert," *The Telegraph*, April 27, 2009, http://www.telegraph.co.uk/news/celebritynews/5226459/Cuts-demanded-in-Keira-Knightleys-anti-domestic-violence-advert.html.

39. I. P. Johnson, "TV's Most Violent Shows," *ShawConnect*, http://www.shawconnect.ca/TV/Galleries/TV_s_most_violent_shows.aspx#!1353422728017_d9e0a41b7141d2fa3c2c9c488d775d26_breaking-bad.

40. See, for example, Jeffry A. Simpson, "The Psychological Foundations of Trust," *Current Directions in Psychological Science*, Vol. 16, Issue 5 (2007): 264–68.

41. Judith Lewis Herman, *Trauma and Recovery* (New York: Basic, 1992), 28.

42. *Plato's Timaeus: With Introduction*, trans. Benjamin Jowett (Rockville, MD: Serenity, 2009), 170.

43. Charlotte Perkins Gilman, *The Yellow Wallpaper* (1899), http://www.library.csi.cuny .edu/dept/history/lavender/wallpaper.html.
44. Herman, *Trauma and Recovery*, 18.
45. Ibid., 18–19.
46. Ibid., 19.
47. Susan Lanser, "Feminist Criticism, 'The Yellow Wallpaper' and the Politics of Color in America," *Feminist Studies*, Vol. 15, Issue 3 (Fall 1989): 422–23, http://www .academicroom.com/article/feminist-criticism-yellow-wallpaper-and-politics-color -america.
48. Ibid., 425.
49. Ibid., 429.
50. Ibid., 433.
51. Patricia Danette Hopkins, "Invisible Woman: Reading Rape and Sexual Exploitation in African-American Literature" (PhD diss., University of Pennsylvania, 2002), http:// repository.upenn.edu/dissertations/AAI3054952/.
52. Neetzan Zimmerman, "Makeup Tutorial Showing Abused Women How to Hide Bruises Is Cleverly Disguised Domestic Violence Awareness Campaign," *Gawker*, July 2, 2012, http://gawker.com/5923320/makeup-tutorial-showing-abused-women -how-to-hide-bruises-is-cleverly-disguised-domestic-violence-awareness-campaign.
53. Maçka Sanat Galerisi, http://www.mackasanatgalerisi.com/index.php?/project/derya -klc-eng/.
54. Jennifer Hattam, "Turkish Artist Paints Cuts, Bruises on Old Masters," *Women's eNews*, February 15, 2013, http://womensenews.org/story/arts/130214/turkish-artist-paints -cuts-bruises-old-masters#.Ul28HY6oJ74.
55. Ibid.
56. Mor Çatı, "About Us," http://www.morcati.org.tr/en/about-us/our-story.
57. Hattam, "Turkish Artist."
58. Ibid.
59. Susan Brooks Thistlethwaite, "Every Two Minutes: Battered Women and Feminist Interpretation," in Roger S. Gottlieb, ed., *Liberating Faith: Religious Voices for Justice, Peace, and Ecological Wisdom* (Lanham, MD: Rowman and Littlefield, 2003), 377–85.
60. Karnika Kohli, "Bruised, Battered Goddesses Feature in Campaign against Domestic Violence," *The Times of India*, September 10, 2013, http://articles.timesofindia .indiatimes.com/2013-09-10/india/41936066_1_goddesses-durga-domestic-violence.
61. World Health Report, ibid. See also "Say No: Unite to End Violence against Women" statistics. http://saynotoviolence.org/issue/facts-and-figures.
62. American Bar Association Commission on Sexual and Domestic Violence, http://www .americanbar.org/groups/domestic_violence/resources/statistics.html.
63. Mary D. Pellauer and Susan Brooks Thistlethwaite, "Conversation on Grace and Healing: Perspectives from the Movement to End Violence against Women," in Susan Brooks Thistlethwaite and Mary Potter Engel, eds., *Lift Every Voice: Constructing Christian Theologies from the Underside* (Maryknoll, NY: Orbis, 1998), 178.
64. Danger Assessment, http://www.dangerassessment.org/about.aspx.
65. Selwyn Crawford, "Black Women at Greater Risk of Becoming Victims of Homicidal Domestic Violence," *Dallas News*, September 21, 2013, http://www.dallasnews.com/ news/crime/headlines/20130921-black-women-at-greater-risk-of-becoming-victims -of-homicidal-domestic-violence.ece.
66. Ibid.
67. Bryan Robinson, "Why Pregnant Women Are Targeted," *ABCNews*, January 7, 2006, http://abcnews.go.com/US/LegalCenter/story?id=522184.

68. Thistlethwaite and Engel, *Lift Every Voice*, 162.
69. "Combatting Acid Violence against Women in Bangladesh, India and Cambodia," Avon Global Center for Women and Justice at Cornell Law School and the New York City Bar Association, 2011, http://www2.ohchr.org/english/bodies/cedaw/docs/cedaw _crc_contributions/AvonGlobalCenterforWomenandJustice.pdf.
70. Ibid., 11, 15.
71. Ibid., 27.
72. *TrustLaw*, "FACTSHEET: The World's Most Dangerous Countries for Women," June 15, 2011, http://www.trust.org/item/20110615000000-hurik/?source=spotlight.
73. Tom de Castella, "How Many Acid Attacks Are There?," *BBC News*, August 9, 2013, http://www.bbc.co.uk/news/magazine-23631395.
74. "'I've Got a Surprise for You': Husband Blindfolds His Wife . . . and Then Chops off Her Fingers to Stop Her Studying for a Degree," *DailyMail*, December 17, 2011, http://www.dailymail.co.uk/news/article-2075435/Husband-chops-wifes-fingers-stop -studying-degree.html.

Chapter 3

1. *Enuma Elish*, Tablet IV: 129–32, 137–40, in Alexander Heidel, *The Babylonian Genesis* (Chicago: University of Chicago Press, 1951), 42.
2. Heidel, *Babylonian Genesis*, 1.
3. Bernard F. Batto, *Slaying the Dragon: Mythmaking in the Biblical Tradition* (Louisville, KY: Westminster/John Knox Press, 1992), 40.
4. *Enuma Elish*, Tablet IV: 96–103, 33–34.
5. *Enuma Elish*, Tablet IV: 98–103, 40.
6. Paul Ricoeur, *The Symbolism of Evil*, trans. Emerson Buchanan (Boston: Beacon, 1969), 180.
7. Ibid., 182–83.
8. Catherine Keller, *From a Broken Web: Sexism, Separation, and Self* (Boston: Beacon, 1986), 77–78.
9. Ibid., 78, citing Mircea Eliade, *The Sacred and the Profane: The Nature of Religion*, trans. W. Trask (New York: Harvest/HJB, 1959), 77.
10. Batto, *Slaying the Dragon*, 76.
11. Susan Brooks Thistlethwaite, "'You May Enjoy the Spoil of Your Enemies': Rape as a Biblical Metaphor for War," *Semeia*, Vol. 61 (1993): 59–78, 66ff.
12. Heidel, *Babylonian Genesis*, chapter III "Old Testament Parallels," and especially 129.
13. Batto, *Slaying the Dragon*, 74.
14. Ibid., 80–82.
15. Scarry, *The Body in Pain*, 183ff.
16. Thistlethwaite, "'You May Enjoy the Spoil of Your Enemies,'" 67.
17. Batto, *Slaying the Dragon*, 82.
18. Isidore Singer, Cyrus Adler, and Susan Rothchild, eds., *Jewish Encyclopedia* [1901–6] (New York: Funk and Wagnalls, 2002), s.v. "Rahab."
19. Thistlethwaite, "'You May Enjoy the Spoil of Your Enemies,'" 68.
20. Ibid.
21. Ibid.
22. Simone Weil, "The Iliad, or, the Poem of Force," *Politics* pamphlet edition, 1945, trans. Mary McCarthy, reprinted by permission of Dwight Macdonald (Wallingford, PA: Pendle Hill, 1967), 1.

23. Ibid., 36.
24. Judith Butler, *Bodies That Matter* (New York: Routledge, 1993), 87.
25. Benjamin Jowett, trans., *Plato's Timaeus: With Introduction* (Rockville, MD: Serenity, 2009), 170.
26. Deborah Tuerkheimer, "Sex without Consent," *Yale Law Journal* (December 1, 2013): http://yalelawjournal.org/the-yale-law-journal-pocket-part/criminal-law-and-sentencing/sex-without-consent/.
27. Butler, *Bodies That Matter*, 117.
28. Ibid., 87.
29. Kelly Brown Douglas, *What's Faith Got to Do with It? Black Bodies/Christian Souls* (Maryknoll, NY: Orbis, 2005), xiv–xv.
30. Black Lives Matter, "About Us," http://blacklivesmatter.com/about/.
31. Aristotle, *On the Soul*, Part 1, 4.
32. Aristotle, *On the Generation of Animals*, book IV.
33. Keller, *From a Broken Web*, 48–50, citing Aristotle, *Genesis of Animals*, 4:2ff.
34. Linda Elizabeth Mitchell, ed., *Women in Medieval Western European Culture* (New York: Garland, 1999), 304.
35. Aristotle, *Politics*, book I, V.
36. Aristotle, *Nicomachean Ethics*, book X.
37. Tacitus, *Agricola*, 30, cited in Roland H. Bainton, *Christian Attitudes Toward War and Peace* (Nashville, TN: Abingdon, 1960), 23.
38. Weil, "The Iliad," 35.
39. Justinus, *Epit. Pompei Trogi*, XXVIII, 2, cited in Bainton, *Christian Attitudes Toward War and Peace*, 23.

Chapter 4

1. Adela Collins, *Harper's Bible Dictionary*, Paul J. Achtemeier, ed. (San Francisco: Harper and Row, 1985), s.v. "Patmos."
2. Josephus, *Jewish War* 5:446–51.
3. Barbara R. Rossing, *The Rapture Exposed: The Message of Hope in the Book of Revelation* (New York: Basic, 2004).
4. Judith Lewis Herman, *Trauma and Recovery* (New York: Basic, 1992), chapter 2, especially 33–42.
5. Ibid., 133.
6. Weil, "The Iliad," 35.
7. Susan Thistlethwaite and Glenn Stassen, "Abrahamic Alternatives to War: Jewish, Christian and Muslim Perspectives on Just Peacemaking," *United States Institute of Peace Special Report 214*, (October 2008): http://www.usip.org/sites/default/files/sr214.pdf.
8. Augustine, *Contra Faustum*, XXII: 74.
9. Augustine, *The City of God*, XV: 4.
10. Ibid., XVI.
11. Ibid., I: 18.
12. Ibid., XIV: 1.
13. Ibid., I: 28.
14. Mary Pellauer, "Augustine on Rape," in Carol J. Adams and Marie M. Fortune, eds., *Violence against Women and Children: A Christian Theological Sourcebook* (New York: Continuum, 1995), 234–35.

15. Chris Hedges, *The Death of the Liberal Class* (New York: Nation, 2010), 56.
16. Chris Hedges, *War Is a Force That Gives Us Meaning* (New York: Anchor, 2002), 162.
17. The Open Society Foundations, *Globalizing Torture: CIA Secret Detention and Extraordinary Rendition* (2013), http://www.opensocietyfoundations.org/reports/globalizing -torture-cia-secret-detention-and-extraordinary-rendition.
18. "Shock and Awe: The Initial Bombing of Baghdad," YouTube video, 2:03, from news coverage televised by CNN, posted August 28, 2009, https://www.youtube.com/watch ?v=NktsxucDvNI.
19. "A Day of Sirens, Bombs, Smoke and Fire," *CNN International*, March 21, 2003, http:// edition.cnn.com/2003/WORLD/meast/03/21/sprj.irq.aday/.
20. Harlan K. Ullman and James P. Wade, *Shock and Awe: Achieving Rapid Dominance* (National Defense University, 1996), xxiv, http://www.dodccrp.org/files/Ullman _Shock.pdf.
21. Kerry Sheridan, "Iraq Death Toll Reaches 500,000 since Start of U.S.-Led Invasion, New Study Says," *The World Post*, October 15, 2013, http://www.huffingtonpost.com/ 2013/10/15/iraq-death-toll_n_4102855.html.
22. "The Three Trillion Dollar War," http://threetrilliondollarwar.org/.
23. Jeena Shah, "Iraq Birth Defects Covered Up?," *The World Post*, October 4, 2013, http:// www.huffingtonpost.com/the-center-for-constitutional-rights/iraqi-birth-defects -cover_b_4046442.html.

Chapter 5

1. This is not the sense of the term as first used by Carl von Clausewitz in his book *On War*. Clausewitz used the term to describe the near impossibility of actually fully knowing what is going on in a war. "War is an area of uncertainty; three quarters of the things on which all action in War is based are lying in a fog of uncertainty to a greater or lesser extent." Military "war games" try to capture the "fog of war" uncertainty idea of Clausewitz, and it has been adopted in military and adventure video and computer games when enemy characters are being hidden from the player. In the 2003 American documentary film, *The Fog of War: Eleven Lessons from the Life of Robert S. McNamara*, about the life and times of the former Secretary of Defense, the term comes closer to my meaning here as creating the conditions where war cannot be clearly seen.
2. Nick Davies and David Leigh, "Afghanistan War Logs: Massive Leak of Secret Files Exposes Truth of Occupation," *The Guardian*, July 25, 2010, http://www.theguardian .com/world/2010/jul/25/afghanistan-war-logs-military-leaks.
3. Tillman had spoken to friends about his opposition to President Bush and the Iraq war, and he had made an appointment with Noam Chomsky, a noted journalist and critic of the wars, for after his return from the military. Destruction of evidence, and the fact that his personal journal continues to be missing, has led several, including his mother, to speculate he was not just accidentally, but deliberately killed. See Mary Tillman and Narda Zacchino, *Boots on the Ground by Dusk: My Tribute to Pat Tillman* (New York: Rodale, 2008); John Krakauer, *Where Men Win Glory: The Odyssey of Pat Tillman* (New York: Random House, 2009).
4. Dave Zirin, "Pat Tillman, Our Hero," *The Nation*, October 24, 2005, http://www .thenation.com/article/pat-tillman-our-hero#.
5. "Mother Questions Tillman's Death in 'Fog of War,'" *NPR*, May 6, 2008, http://www .npr.org/templates/story/story.php?storyId=90203500.
6. Krakauer, *Where Men Win Glory*, 33.

7. Lada Stevanović, "Human or Superhuman: The Concept of Hero in Ancient Greek Religion and/in Politics," Institute of Ethnography, SASA, Belgrade, 8, http://www.doiserbia.nb.rs/img/doi/0350-0861/2008/0350-08610802007S.pdf.

8. Ibid.

9. Ibid., 9.

10. Ibid., 12.

11. Aristotle, *Nicomachean Ethics*, III.6., cited in Stevanović, "Human or Superhuman," 12.

12. Thucydides, *The Peloponnesian War* 2, 43, 2, cited in Stevanović, "Human or Superhuman," 15.

13. Joseph Campbell, *The Hero with a Thousand Faces* (New York: Pantheon, 1949).

14. Ibid., 3.

15. Ibid., 120–26.

16. Stevanović, "Human or Superhuman," 12–13.

17. Seamus Heaney, trans., *Beowulf: A New Verse Translation* (New York: W. W. Norton, 2000), vv. 100–110.

18. Anthony Breznican, "'Maleficent': Angelina Jolie Fires up Her Dragon in New Trailer—VIDEO," *Entertainment*, March 18, 2014, http://insidemovies.ew.com/2014/03/18/maleficent-angelina-jolie-fires-up-her-dragon-in-new-trailer-video/.

19. Hayley Krischer, "The *Maleficent* Rape Scene That We Need to Talk About," *Huffington Post*, May 6, 2014, http://www.huffingtonpost.com/hayley-krischer/the-maleficent-rape-scene_b_5445974.html.

20. Kevin Maness, "Taming the Wild Shieldmaiden: A Feminist Analysis of Tolkien's Heroinism in *The Lord of the Rings*" (Fall 1995), 6, https://www.academia.edu/363083/Taming_the_Wild_Shieldmaiden_A_Feminist_Analysis_of_Tolkiens_Heroinism_in_The_Lord_of_the_Rings.

21. Richard Hamer, ed. and trans., "The Dream of the Rood," in *A Choice of Anglo-Saxon Verse: Selected with an Introduction and a Parallel Verse Translation* (London: Faber and Faber, 1970), lines 36–39, cited in Jeannette C. Brock, "The Dream of the Rood and the Image of Christ in the Early Middle Ages," *Hanover College History Department*, http://history.hanover.edu/hhr/98/hhr98_2.html.

22. Matthew 27:28 (NIV).

23. Kevin Crossley-Holland, *The Battle of Maldon and Other Old English Poems* (Toronto: Macmillan, 1966), cited in Jeannette C. Brock, "The Dream of the Rood and the Image of Christ in the Early Middle Ages."

24. *The Dream of the Rood*, lines 38–41, cited in ibid.

25. J. Denny Weaver, *The Nonviolent Atonement* (Grand Rapids, MI: W. B. Eerdmans, 2001), 16.

26. David Roberts, ed., and Gavin Roberts, il., *Minds at War: The Poetry and Experience of the First World War* (Burgess Hill, UK: Saxon, 1996), 38.

27. David Roberts, ed., *Out in the Dark: Poetry of the First World War* (Burgess Hill, UK: Saxon, 1998), 136.

28. Jessica Ravitz, "Silence Lifted: The Untold Stories of Rape during the Holocaust," *CNN*, June 24, 2011, http://www.cnn.com/2011/WORLD/europe/06/24/holocaust.rape/.

29. "Glendale Memorial Honoring Korean 'Comfort Women' Stirs Controversy," *CBS Local*, July 30, 2013, http://losangeles.cbslocal.com/2013/07/30/glendale-memorial-honoring-korean-comfort-women-stirs-controversy/.

30. Mary Louise Roberts, *What Soldiers Do: Sex and the American GI in World War II* (Chicago: University of Chicago Press, 2013).

31. Edward Tabor Linenthal, "From Hero to Anti-hero: The Transformation of the Warrior in Modern America," JSOR *Soundings: An Interdisciplinary Journal*, Vol. 63, Issue 1 (Spring 1980), 85.
32. Ibid., 86.
33. Ibid., 87.
34. Ibid.
35. Horsley, 297.
36. Susan Thistlethwaite, "Mel Makes a War Movie," in *Perspectives on the Passion* (New York: Miramax, 2004).
37. "Mark Millar's Rape Comments, 'Superheroes' TCA Panel: The Comics World Responds," *The Los Angeles Times*, August 8, 2013, http://herocomplex.latimes.com/comics/mark-millars-rape-comments-superheroes-tca-panel-the-comics-world-responds/.
38. Women in Refrigerators, http://www.lby3.com/wir/.
39. Robin Mcgovern, "Violence against Women in Video Games," YouTube video, 3:30, posted March 31, 2014, https://www.youtube.com/watch?v=9OQldsdVYdM.
40. Susan Brooks Thistlethwaite, "Drone Wars: The Temptation of Automated Conflict," *On Faith*, December 5, 2011, http://www.faithstreet.com/onfaith/2011/12/05/drone-wars-the-temptation-of-automated-conflict/12063.
41. Ibid.
42. Jacob Wood and Ken Harbaugh, "The Limits of Armchair Warfare," *The New York Times*, May 20, 2014, http://www.nytimes.com/2014/05/21/opinion/the-limits-of-armchair-warfare.html?hp&rref=opinion&_r=2.

Chapter 6

1. Pauline Réage, *The Story of O* (New York: Ballantine, 1981). Originally published 1954.
2. Carmela Ciuraru, "The Story of the Story of O," *Guernica*, June 15, 2011, http://www.guernicamag.com/features/ciuraru_6_15_11/.
3. Carolyn Bronstein, *Battling Pornography: The American Feminist Anti-Pornography Movement 1976–1986* (Cambridge: Cambridge University Press, 2011), 289.
4. Ibid., 290–91.
5. Judith Butler, "Against Proper Objects," in Elizabeth Weed and Naomi Schor, eds., *Feminism Meets Queer Theory* (Bloomington: Indiana University Press, 1997), 1.
6. "Research on Pornography," The Aurora Center, University of Minnesota, https://www1.umn.edu/aurora/pdf/ResearchOnPornography.pdf. SEE ALSO http://www.amazon.com/dp/0415523125/ref=rdr_ext_tmb.
7. As National Security Agency leaker Edward Snowden has revealed, "the oversight of surveillance programs was so weak that members of the United States military working at the spy agency sometimes shared sexually explicit photos they intercepted." Michael Schmidt, "Racy Photos Were Often Shared at N.S.A., Snowden Says," *The New York Times*, July 20, 2014, http://www.nytimes.com/2014/07/21/us/politics/edward-snowden-at-nsa-sexually-explicit-photos-often-shared.html?smid=fb-share&_r=0Am.
8. Geraldine Bedell, "I Wrote the Story of O," *The Guardian*, July 24, 2004, http://www.theguardian.com/books/2004/jul/25/fiction.features3.
9. Hugh Thomas, *The Slave Trade* (New York: Simon and Schuster, 1997).
10. Frances Morris and Christopher Green, eds., *Henri Rousseau: Jungles in Paris* (New York: Harry N. Abrams, 2006), 13, 45.

11. Ibid., 97.
12. Audre Lorde, "The Uses of the Erotic: The Erotic as Power," in *Sister Outsider* (New York: Crossing, 1984), 53–59.
13. *Metamorphoses*, I, 438–72, trans. by Daryl Hine.
14. Ibid.; *Metamorphoses*, II, 846–875.
15. Ibid.
16. Harvey Birenbaum, *Myth and Mind* (Lanham, MD: University Press of America, 1988), 123.
17. Guido Reni, *The Rape of Europa*, 1637–39, Oil on Canvas, 177cm x 129.5 cm, The National Gallery, http://www.nationalgallery.org.uk/paintings/guido-reni-the-rape-of-europa.
18. A. W. Eaton, "Where Ethics and Aesthetics Meet: Titian's *Rape of Europa*," *Hypatia*, Vol. 18, Issue 4, "Women, Art, and Aesthetics" (Autumn–Winter, 2003), 159–88.
19. C. D. C. Reeve, "Plato on Friendship and Eros," in Edward N. Zalta, ed., *The Stanford Encyclopedia of Philosophy* (Spring 2011 Edition), http://plato.stanford.edu/archives/spr2011/entries/plato-friendship/.
20. Rosemary Radford Ruether, "Foundations for a Theology of Liberation," in *Liberation Theology: Human Hope Confronts Christian History and American Power* (New York: Paulist, 1972), 16–17.
21. Phyllis Trible, *Texts of Terror* (Philadelphia: Fortress, 1984), 39.
22. Dave Itskoff, "For 'Game of Thrones,' Rising Unease over Rape's Recurring Role," *The New York Times*, May 2, 2014, http://www.nytimes.com/2014/05/03/arts/television/for-game-of-thrones-rising-unease-over-rapes-recurring-role.html?_r=0.
23. Trible, *Texts of Terror*, 65.
24. Ibid., 68–69.
25. Ibid., 83.
26. Barbara R. Rossing, *The Rapture Exposed: The Message of Hope in the Book of Revelation* (New York: Basic, 2004), 199.
27. Hal Lindsey, *The Late Great Planet Earth* (Grand Rapids, MI: Zondervan, 1970), 168.
28. Susan Thistlethwaite and Glenn Stassen, "Abrahamic Alternatives to War: Jewish, Christian and Muslim Perspectives on Just Peacemaking," *United States Institute of Peace Special Report 214*, (October 2008), http://www.usip.org/sites/default/files/sr214.pdf.
29. Augustine, *City of God*, I: 28.
30. Joseph Campbell, *The Hero with a Thousand Faces* (New York: Pantheon, 1949), 122.
31. Julie B. Miller, "Eroticized Violence in Medieval Women's Mystical Literature: A Call for a Feminist Critique," *Journal of Feminist Studies in Religion*, Vol. 15, Issue 2 (Fall 1999): 25–49, http://www.jstor.org/stable/25002364.
32. *Summa Theologica*, I, Q. 51, Art. 3.
33. Anne Llewellyn Barstow, "On Studying Witchcraft as Women's History: A Historiography of the European Witch Persecutions," *Journal of Feminist Studies in Religion*, Vol. 4 (Fall 1988): 7–20.
34. See, for example, Barbara Becker-Cantario, "'Feminist Consciousness' and 'Wicked Witches': Recent Studies on Women in Early Modern Europe," *Signs*, Vol. 20 (Autumn 1994): 170, and also the comment in Ute Frevert, Heide Wunder, and Christina Vanja, "Historical Research on Women in the Federal Republic of Germany," in Karen Offen, Ruth Roach Pierson, and Jane Rendall, eds.,*Writing Women's History: International Perspectives* (Bloomington: Indiana University Press, 1991): "[R]esearch on this topic (witch trials) has become mainly a 'men's subject', as it deals with territory, collectivities,

the creation of modern states, and the consolidation of legal and juridical authority, and the development of theological and learned discourses."

35. Yuval Taylor, ed., *I Was Born a Slave: An Anthology of Classic Slave Narratives* (Chicago: Lawrence Hill, 1999), 160.

36. Ibid.

37. Lucille Davie, "Sarah Baartman, at Rest at Last," *SouthAfrica.info*, May 14, 2012, http://www.southafrica.info/about/history/saartjie.htm#.U-DONI6oJ75.

38. Cheryl Townsend Gilkes, "The 'Loves' and 'Troubles' of African American Women's Bodies," in Emilie M. Townes, ed., *A Troubling in My Soul: Womanist Perspectives on Evil and Suffering* (Maryknoll, NY: Orbis, 1993), 233–34.

39. Ibid., 242.

40. Rita Nakashima Brock and Susan Brooks Thistlethwaite, *Casting Stones: Prostitution and Liberation in Asia and the United States* (Minneapolis, MN: Fortress, 1996), 178–81.

41. "Sexual Abuse in Immigration Detention," American Civil Liberties Union (October, 2011) https://www.aclu.org/sexual-abuse-immigration-detention. Be sure to look at the resources in the article for immigrant rights.

42. Peter Wagner, *Eros Revived: Erotica of the Enlightenment in England and America* (London: Secker, 1988); see also Robert Purks Maccubbin, ed., *'Tis Nature's Fault: Unauthorized Sexuality during the Enlightenment* (Cambridge: Cambridge University Press, 1988), and Felicity Nussbaum and Laura Brown, *The New Eighteenth Century: Theory, Politics, English Literature* (New York: Methuen, 1987).

43. Thomas Crow, "Tensions of the Enlightenment: Goya," in Stephen Eisenman, Thomas Crow, Brian Lukacher, Linda Nochlin, David L. Phillips, and Frances K. Pohl, eds., *Nineteenth Century Art: A Critical History* (London: Thames and Hudson, 2011), 80.

44. Ibid., 79, https://www.msu.edu/course/ha/445/crowgoya.pdf.

45. Michelle Fine and Lois Weis, "Disappearing Acts: The State and Violence against Women in the Twentieth Century," *Signs*, Vol. 25, Issue 4, "Feminisms at a Millennium" (Summer 2000): 1139–46. http://www.jstor.org/stable/3175501.

46. Reva B. Siegel, "A Short History of Sexual Harassment," in Catherine MacKinnon and Reva B. Siegel, eds., *Directions in Sexual Harassment Law*, http://www.law.yale.edu/documents/pdf/Faculty/Siegel_Directions_in_Sexual_Harassment_Law.pdf.

47. See *Killing Us Softly 4*, full online video, for educational purposes only: http://www.dailymotion.com/video/x1n3d88_killing-us-softly-4_news; See also http://www.jeankilbourne.com/videos/.

48. Smriti Sinha, "The Internet Is Furious over This Disturbing Indian Fashion Photoshoot," *Identities.mic*, August 6, 2014, http://mic.com/articles/95668/the-internet-is-furious-over-this-disturbing-indian-fashion-photo-shoot?utm_source=policymicFB&utm_medium=main&utm_campaign=social; "Sexism and Racism Permeate Music Videos, According to New Report," *The Guardian*, August 8, 2014, http://www.theguardian.com/music/2014/aug/08/sexism-and-racism-permeate-music-videos-new-report?CMP=ema_630.

49. Arturo Garcia, "Feminist Video Game Critic Forced to Leave Her Home after Online Rape and Death Threats," *Raw Story*, August 27, 2014, http://www.rawstory.com/rs/2014/08/27/feminist-video-game-critic-forced-to-leave-her-home-after-online-rape-and-death-threats/.

50. Amanda Hess, "A Former FBI Agent on Why It Is So Hard to Prosecute Gamergate Trolls," *Slate*, October 17, 2014, http://www.slate.com/blogs/xx_factor/2014/10/17/gamergate_threats_why_it_s_so_hard_to_prosecute_the_people_targeting_zoe.html.

51. Mary Elizabeth Williams, "Horrifying New Trend: Posting Rapes to Facebook," *Salon*, May 20, 2013, http://www.salon.com/2013/05/20/worst_horrifying_new_trend _posting_rapes_to_facebook/.

52. Paul Bentley, "'Mummy Porn' Fifty Shades of Grey Book Outstrips Harry Potter to Become Fastest Selling Paperback of All Time," *MailOnline*, June 17, 2012, http://www .dailymail.co.uk/news/article-2160862/Fifty-Shades-Of-Grey-book-outstrips-Harry -Potter-fastest-selling-paperback-time.html#ixzz1y9SHlzQU.

53. Ibid.

54. "50 Shades of Grey and the Erotization of Male Domination," *The Liberation Collective*, April 12, 2012, http://liberationcollective.wordpress.com/2012/04/02/on-50 -shades-of-grey-and-the-erotization-of-male-domination/.

55. Eva Illouz, *Hard-Core Romance: "Fifty Shades of Grey," Best-Sellers and Society* (Chicago: University of Chicago Press, 2014).

Chapter 7

1. Tom Boggioni, "Bob Jones University Told Rape Victims to Repent and to Look for 'Root Sin' That Caused Their Attack," *The Raw Story*, June 18, 2014, http://www .rawstory.com/rs/2014/06/18/bob-jones-university-told-rpe-victims-to-repent-and -look-for-root-sin-that-caused-their-rpe/?onswipe_redirect=no&oswrr=1.

2. A. G. Sulzberger, "Facing Cuts, a City Repeals Its Domestic Violence Law," *The New York Times*, October 11, 2011, http://www.nytimes.com/2011/10/12/us/topeka-moves -to-decriminalize-domestic-violence.html?_r=3&.

3. "Quotes from the War on Women," *Alex Leo*, August 30, 2012, http://alexleo.tumblr .com/post/30553490224/quotes-from-the-war-on-women.

4. Just Peace theory is a latecomer to this list and is barely a quarter of a century old, while Crusade is rarely referenced in a secular age. The terror attacks in Norway by Anders Breivik, however, may signal a return of "Crusade." See "Anders Breivik Trial: 21st Century Crusader Battling against Islam in Europe," *Huffington Post*, April 16, 2012, http://www.huffingtonpost.co.uk/2012/04/16/anders-breivik-trial -crusader-battling-against-islam_n_1427591.html?just_reloaded=1.

5. Rosemary Radford Ruether, "The Western Tradition and Violence against Women," in Joanne Carlson Brown and Carole R. Bohn, eds., *Christianity, Patriarchy, and Abuse: A Feminist Critique* (New York: Pilgrim, 1989), 32.

6. Ibid., 33.

7. Ibid., 33–34.

8. Ibid., 34–35.

9. Katie Geneva Cannon, *Black Womanist Ethics* (Atlanta: Scholars, 1988); Dolores Williams, *Sisters in the Wilderness: The Challenge of Womanist God-Talk* (Maryknoll, NY: Orbis, 2004), originally published in 1993.

10. Alice Walker, *In Search of Our Mothers' Gardens: Womanist Prose* (New York: Harcourt, 1983).

11. Williams, *Sisters in the Wilderness*, x.

12. M. Shawn Copeland, *Enfleshing Freedom: Body, Race, and Being* (Minneapolis, MN: Fortress, 2009).

13. Mary Potter Engel, "Historical Theology and Violence against Women: Unearthing a Popular Tradition of Just Battery," in Joanne C. Brown and Carole R. Bohn, eds., *Christianity, Patriarchy, and Abuse: A Feminist Critique* (New York: Pilgrim, 1989), 248.

14. Ibid., 249.
15. Ibid.
16. Ibid., 250. Italics in original.
17. Kathryn Joyce, "Biblical Battered Wife Syndrome: Christian Women and Domestic Violence," *Religion Dispatches*, June 18, 2009, http://religiondispatches.org/biblical-battered-wife-syndrome-christian-women-and-domestic-violence/.
18. Aristotle, *Politics*, book I, V.
19. Augustine, *City of God*, XV: 4.
20. "The Bush Doctrine," http://www.princeton.edu/~achaney/tmve/wiki100k/docs/Bush_Doctrine.html. "Bush Doctrine" concept, first used by Charles Krauthammer, "Charlie Gibson's Gaffe," *Washington Post*, September 13, 2008, http://www.washingtonpost.com/wp-dyn/content/article/2008/09/12/AR2008091202457.html.
21. Engel, "Historical Theology and Violence against Women," 251.
22. Nathaniel Vinton, "ESPN Suspends Stephen A. Smith for One Week Following Domestic Abuse Rant," *NYDailyNews*, July 29, 2014, http://www.nydailynews.com/sports/football/stephen-smith-suspended-espn-domestic-abuse-rant-article-1.1884632.
23. David Folkenflik, "The Video, The Tabloid Site and the NFL's Unwanted Reckoning," *National Public Radio*, September 9, 2014, http://www.npr.org/2014/09/09/347140605/the-video-the-tabloid-site-and-the-nfls-unwanted-reckoning.
24. Matt Saccaro, "It Wasn't Ray Rice's Fault: The Sick, Twisted Logic of Men's Rights Activists on Domestic Violence," *Salon*, September 9, 2014, http://www.salon.com/2014/09/09/it_wasnt_ray_rices_fault_the_sick_twisted_logic_of_mens_rights_activists_on_domestic_violence/.
25. Simone Sebastian and Ines Bebea, "For Battered NFL Wives, a Message from the Cops and the League: Keep Quiet," *Washington Post*, October 17, 2014, http://www.washingtonpost.com/posteverything/wp/2014/10/17/for-battered-nfl-wives-a-message-from-the-cops-and-the-league-keep-quiet/?TID+SM_FB.
26. Estelle B. Freedman, *Redefining Rape: Sexual Violence in the Era of Suffrage and Segregation* (Cambridge, MA: Harvard University Press, 2013), 1.
27. Ibid.
28. Ibid., 1–2.
29. "The Growth of Slavery in North America," *Africans in America: The Terrible Transformation*, PBS, http://www.pbs.org/wgbh/aia/part1/1narr5.html.
30. Rita Nakashima Brock and Susan Brooks Thistlethwaite, *Casting Stones: Prostitution and Liberation in Asia and the United States* (Minneapolis, MN: Fortress, 1996).
31. Cristan Williams, "Trans People Added to Violence against Women Act," *TransAdvocate*, April 22, 2014, http://www.transadvocate.com/trans-people-added-to-violence-against-women-act_n_13521.htm.
32. Eileen Graef, "Rush Limbaugh: Women Actually Are Consenting When They Say 'No,'" *UPI.com*, September 16, 2014, http://www.upi.com/Top_News/US/2014/09/16/Rush-Limbaugh-Women-actually-are-consenting-when-they-say-no/4851410893932/.
33. Andrea Smith, "Sexual Violence and American Indian Genocide," in Nantawan Boonprasat Lewis and Marie Fortune, eds., *Remembering Conquest: Feminist/Womanist Perspectives on Religion, Colonization, and Sexual Violence* (New York: Haworth Pastoral, 1999), 32.
34. Ibid., 35.
35. Ibid.
36. Ibid.

37. The Stream Team, "Native Americans Speak up about 'Redskins' Name Controversy," *America.Aljazeera.com*, October 18, 2013, http://america.aljazeera.com/watch/shows/the-stream/the-stream-officialblog/2013/10/18/native-americansspeakupaboutredskinsnamecontroversy.html.

38. Andrea Smith, "Sexual Violence and American Indian Genocide," 37–38.

39. "General Retreat/Westward Ho," *IGN Entertainment*, http://www.ign.com/games/general-retreat-westward-ho/2600-4775.

40. Brock and Thistlethwaite, *Casting Stones*.

41. Andrea Smith, "Sexual Violence and American Indian Genocide," 38.

42. Ainab Rahman, "The War for Afghan Women," *South Asia Journal*, Issue 3 (January 4, 2012): http://southasiajournal.net/2012/01/the-war-for-afghan-women/.

43. Ibid.

44. "Would the Invasion of Iraq Be a 'Just War'?," *United States Institute of Peace Special Report 98*, January 2003, http://www.usip.org/sites/default/files/sr98.pdf.

45. Augustine, *Contra Faustum*, XXII: 74.

46. Robert Parry, "Blair Reveals Cheney's War Agenda," *consortiumnews.com*, September 6, 2010, http://www.consortiumnews.com/2010/090610.html.

47. See Joseph Nye, *Bound to Lead: The Changing Nature of American Power* (New York: Basic, 1991).

48. David Henderson, "Was the Iraq War about Oil?," *Library of Economics and Liberty*, March 19, 2013, http://econlog.econlib.org/archives/2013/03/was_the_iraq_wa.html.

49. Jason Stearns, *Dancing in the Glory of Monsters: The Collapse of the Congo and the Great War of Africa* (New York: PublicAffairs, 2011), 25.

50. Judith Butler, *Bodies That Matter* (New York: Routledge, 1993), 117.

51. Butler, *Bodies That Matter*, 87.

Chapter 8

1. Rita Nakashima Brock and Susan Brooks Thistlethwaite, *Casting Stones: Prostitution and Liberation in Asia and the United States* (Minneapolis, MN: Fortress, 1996), 81.

2. Susan Thistlethwaite, "Tweeting for Justice," *On Faith*, March 8, 2012, http://www.faithstreet.com/onfaith/2012/03/08/tweeting-for-justice-why-social-media-is-the-new-face-of-feminism/10030.

3. Brock and Thistlethwaite, *Casting Stones*, 82.

4. Dr. Martin Luther King Jr., "Beyond Vietnam—A Time to Break Silence," *American Rhetoric: Online Speech Bank*, April 4, 1967, http://www.americanrhetoric.com/speeches/mlkatimetobreaksilence.htm.

5. Tiffany D. Joseph, "Black Women in the Civil Rights Movement: 1960–1970," Brown-Tougaloo Exchange, http://cds.library.brown.edu/projects/FreedomNow/tiffany_joseph_thesis.html.

6. Ibid.

7. Roland H. Bainton, *Christian Attitudes toward War and Peace: A Historical Survey and Critical Re-Evaluation* (Nashville, TN: Abington, 1960), 20.

8. Ibid., 67–68.

9. Ibid., 71–72.

10. Ibid., 72–73.

11. Ibid., 76–77.

12. *Urban II: Speech at Council of Clermont, 1095, according to Fulcher of Chartres.* Fordham University, Medieval Sourcebook, http://www.fordham.edu/halsall/source/urban2-fulcher.html.

13. Desiderius Erasmus, *The Complaint of Peace. Translated from the Querela Pacis (A.D. 1521) of Erasmus* (Chicago: Open Court, 1917), http://oll.libertyfund.org/titles/87.

14. Martin Luther, Reformer (1483–1546), *Works 12.94.*

15. Jaroslav J. Pelikan and Hilton C. Oswald, *Luther's Works,* 55 vols. (St. Louis, MO: Concordia and Fortress, 1955–86), 46: 50–51.

16. Margaret E. Hirst, *The Quakers in Peace and War* (London: George Allen and Unwin, 1923), 57.

17. Ibid., 213.

18. George Fox, *Gospel Family Order,* http://gallery.nen.gov.uk/image77434-.html.

19. Sandra Stanley Holton, *Quaker Women: Personal Life, Memory and Radicalism in the Lives of Women Friends, 1780–1930* (New York: Routledge, 2007), chapters 6, 13.

20. Ibid., 5–6.

21. "The Schleitheim Confession," February 24, 1527, http://www.anabaptists.org/history/the-schleitheim-confession.html.

22. See links to the articles in Ted Grimsrud, "John Howard Yoder's Sexual Misconduct (1992 Elkhart Truth Articles)," *Peace Theology Blog,* http://peacetheology.net/john-h-yoder/john-howard-yoder's-sexual-misconduct—part-five-2/.

23. Religion News Service, "Mennonite Theologian Disciplined," *Chicago Tribune,* August 28, 1992, http://articles.chicagotribune.com/1992-08-28/news/9203180387_1_john-howard-yoder-sexual-misconduct-mennonite-church.

24. Mark Oppenheimer, "A Theologian's Influence, and Stained past, Lives On," *The New York Times,* October 11, 2013, http://www.nytimes.com/2013/10/12/us/john-howard-yoders-dark-past-and-influence-lives-on-for-mennonites.html?pagewanted=all&_r=0.

25. David Cramer, Jenny Howell, Jonathan Tran, and Paul Martins, "Scandalizing John Howard Yoder," *the other journal.com,* July 7, 2014, http://theotherjournal.com/2014/07/07/scandalizing-john-howard-yoder/.

26. Elizabeth G. Yoder, ed., *Peace Theology and Violence against Women,* Occasional Papers Issue 16 (Elkhart, IN: Institute of Mennonite Studies, 1992), 1.

27. Ibid., 7.

28. Ibid., 99ff.

29. Ibid., 119–21.

30. *Our Stories Untold,* http://www.ourstoriesuntold.com.

31. The Nobel Prize official website, "Nobel Prize Awarded Women," *Nobelprize.org,* 2014, http://www.nobelprize.org/nobel_prizes/lists/women.html.

32. "Jane Addams—Facts," ibid.

33. Jane Addams, *Peace and Bread in Time of War* (New York: Macmillan, 1922), 135–51. http://pds.lib.harvard.edu/pds/view/3545799?n=163&s=4&printThumbnails=no.

34. R. A. R. Edwards, "Jane Addams, Walter Rauschenbusch, and Dorothy Day: A Comparative Study of Settlement Theology," in Wendy J. Deichmann Edwards and Carolyn De Swarte Gifford, eds., *Gender and the Social Gospel* (Urbana: University of Illinois Press, 2003), 151–57.

35. Ibid., citing Christopher Lasch, *The New Radicalism in America, 1889–1965* (New York: Knopf, 1965), 11.

36. Jean Bethke Elshtain, *Jane Addams and the Dream of American Democracy: A Life* (New York: Basic, 2002), 35.

37. Leymah Gbowee, *Mighty Be Our Powers: How Sisterhood, Prayer, and Sex Changed a Nation at War, A Memoir* (New York: Beast, 2011), chapter 13.

38. Ibid., chapter 14.

39. Ibid., 76.

40. Glen H. Stassen, ed., *Just Peacemaking: Transforming Initiatives for Justice and Peace* (Louisville, KY: Westminster/John Knox, 1992).

41. Glen H. Stassen, *Just Peacemaking: The New Paradigm for the Ethics of Peace and War* (Cleveland, OH: Pilgrim, 2008), 34–35.

42. Michael Walzer, *Just and Unjust Wars: A Moral Argument with Historical Illustrations* (New York: Basic, 2000), 42. Originally published in 1977.

43. Susan Brooks Thistlethwaite, ed., *Interfaith Just Peacemaking: Jewish, Christian, and Muslim Approaches to the New Paradigm of Peace and War* (New York: Palgrave Macmillan, 2012).

Chapter 9

1. Federico Finchelstein, *The Ideological Origins of the Dirty War: Fascism, Populism, and Dictatorship in Twentieth Century Argentina* (New York: Oxford University Press, 2014), http://ukcatalogue.oup.com/product/9780199930241.do.

2. William Countryman, *Dirt, Greed, and Sex: Sexual Ethics in the New Testament and Their Implications for Today*, revised edition (Minneapolis, MN: Fortress, 2010), originally published 1988.

3. Ibid., 12, citing Mary Douglas, *Purity and Danger: An Analysis of Concepts of Pollution and Taboo* (London: Routledge and Kegan Paul, 1966), 2, 35.

4. Aristotle, *Politics*, book I, V.

5. Kay Marshall Strom, *In the Name of Submission: A Painful Look at Wife Battering* (Eugene, OR: Wipf and Stock, 2007).

6. Susan Brooks Thistlethwaite, *#Occupy the Bible: What Jesus Really Said (and Did) about Money and Power* (Eugene, OR: Wipf and Stock, 2013).

7. John-Paul Flintoff, "Gene Sharp: The Machiavelli of Non-Violence," *The New Statesman*, January 3, 2013, http://www.newstatesman.com/politics/your-democracy/2013/01/gene-sharp-machiavelli-non-violence.

8. Judith Lewis Herman, *Trauma and Recovery* (New York: Basic, 1992), 33.

9. Ibid., 43.

10. Leymah Gbowee, *Mighty Be Our Powers: How Sisterhood, Prayer, and Sex Changed a Nation at War, A Memoir* (New York: Beast, 2011), 69ff.

11. Herman, *Trauma and Recovery*, 41–42.

12. Audre Lorde, "The Uses of the Erotic: The Erotic as Power," in *Sister Outsider* (New York: Crossing, 1984), 55.

13. Jacqui True, *The Political Economy of Violence against Women* (New York: Oxford University Press, 2012), 53.

Conclusion

1. "History of Marches and Mass Actions," *National Organization for Women*, 2015, http://now.org/about/history/history-of-marches-and-mass-actions/; see also Susan Brooks Thistlethwaite, *#Occupy the Bible: What Jesus Really Said (and Did) about Money and Power* (Eugene, OR: Wipf and Stock, 2013).

2. Ibid.
3. Jacqui True, *The Political Economy of Violence against Women* (New York: Oxford University Press, 2012), 88.
4. Laura Bassett, "Republicans Introduce Five Anti-Abortion Bills in First Days of New Congress," *Huffington Post*, January 8, 2015, http://www.huffingtonpost.com/2015/01/08/republicans-abortion_n_6438522.html.
5. Erica Hellerstein, "The Rise of the DIY Abortion in Texas," *The Atlantic*, June 27, 2014, http://www.theatlantic.com/health/archive/2014/06/the-rise-of-the-diy-abortion-in-texas/373240/.
6. Alicia Garza, "A Herstory of the #BlackLivesMatter Movement," *The Feminist Wire*, October 14, 2014, http://thefeministwire.com/2014/10/blacklivesmatter-2/.
7. Katie Van Syckle, "The Tiny Police Department in Southern Oregon That Plans to End Campus Rape," *New York Magazine*, November 9, 2014, http://nymag.com/thecut/2014/11/can-this-police-department-help-end-campus-rape.html.
8. Vanessa Grigoriadis, "Meet the College Women Who Are Starting a Revolution against Campus Sexual Assault," *New York Magazine*, September 21, 2014, http://nymag.com/thecut/2014/09/emma-sulkowicz-campus-sexual-assault-activism.html.
9. Susan Brooks Thistlethwaite, *Interfaith Just Peacemaking: Jewish, Christian, and Muslim Approaches to the New Paradigm of Peace and War* (New York: Palgrave Macmillan, 2012), 84.
10. This is a complex and varied field. See this excellent review of the literature: Kevin Avruch and Beatriz Vejarano, "Truth and Reconciliation Commissions: Review Essay and Annotated Bibliography," School for Conflict Analysis and Resolution, George Mason University (2001): http://scar.gmu.edu/sites/default/files/Avruch%20and%20Vejarano%20-%202001%20-%20Truth%20and%20reconciliation%20commissions%20a%20review%20ess.pdf.
11. Leymah Gbowee, *Mighty Be Our Powers: How Sisterhood, Prayer, and Sex Changed a Nation at War, A Memoir* (New York: Beast, 2011), 144.
12. Amnesty International, "Violence Against Women," 2015, http://www.amnestyusa.org/our-work/issues/women-s-rights/violence-against-women.
13. Ibid.
14. Rachel Reid, *"We Have the Promises of the World": Women's Rights in Afghanistan* (New York: Human Rights Watch [HRW], 2009), http://www.hrw.org/sites/default/files/reports/afghanistan1209web_0.pdf.
15. True, *Political Economy*, 235.
16. Ibid., 236–37.
17. Sidney Ruth Schuler, Syed Hashemi, and Huda Badal Shamsul, "Men's Violence against Women in Rural Bangladesh: Undermined or Exacerbated by Microcredit," *Development in Practice*, Vol. 8, Issue 2 (May 1, 1998): http://policy-practice.oxfam.org.uk/publications/mens-violence-against-women-in-rural-bangladesh-undermined-or-exacerbated-by-mi-130309.
18. "MIF and Finca Peru Seek to Prevent Violence against Women through an Innovative Microfinance Program," Press release, *Multilateral Investment Fund*, January 15, 2014, http://www.fomin.org/en-us/HOME/News/Press-Releases/ArtMID/3819/ArticleID/1043/MIF-and-Finca-Peru-seek-to-prevent-violence-against-women-through-an-innovative-microfinance-program.
19. A list of some of these organizations can be found here: http://www.accessingsafety.org/index.php/main/right_menu/resources/links_to_organizations/violence_prevention_organizations.

20. Natalie Gyte, "Why I Won't Support One Billion Rising," *Huffington Post*, February 14, 2014, http://www.huffingtonpost.co.uk/natalie-gyte/one-billion-rising-why-i-wont -support_b_2684595.html.

21. Lauren Chief Elk, "There Is No 'We': V-Day, Indigenous Women, and the Myth of Shared Gender Oppression," *Model View Culture*, February 3, 2014, https:// modelviewculture.com/pieces/there-is-no-we-v-day-indigenous-women-and-the -myth-of-shared-gender-oppression.

22. Gbowee, *Mighty Be Our Powers*, 139.

23. Gerald Caplan, "Peacekeepers Gone Wild: How Much More Abuse Will the UN Ignore in Congo?," *The Globe and Mail*, August 3, 2012, http://www.theglobeandmail.com/ news/politics/second-reading/peacekeepers-gone-wild-how-much-more-abuse-will -the-un-ignore-in-congo/article4462151/.

24. Steven Hsieh, "States Move to Keep Guns out of the Hands of Domestic Abusers," *The Nation*, May 8, 2014, http://www.thenation.com/blog/179761/states-move-keep-guns -out-hands-domestic-abusers.

25. Alice Dahle, "Gender Based Violence and the Arms Treaty," *Amnesty International*, December 9, 2014, http://blog.amnestyusa.org/women/gender-based-violence-and -the-arms-trade-treaty/.

Index